ENGLAND'S GREAT TRANSFORMATION

ENGLAND'S GREAT TRANSFORMATION: LAW, LABOR, AND THE INDUSTRIAL REVOLUTION

MARC W. STEINBERG

THE UNIVERSITY OF CHICAGO PRESS
CHICAGO AND LONDON

MARC W. STEINBERG is professor of sociology at Smith College.

The University of Chicago Press, Chicago 60637
The University of Chicago Press, Ltd., London

Printed in the United States of America

25 24 23 22 21 20 19 18 17 16   1 2 3 4 5

ISBN-13: 978-0-226-32981-9 (cloth)
ISBN-13: 978-0-226-32995-6 (paper)
ISBN-13: 978-0-226-33001-3 (e-book)
DOI: 10.7208/chicago/9780226330013.001.0001

Library of Congress Cataloging-in-Publication Data

Steinberg, Marc W. (Marc William), 1956– author.
England's great transformation : law, labor, and the Industrial Revolution / Marc W. Steinberg.
pages cm
Includes bibliographical references and index.
ISBN 978-0-226-32981-9 (cloth : alk. paper)—ISBN 978-0-226-32995-6 (pbk. : alk. paper)—ISBN 978-0-226-33001-3 (e-book) 1. Industrial relations—England—History—19th century. 2. Industrial relations—England—Case studies. 3. Labor laws and legislation—England—History—19th century. 4. Industrial revolution—England. I. Title.
HD8390.S795 2016
331.0942'09034—dc23

2015024879

♾ This paper meets the requirements of ANSI/NISO Z39.48–1992 (Permanence of Paper).

For Charles Tilly, who patiently taught me the fine arts and big problems of historical sociology, and who always encouraged me to forge my own path,

and

David Spring who brought me into the world of English history

CONTENTS

PREFACE

A couple decades ago I was busily at work writing a dissertation that would eventually see the light of day as my first book, *Fighting Words*. My investigations ultimately led to an argument concerning how class struggle was expressed, conditioned, and channeled through discourse. Back then I was deeply steeped in British Marxist history of class formation during the Industrial Revolution. My friend and, at the time, mentor, Peggy Somers, politely suggested that I was more than steeped; I displayed a certain inebriation in sometimes purple prose concerning the heroic efforts of workers battling against the dark forces of capitalism. It offered exhilaration, but she was correct, of course, as was my adviser Charles Tilly, who pushed me to consider the ways in which my analyses moved beyond the classic and dominant account of Thompson's *The Making of the English Working Class*.

Abandoning the prose was one matter, but focusing on particular forms of class struggle was another. British Marxist historians offered a remarkably rich account of how workers struggled against emergent forms of capitalist subjugation through machine breaking and property destruction, anonymous threatening letters, emergent forms of strikes, underground radical politics, and other captivating forms of dramatic resistance. They also highlighted the ways in which capitalists turned to state repression and violence to meet and defeat these workers.

Indeed, one of the two case studies that made up the dissertation and subsequent book had all these trappings. In my analysis of the struggles of the cotton spinners of Ashton-under-Lyne and surrounding towns in Lancashire I found huge strikes, attacks on strike breakers, assaults on mills, and even an assassination of a mill owner's son. Cotton manufacturers turned to the local magistrates who, with the support of Westminster, sent in troops to quell what they saw as the start of a possible rebellion. This was class warfare!

And then I turned to my second case, the silk weavers of the Spitalfields district of London, and matters got complicated. Yes, the silk weavers, in their attempts to resist the dismantling of the legal protections of their trade and the precipitous debasement of their wages and community status turned to some pretty dramatic collective actions. They held mass demonstrations in front of Parliament in an unsuccessful effort to prevent the repeal of laws that had provided them with a modicum of material security for a half century. In the face of dramatic cuts in the piece rates paid by the large masters that dominated the trade, they responded with readily recognizable forms of resistance. Weavers engaged in a large-scale strike action in which many sealed their looms with wax, demonstrating that they had not and would not work on the materials already in production until their masters relented. Weavers who refused to participate were furtively visited at night and their work was slashed into worthlessness. And yes, the London police were called upon to hunt down the perpetrators of this destruction.

As I pored over the daily magistrates' court reports to find prosecutions of weavers who had committed silk cutting, I noticed that the silk masters regularly engaged in an activity to control and discipline weavers that was nowhere on the class struggle roadmap that I had constructed. I began to notice cases of silk masters prosecuting weavers for neglect of work for not finishing their assignments on time. Paging through the daily records I found dozens of such cases. Sometimes masters seemed to rely on the law to break strikes, forcing weavers back to work under threat of prosecution; at other times they simply used the law to force weavers who had taken in work to bring their task to completion. Poking around I learned that the statutes on which they relied fit under the category of the Master and Servant Acts and that the offenses being prosecuted were defined by the law as criminal. This seemed both an oddity and a puzzle. It was an ongoing class struggle without all of the heat and hoopla of public contention that were this graduate student's romanticized reading of the making of the English working class. And where strikes and property destruction I documented were episodic and often dramatic, this class struggle was more a continuous and quiet grind. I read a contemporary treatise or two on labor laws, developed a basic understanding of the Master and Servant Acts, and moved on, since this was outside the boundaries of my focus on discourse and working-class collective action.

But the questions from this encounter with the court reports dogged me, and eventually I returned to role of the law on class conflict, developing the current project that is this book. My attention turned to mid-Victorian England because that is when annual parliamentary reports on the number of prosecutions under master and servant law first became available. As I was developing my project several historians—most especially Douglas Hay and Paul Craven, Robert J. Steinfeld and Christopher Frank—were publishing signal studies on the uses of master and servant law in eighteenth- and nineteenth-century England that oriented and sharpened my focus.

As a student of Chuck Tilly I took it as my broadest purpose to offer an analysis of processes of structured inequality through time. In this sense I ask the same question he did in *Big Structures, Large Processes, Huge Comparisons*: "How can we improve our understanding of large-scale structures and processes that were transforming the world of the nineteenth century and those transforming our world?" (1984, 2). That is in part why I return to mid-Victorian England and the Industrial Revolution. In writing about European revolutions Tilly remarked that the British case was "a much-thumbed manual" for their avoidance (1993, 104). In many respects the British industrial revolution became too much-thumbed, as historians and social scientists lefts their prints all over its pages in the search for the manual for "development." My following analysis takes the mid-Victorian case as no such manual. Instead, I hope I provide a lens on durable structures of exploitation endured by groups of working people in factories, workshops, and at sea in this historical moment.

That is a historical project. In addition, the sociological project focuses on the partnering of historical materialism and historical institutionalism. Some scholars who have nurtured the latter see it as a means of supplanting the former. My aim is to convince readers that this coupling improves our understanding of large-scale structures and processes that were and are transforming the world, in this case processes of exploitation. This goal lies behind both the lengthy discussions of the analysis of the labor process and the historical development of legal institutions. On the one hand I discuss how studies of the labor process require an intensive interrogation of the institutions within which they are embedded, a subject that remains somewhat peripheral in the Marxist tradition. On the other hand I suggest that the historical analysis of economic and legal institutions benefits from a renewed focus on exploitation and class struggle, using a dialogue with Karl Polanyi's *The Great Transformation* to make this case. This is a limited agenda that insufficiently broaches gendered structures for reasons that I explain in discussing the development of the case studies that follow. However, in pursuing Tilly's encompassing question I hope I provide some strands of analytic thinking that have purchase in examining processes of structured inequality through time that inevitably involve more than class. If I meet with some success, then, this is a book about class struggle in Victorian England in a social world of (largely) adult white males actors, but *not* only about that process. In the conclusion I briefly discuss the contemporary sweep and insinuation of global capital in Asia to remind myself and suggest to readers that institutional analyses of exploitation are needed in the twenty-first century as well. The brief vignettes of the trials of Charles Taylor and George Tittensor with which I open the book have millions of contemporary counterparts around the globe that require our recognition and critical scrutiny.

This study was conceived in the late 1990s, and given the speed of bringing it to fruition at times I have felt much affinity with the *Chelonoidis nigra* or giant tortoise. Moving slowly, slowly I have accumulated many debts atop my shell.

For an understanding of labor law in general and master and servant law more particularly I owe significant gratitude to Christopher Frank, Barry Godfrey, Douglas Hay, James Jaffe, John Orth, Robert Steinfeld, and Christopher Tomlins, who responded to my many naïve inquiries. Over the years conversations with Mary Vogel expanded my knowledge of the sociological and historical analysis of the law. Patty Ewick, Susan Silbey, and Austin Sarat were patient mentors in sociolegal studies. Fred Block and Margaret Somers were my indispensable guides to Karl Polanyi. Through the years Colin Barker has provided inspired conversation and commentary on Marxism. Robb Robinson schooled me in the history of Hull and its sea industries, and David Starkey, Laura Tabili, and Martin Wilcox also supplied welcome counsel on maritime history. S. R. H. Jones provided valuable assistance in understanding the history of the Redditch needle industry. Carol Morgan offered her deep understanding of the Black Country metal trades. Marguerite W. Dupree, Derek Phillips, and Richard Whipp graciously provided insights on the pottery industry and the Black Country. J. A. Yelling offered his vast knowledge of East Worcestershire agriculture.

Those readers who have done historical research know that archivists are the lynchpins of success. I have legions of them to thank. Staffs at the following libraries and archives made my primary historical work possible: the British Library Newspaper Library, the British Public Record Office, the Harvard Business School Baker Library, the Keele University Library, the Kingston upon Hull City Archives, the University of London Goldsmiths' Library, the London School of Economics British Library of Economic and Political Science, the Redditch Library, the Staffordshire County Public Record Office, the Stoke-upon-Trent City Archives, Walsall Local History

Centre, and the Worcestershire County Public Records Office. I also want to express my appreciation for the ready assistance provided by the Mount Holyoke College Library, the University of Massachusetts DuBois Library, the Oxford Bodleian Libraries, the Smith College Neilson Library and the Stoke-upon-Trent Central City Library. I am also grateful to the directors of the Wedgwood Museum for access to the Wedgwood papers at Keele University.

A semester at the Centre Socio-Legal studies at Oxford offered me a valuable opportunity to complete my historical studies. A generous fellowship from the American Council of Learned Societies and the support of the Smith College Faculty Development Fund made this research possible.

The support of friends and family kept me going. My dear friend Sabina Knight was my indefatigable supporter. Grad school friends Nicki Beisel and Irene Padavic have offered sustenance over the years. My colleagues in the sociology department at Smith have kept me buoyant. My family—mother Beverly, late father Erwin, and brother Alan—have been everything that family should be, and were with me every step of the way.

Doug Mitchell at the University of Chicago Press made initial inquiries into this project and provided enthusiastic support. He, Tim McGovern, and Kyle Wagner guided me through the publication process. Anonymous readers for the manuscript provided both encouragement and helpful critique.

This book is dedicated to two mentors. David Spring was my history thesis adviser at Johns Hopkins University. He warmly took me in when I was full of energy but not direction and patiently introduced me to modern English social history. Chuck Tilly was my graduate adviser and dissertation chair at Michigan. He introduced me to deep systematic thinking on the large-scale structures and processes that transform the world. And Chuck enthusiastically supported my research agenda when I moved in a different direction from his monumental Great Britain Study. I hope that readers can see the mark of these two mentors in this work.

PART I

CHAPTER ONE

Introduction

Charles Taylor stood defiant in front of Hull (East Yorkshire) magistrate Thomas Travis. The twenty-year-old fishing apprentice, having already been directed once by the magistrate to serve his master, Brazillai Cook, and board his ship, had been brought back by his master for his persistent refusal. Taylor, who had a wife and child to support, insisted that Cook provide him with wages so that he could keep them out of the poorhouse. Travis urged Taylor, who by the terms of his indenture had no claim to wages, "to go to sea like a good lad." But the apprentice responded that "England was a free country, and he would not be treated like a slave." Although the magistrate applauded Taylor's decision to marry the mother of his child, and admonished the master to cease hitting his apprentice to compel his labor, he nonetheless would have none of what he perceived as the apprentice's clear obstinacy. His swift justice was forty days in prison.[1]

Not long after Taylor had suffered his day in court to the east in Hanley, Staffordshire George Tittensor stood before the town's magistrates charged by Joseph Clementson, a prominent pottery manufacturer, with missing a day of work. Like Taylor, Tittensor too found himself before the bench for his second time. He, perhaps somewhat contritely, admitted his transgression and that his inability to engage in his work the following morning was due to his being drunk. He was found guilty and the court ordered that he return to work and that a total of 19 shillings 6 pence (perhaps a week's worth of wages) be deducted from his wages in the coming weeks.[2]

Both Taylor and Tittensor likely were prosecuted under the Master and Servant Act of 1823, and under this and related statues the charges against them were criminal, not civil. Workers under a contract of service could be prosecuted for being absent from work, disobeying an employer's orders, not committing full effort to their jobs, leaving work without proper notice (which covered much strike activity), and a number of other "offenses." And Taylor's and Tittensor's experiences with the law were not rare or unusual. We will see in chapter 3 that working people in mid-Victorian England were about as or more likely to be prosecuted as criminals for such work issues as they were for breaches of local acts, vagrancy, and begging. As important, these laws were not relics of a feudal past to be supplanted by more "modern" forms of control: they were developed and consolidated during the Industrial Revolution in response to employers' demands.

This study focuses on the experiences of Taylor, Tittensor, and hundreds of other such workers to take a fresh look at capitalist development and labor control in the English Industrial Revolution. I examine the ways in which capitalists in a number of different industries and regions turned to the law as a staple of their control of the labor market and workplace. I pursue six related questions as to how and why these capitalists found in a series of statutes, termed master and servant law, an effective means of exerting this power. Why did pottery manufacturers, fishing trawler owners, and other employers adopt strategies of labor control that significantly depended on the law? In what ways did the specifics of the production processes in their industries set the conditions by which the law became a strategy of choice? What were the economic, political, and social circumstances in their locales that led them to see the law as an important tool for labor discipline? How did recourse to the law for workplace control become embedded in the routine governance and organization of the production process? To what extent did these capitalists' reliance on the law affect the ways in which they considered alternatives to the organization of the production and ultimately changes in the law itself? And to what degree and in what ways did these legal strategies of labor control affect the trajectory of these enterprises within their industries?

Such questions matter not only for the analysis industrial development, labor control, and class conflict in nineteenth-century England, but also for more encompassing concerns shared by historians and social scientists involving both capitalist development and power and exploitation in the workplace. An enduring metanarrative of the rise of Great Britain as the first industrial nation has deep roots stretching back into the nineteenth century, both in historiography and social theory. Marx's trenchant theorizing of the rise of modern capitalism, of course, depended heavily on his analyses of "England, the native land of large-scale industry," but so too for many other classical theorists of Western industrial society and modernity to which we still turn (1976, 390). As Rebecca Emigh observes, echoes of this historical template of an "inevitable and natural rise of English capitalism" in which the British case provides a path for development "through which all countries march" can still be found in scholarly debates on the transition to capitalism (2005, 356).

Marx's theorizing of the capitalist labor process depended heavily on his examination of the British case. Within his historical materialist perspective the two were intertwined in his pursuit of unmasking the exploitative core of capitalism. In *Capital* and other works Marx offered a picture of how capitalists, compelled by the ceaseless quest for capital accumulation, transformed the social relations in and of production for ever greater exploitation of their workers. This drive to wring more value out of workers' labor led capitalists down a long path of reorganizing the labor process to wrest control of work from the workers themselves. His panoramic vision started with the humble agricultural laborer and artisan and ended with the enchained factory worker. Marx's account of this process charted the successive strategies capitalists employed to exert complete domination in the workplace. Collecting workers in workshops for direct supervision, the lengthening of the work day, the imposition of piece rates, an increasing division of labor, and ultimately the use of machinery were part of a progression through which capitalists eventually subsumed workers under their control. In Great Britain's "dark satanic mills" Marx found the destination of this path; an organization of production in which workers had been stripped of all autonomy and agency, degraded into bearers of labor power in the complete service of capitalists.

One of Marx's abiding questions throughout these analyses was how capitalist control of the labor process was achieved and transformed. In answering this question the sociologist Michael Burawoy, in accord with many others, replies with a straightforward admonition: "we must go beyond Marx" (1985, 29). He does so by offering a theory of how distinct political apparatuses of production are combined with the labor process itself, creating historically contingent ways in which capitalists structure coercion and consent in the workplace. Burawoy's emphasis on how both production and state politics combine with the social relations in production points to an opening to the ways in which law structures the power dynamics of the workplace.

Casting a historian's eye over nineteenth-century England Richard Price also goes beyond Marx in analyzing how chains of authority in and outside the workplace converged to produce forms of control and resistance at work. Price argues that for most of the century workers maintained significant autonomy at the "frontiers of control" and that capitalists drew on both tradition and the law to exert control. His focus on the law in particular substantially reorients our vision of its role as a means through which capitalists wielded power in the production process.

Feminists also go beyond Marx by explaining how the social relations in and of production are organized through gender difference. Institutionalized practices of gender difference shaped divisions between household and workplace, constructions of skill and autonomy and the organization of authority in the workplace. Law was increasingly part of these practices in some industrial sectors in nineteenth-century Britain. It was layered on existing gender organization to define how women and children were "unfree agents" requiring state protection, and created dilemmas for adult male workers concerning their true "independence" both at work and in the polity.

Burawoy thus recognizes varying institutional structures through which coercion and controls are organized but does not wholly see the embeddedness of law within the production process. Price highlights the centrality of law on continuing struggles to exercise authority, but does not pursue systematically an institutional perspective on how and why some capitalists turned to the law. Feminists foreground the role of gender difference in constituting the labor force and workplace governance, though there is additional ground to cover on how the law variably contributed to these processes. All complement one another in the efforts to go beyond Marx but, as I argue below, we should go somewhat further.

The "further" that I offer involves several theoretical and analytical steps. The first is a reading of Marx's theory that recognizes the materiality of the law. By this I mean that the law is not just part of a "superstructure" that provides ideological legitimation for an economic "base": it is a set of social practices that plays an important constitutive role in the organization of the social relations in and of production. "Capitalism," Philip Corrigan and Derek Sayer remark, "is not just an economy, it is a regulated set of social forms of life" (1985, 188). The argument I pursue in this book is that the contests over the "social forms" of the workplace in nineteenth-century Britain could be shaped as much by legal practice as they were by the division of labor or the use of machinery.

Among the legal factors examined here, particular consideration is given to the labor contract. The labor contract organizes power in both directions in labor relations, that is, outward in the labor market and inward into the workplace. Because of this potential to coordinate power in both directions, it was and is a critical legal site for the struggle over labor subjugation and autonomy. Moreover, as we will see in the historical analyses to come, the labor contract through master and servant law provided capitalists the opportunity to reinforce their authority in the workplace with their control of or access to local political and legal institutions.

Thus, my second step is to develop a more concerted institutional analysis of class power and the ways its organization and distribution in space and place beyond the point of production impact struggles over control in the workplace itself. Concurring with Jeffrey Haydu (1988, 1998, 2008) I argue that we need to map the institutional configurations of power and authority in workplace locales to understand the ways in which political and economic institutions could be tied together to organize judicial authority. These configurations made the law a viable, reliable, and sometimes preferable option for capitalist exertion of control of the workplace. In order to understand the workings of the law not merely or largely as the overlaying of "state" authority on local practice, I focus on local institutional configurations of power that provided opportunities for such legal practices. As George Steinmetz (1993), Bob Jessop (2008), and many geographers maintain, what we often view in shorthand terms as the working of the state is given form and content through the micropolitics of local practices. And as sociolegal scholars have for many years taken for granted, legal practice does not emerge fully formed from law on the books. The nineteenth-century parliamentary statutes and common law governing labor relations lived in the local courts.

A third step is to combine insights from historical materialism and historical institutionalism in an analytic framework. The former provides analytic tools for interrogating the processes of capitalist exploitation, while the latter emphasizes the ways in which historical configurations of institutions provide the social and political structures through which power and resources are routinely mobilized. Some members of the latter camp have offered their institutional perspective as alternatives to the former. However, I see important affinities that can add to class analyses of the historical structuring of the labor process. Both centrally concern how durable social structures construct and maintain asymmetries of power. In doing so both focus on chains of historical processes. For the purposes of this study historical institutionalism offers a key set of conceptual insights. I will draw on them to analyze the reliance of some capitalists on the law for labor control. The first is an attention to how actors make pragmatic choices within institutional constraints at critical conjunctures, as well as the lasting consequences of these choices. The second is to examine how such choices become embedded in specific institutional orders, and thus become accepted and often beneficial paths for ongoing action, but perhaps also create an inertial drag on change. The case studies present three specific contexts in which employers in each of the industries turned to the law and made it an accepted practice for labor control. They highlight particular configurations of the production process, the social relations in them, the shape of labor markets, and the local organization of power, among several factors. As I argue in the following chapters, it is the combination of these perspectives that offers fuller insights into how and why some capitalists in Victorian England turned to the law.

Exactly how and why some capitalists turned to the law in constructing labor control regimes will be examined in the three case studies of Hanley, Hull, and Redditch. In three quite distinct towns and industries groups of employers relied in part on the law for labor market and workplace discipline. In each case we will examine how a conjuncture of the dilemmas of labor control and opportunities for routine deployment led to its pragmatic adoption as a solution. These studies highlight how the configuration of power in local political and legal institutions, in addition to the "law on the books," provided the openings for such strategies. These conjunctures of needs and opportunities varied significantly across England: in many parts of the industrial and agricultural theaters, law was only a bit player in the everyday drama of autonomy and control. The case studies give us specific though incomplete answers to the questions I have raised above. They are not nor can they be definitive for even the English case. As I discuss in their preface the analyses do not rely on a well-structured comparative-historical methodology, but frankly rather on a *carpe diem* opportunism to gain some purchase on the past. In the end, following Burawoy, they are an invitation to "go beyond."

In the last section of the book, having joined historical institutionalism and historical materialism to sharpen the analysis of labor control, I turn to the former to revise an important institutionalist analysis of the Industrial Revolution. Karl Polanyi's *The Great Transformation* has received significant renewed attention, both by critics of neoliberal globalization and the academics who study movements against it, for his analysis of the institutional embeddedness of economy within society. More particularly they draw on Polanyi's analysis of the "double movement" in nineteenth-century England when the market was disembedded from its societal moorings, creating a laissez-faire "market society," only to be re-embedded in response to a general societal countermovement against the destruction of unrestrained markets.

I revisit this narrative of the double movement in order to pose a reinterpretation. Drawing on examinations of labor law and juridical institutions from earlier in the volume, I argue that labor remained embedded in a legal system structured to serve capitalists' interests. Indeed, to the extent that there was attenuation between political and economic institutions, it was ultimately accomplished at the hands of labor unions and their allies. Deeply skeptical of the role of the courts in the governance of labor relations, working-class leaders sought to remove their affairs from juridical oversight. Given the institutional constraints these leaders faced, the result was to opt for a liberal model of labor relations in which government was kept at arms' length from their relations and conflicts with capital. My revised narrative, therefore, presents the continued embeddedness of labor relations under common and statutory law favorable to capitalists until the last quarter of the nineteenth century, when working-class leaders pursued legislative reform more clearly separating labor relations from state intervention.

The empirical contours of this study are fairly constrained: my foci are on the law and labor control and how the former became, for some capitalists, a strategy for the latter in mid-Victorian Britain. Yet such a study ultimately involves the analysis of power and inequality. In books and papers propounding his relational perspective on these core social issues, Charles Tilly (1998, 2002, 2008) advised his readers that they could only be understood by combining top-down and bottom-up analyses. Both in the institutional history of master and servant laws and my revisiting of Polanyi's narrative I focus on the machinations of state politics and national economic transformation that gave rise to and ultimately sealed the demise of master and servant and other labor laws. In three case studies I go local, analyzing how particular industries drew on the law to control the workplace given specific organizations of the production process and the immediate institutional orders through which the law was administered. The top-down and bottom-up analyses yield different insights, and I hope that the combination of the two, as Tilly recommended, give a fuller accounting of the workings of resistance to structures of power and inequality.

This volume starts with theoretical considerations. In chapter 2 I focus on theories of the labor process, starting with Marx's perspective and his somewhat scattered reflection on the role of the law. I then discuss the ways in which Burawoy, Price, and feminist analysts successfully move beyond Marx, while highlighting aspects of law and the labor process that remained to be pursued. In chapter 3 I take up these issues by discussing the materiality of the law as part of the social relations in and of production. I make the case for stitching together historical materialism and historical institutionalism for a more comprehensive analytic framework. This chapter also presents a history of the rise of master and servant and other labor law, focusing on how the law emerged as a new form of capitalist labor control during the Industrial Revolution. The succeeding three chapters are case studies, which I preface with an overview of their selection, the compiling of data on master and servant cases for each, and some cautionary notes on their limits. Each case study focuses on quite distinct industries and locales. The first, chapter 4, examines earthenware manufacturing in the famous Potteries district of the Midlands and analyzes the use of the law in Hanley, Staffordshire. Hanley was one the largest of six towns that composed the district, and was the home of a mix of both quite large and modest manufactories. Next, chapter 5 turns to the northeast coast and Kingston-upon-Hull, East Yorkshire. Hull was one of the three largest English ports at the time and contained a number of manufacturing industries that complemented a substantial Baltic trade in raw materials. For all of this range of economic activity it was the fish trawling industry that far and away occupied the local court the most, and I examine why this trade was so heavily dependent on the law. Finally, in chapter 6 I move back to the lower Midlands and Redditch, Worcestershire. Redditch was a small town that was the center of a needle manufacturing industry with international reach. It also was a market center for livestock, dairy and related farming which serviced Birmingham and other nearby cities of greater size. Master and servant prosecutions consumed more of the local court's time than in many other towns in England, and I examine how both needle manufacturers and farmers gravitated to it in their efforts to control their labor forces. Chapter 7 returns to the national level to revisit Polanyi's analysis of the Great Transformation, and I offer concluding remarks collecting the results of both top-down and bottom-up analyses in chapter 8.

With some modest exceptions Marx saw public law stopping at the factory and workshop gates, viewing the interior as a domain in which capitalists exercised their own private laws for exploitation. This study demonstrates how such gates were not only *not* secured but also often wide open. The book thus offers what I hope readers will find to be a fresh analysis of the role of the law in labor control. Going beyond Marx necessitates an institutional analysis not contained in his theory or fully explicated in contemporary revisions of his work. I invite readers to go beyond with me, both to see how law and labor were intertwined in the English Industrial Revolution and to reflect more generally on their relationship in structuring power in the workplace.

CHAPTER TWO

The Labor Process and Beyond

The central questions motivating this study ask how law became an important part of labor control regimes in several different locales and industries. In answering them we will enter the world of mid-Victorian England and examine complex institutional relationships that go beyond the workplace, though our focus in this chapter is squarely on it. Social scientists and historians have been investigating authority and control at work for many decades, and for much of the twentieth century these analyses of the workplace and labor relations rarely had recourse to Marx's theory. Social and economic historians offered accounts centered on the development of "modern" labor unions, with a story centered on the institutionalization of labor relations between employers and workers. Social science generally concentrated on organizational studies of efficiency and the social psychology of workplace relations. Underlying many of these analyses was a story that foregrounded patterns of accommodation and conciliation based in a master narrative of modernity's advancement.

By the 1970s the analysis of work veered substantially, rediscovering Marx's emphases on domination and exploitation. Class analysis was back, and in a big way. Ignited in part by Harry Braverman's *Labor and Monopoly Capital*, social scientists and historians burrowed into the dynamics of the workplace to analyze the control of workers in the labor process. Historians inspired by Eric Hobsbawm, E. P. Thompson, and other "new social historians" illuminated the ways in which the light cast by capitalist development and class struggle bathed all aspects of everyday life, including the world of work, in its hue. Marxist-inspired accounts of exploitation proliferated to explain the capitalist assault on the workplace. In this narrative capitalists wrested away knowledge and skill from workers. Capitalists disempowered workers through grasping at the roots of the labor process as they reorganized the workplace, and workers in turn struggled against increasing control. The accumulation of these studies offered readers an increasingly panoramic historical vision of a class control and struggle forged in successive battles at work and beyond.

Over the succeeding decades numerous analysts have extended and critiqued this work, and some have moved in quite different (even antagonistic) directions from its professed Marxist roots. In this chapter we will be moving through labor process theory founded on Marx's vision and the accretion of amendments and challenges to it, with the ultimate goal of understanding of how legality is part and parcel of the labor process.

To start this journey, however, we first return briefly to Karl Marx and his critical vision of modern capitalist development. Marx's writings serve as the foundation upon which labor process theory ultimately rests. His commentary—and more vitally his silence—on the place of the law in the processes that consumed his intellectual attention also represent critical sign posts for our subsequent theory building and analysis.

IN THE BEGINNING

One of Marx's foremost concerns was to unearth the underlying historical development of the capitalist mode of production. His subterranean investigations, below the world of what he deemed distorted appearances, led him to analyze the processes that not only birthed this system but also impelled its development. Marx investigated the labor process to account for how capitalists devised strategies to intensify surplus extraction, the process by which capitalists exploited workers by retaining the surplus value that went beyond meeting their needs. While capitalist ideology mystified the exchange of work for wages as an exchange in the market like any other, in reality it was distinctive. The deal enacted between capitalist and worker was for potential labor power, whose value was only realized in its ongoing exercise for the period of contract. While under contractual agreement the labor power belonged to the capitalist, his quandary was that the worker still exercised immediate functional control. What the capitalist actually owned after the initial transaction remained indeterminate, creating an irresolvable and fundamental conflict between capitalist and worker. This was the impetus for the capitalist's quest for control of the social and technical relations of production.

Marx schematically analyzed the capitalist's dilemma of insuring surplus extraction through two phases in an historical tour of the English industrial revolution. Under absolute surplus extraction (or formal subsumption) capitalists became the direct managers of the labor process and labor became "socialized."[1] During the "period of cooperation" they first extended supervisory control by bringing previously independent artisans together in larger workshops to stiffen work discipline. In the subsequent "period of manufacture" in the latter part of the eighteenth century, capitalists ratcheted up the intensity of the labor process still further by refining the division of labor and thus quickening the pace of production. They also lengthened the workday without additional pay or paid piece rates rather than day wages to force greater productivity.[2] All of these schemes, Marx concluded, had limited utility, and ultimately capitalists turned to other means.

Compelled by competition, capitalists moved into a second phase of relative surplus extraction (or real subsumption). Once the labor process entered the period of "modern industry" with the dawn of the factory, it was truly revolutionized. With the "direct application of science and technology" capitalists seized complete control of the knowledge, organization, and pace of production and thoroughly transformed the labor process (Marx 1976, 1035; 1994, 106). Steam power and geared taskmasters completely dominated workers—stripping all discretion and control—reducing them to the simple "homogenous" labor power compelled to attend the dictates of the machine. For Marx this was the first "specifically capitalist mode of production" and he provided readers with graphic accounts of the hulking cotton mills to illustrate its tragic human impact (1976, 1021).

Marx's thoughts on the role of law in these changes, and concerning labor control more generally, are unsystematic and somewhat contradictory. He noted that a secure legal construction of private property and its unencumbered circulation and "free" individuals were the foundations for successful capitalism in general and the exchange of labor in particular (1976, 178).[3] In his initial reflections on capitalist development and law the latter appeared largely as a fraying feudal restraining tie on the energies of a maturing capitalism, strands successively snapping with each tug of expansion: "the capitalist mode of production itself raises obstacles in the way of its own tendency, but it pushes to one side all *legal* and other *extra-economic* obstructions standing in the way of this versatility" (1976, 1013; emphasis in original).[4]

In considering the labor contract Marx focuses his attention on the sphere of commodity exchange, the "surface" dynamics of capitalism, rather than that of production. This is the realm of distortions in which relations between capitalist and worker appear as a matter of complete equality. "They contract as free persons, who are equal before the law. Their contract is the final result in which their joint will finds a common legal expression.

Equality, because each enters into relation with the other, as with a simple owner of commodities, and they exchange equivalent for equivalent. Property, each disposes only of what is his own" (1976, 280).[5] But in focusing on the economic basis of the labor contract as part of the mystifying order of appearances Marx largely loses the opportunity to analyze how legal practices and state institutions can structure power in the sphere of production.

This can be seen in his analysis of factory production. In Marx's analysis of modern industry the factory wall represented a social boundary to state interference as well as physical barrier. The interior of the factory was a world unto itself, one in which the capitalist was lord and master, and who therefore established the laws of his kingdom. "In the factory code, the capitalist formulates his autocratic power over his workers like a private legislator, and purely as an emanation of his own will, unaccompanied by either that division of responsibility otherwise so much approved by the bourgeoisie, or the still more approved representative system. This code is merely the capitalist caricature of the social regulation of the labour process which becomes necessary in co-operation on a large scale and in the employment of common instruments of labour, and especially machinery" (1976, 549–50; see also 902). In this sense factory politics was basically autonomous from the law of the realm.

The one significant exception to this analysis of the law comes in his discussion of the factory acts, which were passed ostensibly for the protection of children and women. "Nothing," Marx observed, "characterizes the spirit of capital better than the history of English factory legislation from 1833 to 1864" (1976, 390). Marx depicted the push for the acts as a "protracted and more or less concealed civil war between the capitalist class and the working class" in which the latter countered the former in political society because of capitalists' utter domination within the factory.[6] After three decades of resistance the great capitalists relented not out of recognition for workers' rights, but because of a pragmatic realization that such state interference disadvantaged their smaller competitors and allowed them further consolidation of control. In a paradoxical fashion the acts also prodded laggard industries to overcome perceived impediments to modernization and hasten capital concentration. "No poison kills vermin with more certainly," he caustically noted, "than the Factory Act removes such 'natural barriers'" (1976, 605). On the whole, then, Marx pronounced the factory acts as a hard-fought but modest victory for workers. Most important, his analysis suggested little of the ways in which legality impacted the labor process beyond accelerating the underlying tendencies of a maturing capitalism toward modern industry.

Marx's legacy with regards to the analysis of the capitalist control of work is in some ways foundational, but in other ways problematic. In his theory of capitalist development he explained why capitalist control of the labor process was essential and provided truncated historical perspectives on how it evolved. Yet Marx the dialectician, the theorist who saw contradiction and conflict at the heart of social transformation, shed little light on these aspects of the transformation. He expended relatively little attention on the actual processes by which skill, discretion, and control were wrested from workers or how the latter resisted and shaped these processes. More generally—and this is an issue that we will be engaging throughout this book—Marx did not fully explore the social dynamics of exploitation he saw as so central to the capitalist system.

Of course, Marx's fundamental point was that any mode of production is a system of social relations, and that capitalism was not the natural order of political economy's acclaim. To introduce a concept we will be deploying later, Marx argued that the productive activity of the "economy" was necessarily *embedded* in social relations. For this reason some social scientists portray Marx as an early institutionalist.[7] However, in his latter works (those in which he provided his most complete discussions of exploitation), Marx's focus was on burrowing into what he understood as the interior of the capitalist system to discover its inner logic. This was an exercise in structural excavation, and in conducting this foundational analysis social relations receded in his vision. Michael Burawoy (2003), whose perspective we will engage below, suggests that Marx never really resurfaced to offer a full-fledged analysis of society under capitalism. From the vantage point of this study I think it more appropriate to suggest that, in pursuing the inner logic of capitalism, Marx advanced his analysis of the inner logic of capitalism's deep structures without a corresponding investigation of its institutional dynamics.[8] His discussion of the separation of the world of the factory from the world outside the wall provides an apt metaphor from what transpires in his own work: it is why Marx provides us with occasional and uneven insights into the place of law in the social relations of production.[9] A key object of this study is to make such connections.

THE LEGACY

After almost a century of neglect, historians and social scientists reengaged Marx's work on the labor process. The return to Marx was motivated by dissatisfaction with the dominant narratives of the Industrial Revolution and economic development in which technological innovation was the bright star that guided industrial transformation, yielding bounties of greater efficiencies and prosperity. Scholars returned to Marx's theory of capitalist subjugation and his account of the rise of modern industry, reversing the causal ordering between social and technical transformations. At times this reengagement involved new chapters and headings for this story, updating and refining the broad outlines of characters and plot concerning skill and work discipline. Some theorists pursued lines of analysis that abandoned one or more of Marx's core assumptions, such as class struggle as the progressive dynamic of history or dialectic transformation, but retained his materialist framework and emphasis on fundamental conflicts in the workplace.[10] Most studies drawing on what is now termed labor process theory (LPT) analyze control of the workplace in the sweep of history beyond Marx's lifetime, and highlight some dynamics less relevant to the case studies reviewed in this volume. In this section I briefly review the work of Harry Braverman, who reignited debates on the labor process, and then turn to two scholars who offer historical perspectives that particularly relate the theoretical and empirical concerns of this study, Michael Burawoy and Richard Price.

In *Labor and Monopoly Capital*, Harry Braverman sought to renew Marx's analysis of real subordination by focusing on the degradation and transformation of craft work under systems of mass production, or, as it frequently termed in shorthand, deskilling. He consciously anchored his perspective in an "objective" analysis of the labor process (1974, 27). In his analytic narrative of the nineteenth-century US capitalists sought to gain control over the labor process by subcontracting and the proliferation of alternative schemes of remuneration such as piecework (see also Clawson 1980). However capitalists continued to confront the problem of indeterminacy and, impelled by the imperatives of capitalism's inner logic of accumulation, they pressed forward with the deskilling process.

This undermining of craftworker control and the complete alienation of labor involved three core principles. The first was to disassociate the labor process from workers' skills. Then conception and execution were separated so that capitalists monopolized the mental labor in the production process. Finally, the labor process was reassembled, but with capitalists commanding exclusive understanding and decision making, with workers reduced to mere bodies of execution. Capitalists pursued the development of machinery to the extent that it offered a path to full exploitation. Science and technology were handmaidens of subordination, not masters (Braverman 1974, 115–19, 193–95, 227–30; Clawson 1980, 231–32).

The work by Braverman and others (for the US context) shifts the advent of real subordination from Marx's age of modern industry to the rise of monopoly capitalism in the late nineteenth and early twentieth centuries.[11] With the onset of large-scale mass production, and techniques of "scientific management" pioneered by the engineer Frederick Taylor, capital developed the resources, managerial capacities, and imperatives to seize the labor process at it roots (Braverman 1974, 53, 63, 90, 171, 181, 252; Clawson 1980, chap. 6). These transformations were neither simple nor linear. Braverman emphasized that while this followed a general underlying determinacy, the process was a "thread-by-thread weaving of the fabric of history, not the imposition of external formulas" (1974, 21).

Labor and Monopoly Capital prompted a number of studies of work degradation, but it also generated a standard set of critiques. Critics objected that deskilling analyses overlooked worker agency and resistance; failed to recognize the "subjective" aspects of the labor process including the cultural and institutional bases of management and labor control; lacked an appreciation for the uneven and contradictory development of capitalism; was based on too narrow or ambiguous a concept of skill and obscured its gendered bases; romanticized "craft" work and failed to offer a sustained analysis of the early industrial labor process; and neglected to analyze the social organization of capitalists themselves as a factor.[12] Among these critics were Michael Burawoy and Richard Price, who offered solutions to these shortcomings.

Burawoy acknowledges the achievements of Braverman and Marx, but also focuses on their incompleteness.[13] He argues that Marx errantly generalized the specific production politics of the contemporary English factory system as the singular means of capitalist domination as did Braverman for the rise of US monopoly capitalism. With this misstep both Marx and Braverman developed theories of how the social relations in production create a deterministic path for capitalist exploitation, while failing to recognize how the broader social relations of production equally affect these relations. As a result they missed how historical struggles contingently shape the capitalist production process and how coercion and consent, the political and ideological, are intertwined in these developments.[14]

To address these issues Burawoy starts with two fundamental distinctions. The first is between the labor process ("the coordinated set of activities and relations involved in the transformation of raw materials into useful products") and the political apparatuses of production ("the institutions that regulate and shape struggles in the workplace"). These two vary independently of one another and both shape the interests and capacities of workers to respond to capitalists (1985, 87, 123; 1984a, 274). Second, he identifies two forms of politics that shape specific forms of domination and exploitation, a specific production politics forged in that area and state politics.[15] Burawoy's purpose in making these distinctions is twofold. The first is to recognize that any "production process must itself be seen as an inseparable combination of its economic, political and ideological aspects," and that each has a relative autonomy in shaping labor control regimes. Relations within any production apparatus are based both in coercion and consent—the ways in which capitalists, managers, and workers recognize their interests in the workplace and organize themselves to these ends—and the labor process itself is only one of several determinants of how class relations in the workplace are configured (1985, 24–25, 59).

Second, both production and state politics have independent effects on the development of any historically specific production apparatus and they mutually condition one another. The structure of power within the social relations of production shapes the ways in which capitalists, managers, and workers understand and pursue their interests in the arena of state politics. State policies affect workers' dependence on the wage bargain for their livelihood and limit the ways in which capitalists and managers exercise domination in the workplace. This interaction is time and place dependent: there is no single inner logic that drives the configuration or transformation of the production process (Burawoy 1985, 125–26, 260). In this scheme the law makes independent contributions to domination: "The legal structure, for example, has a coherence and dynamic of its own, and its precepts cannot be arbitrarily changed by external forces. Moreover, it performs a 'legitimating' function by masking relations of production, in particular by creating distinctions between people and things, by blurring distinctions between different types of things (things consumed productively—machines—and things consumed unproductively—shirts) and different types of people (those who must sell their labour power and those who own the means of production) as 'free and equal' citizens" (1985, 60).

On this basis Burawoy developed a comparative-historical perspective on what he later termed factory or production regimes (1985, 2001). He identifies four factors that contribute to the constitution of a production regime. First, the degree of intra-industrial capitalist competition determines the introduction of new technologies and work intensification. Second is Marx's distinction between the formal and real subordination of labor. Third is the degree to which workers rely on their subsistence completely by the sale of their labor power to the capitalist, and the ways in which their maintenance and reproduction through ties of kin and community affect the sale of labor power. Finally, Burawoy differentiates between external and internal state intervention. In the former the state insures the free play of market forces but does not inject itself directly into the workplace or workers' economic security. In the latter the state intercedes directly by placing constraints on the exercise of capitalists' power in the workplace and by offering workers forms of economic and social insurance that mediate their relationships with capital (1984, 28, 31).

Using these dimensions to construction a typology of production regimes Burawoy identifies two ideal-type capitalist regimes, the despotic—in which domination in principally enacted through managerial and economic coercion—and the hegemonic, in which workers are ideologically consent to domination through what is seen as a mutually understood bargain or system of reciprocity (though coercion is not entirely absent) (Burawoy and Wright 1990, 254). There is an overall logic by which capitalist systems evolve from despotic to hegemonic regimes, and by which the state intrudes into the political apparatuses of production, but the exact mechanisms by which this is accomplished vary significantly by time and place (Burawoy 1985, 127–28, 138).

Reconceptualizing the history of the English Industrial Revolution and its "dark satanic mills" Burawoy argues that Marx inappropriately generalized a particular ideal-type of factory regime of the contemporary cotton factories, the relatively rare market despotism. This exists when the "regulation of the labor process is constituted by the whip of the market" (1985, 12, 251–52). Stripped of any other possibility of producing a means of subsistence, workers are at the mercy of capitalists, the workplace is under the latter's total control, and in the throes of competitive capitalism capitalists constantly seek new ways of intensifying exploitation.[16]

Charting the larger course of labor control in these mills, Burawoy examines a series of despotic regimes, the company state, patriarchal despotism, and paternalistic despotism. He finds the last two most prevalent. Under patriarchal despotism adult males workers retained some control in the workplace as subcontractors of the labor of women and children (who were often family members). With paternalistic despotism the factory owner sought to construct an encompassing personal dependence that covered the workplace, family, and community. In this last shift Burawoy argues that the patriarchal regime of factory labor shaped larger class interests, as it provided the rationale for male workers to press for state regulation of working hours under the guise of protecting women and children in the push for a ten-hour day. The resultant passage and struggle over a series of factory acts, with their state-mandated limits of the workday, in part led to the gradual transformation from a despotic to a hegemonic regime. Overall, though, Burawoy concludes, "In England the extension of political concessions to the working class during the second half of the nineteenth century—voting rights, trade union recognition, regulation of the working day, the repeal of the Masters and Servants Laws—tended to insulate production politics from state politics" (1985, 275). In the English case the greater involvement of the state in the arena of production politics and the rise of the hegemonic regime waited until the new century.

William Staples (1987; Staples and Staples 2001) provides a more explicit theoretical framework for the transformation of factory regimes. Based in an analysis of a transformation in hardware production for the period, Staples argues that "significant changes in the technical and social organization of work occur during critical historical periods in which either capital or labor is required to respond to contradictions emerging from the mode of production" (1987, 85). This depends on the historical sequencing of changes in the four factors of production politics outlined by Burawoy. In the specific case of the Kenrick's hardware firm analyzed by Staples, state regulation of child labor, followed by their growing market power and a deflationary period that squeezed profit margins, prompted the company to adopt mechanized production techniques and to wrest production control from the skilled male workers. This was coupled with the exchange of greater welfare provisions in return for worker loyalty and it greased the transition to the complete subordination of labor under a paternalistic regime (1987, 72–80).

In developing his historical perspective on labor control Richard Price concurs with Burawoy on the inadequacies of Marx's and Braverman's shared economic determinism (Price 1984a, 217; 1984b, 120–21; 1984c, 91–93). Price also argues for a perspective on labor control that expands beyond the confines of the labor process, but from a different analytic orientation to control and resistance. Workplace collaboration (that serves the material interests of both capitalists and workers) is founded fundamentally in an ongoing dynamic of subordination and resistance, acquiescence, and dissent.[17] For Price it is "the search for authority that integrates various aspects of the [labor] process" and the indeterminacy of this authority that underlies workplace conflict (1984b, 119; 1986, 72). He too emphasizes the organization of power outside the immediate labor process, but does not make specific distinctions between production and state politics. Rather he urges us to analyze the configuration of "chains of connection" between work systems and authority, the ways in which they converged in the workplace, and how these patterns changed over time (1986, 43). Authority was organized in institutions that gave material forces their particular social forms: in organizations of workers and capitalists, labor and production markets, communities, families, and multiple levels of politics and state authority. The technical and material dimensions of the labor process set the conditions for the mobilization of authority by both sides, but they led to quite different forms of accommodation and struggle given this circulation of authority in and outside of the workplace.[18] We can start with the inner logic of capitalism, but our analyses ultimately rest on the hard work of historical excavation to unearth the dynamics of the workplace.

Price suggests that if we set our sights on everyday life in the workplace we find the ongoing contradictions between accommodation and opposition at the "frontiers of control," as capitalists and workers tested the limits of their relations. Crises of accumulation often accentuated the contradictions and impelled capitalists toward new solutions, but didn't necessarily lead to wholesale transformation. Moreover, traditions of the workplace shaped any new order. Workers carried with them forms of organization, techniques of labor, collective understandings of independence, and other aspects of social relations that they used as the bases of continued resistance, and shaped new forms of labor control in turn (1980, 148; 1983, 58–60, 65; 1984b, 12; 1986, 72, 81).

Drawing on this framework Price offers a history of labor control in nineteenth-century England that focuses on the continuing struggles within systems of formal subordination. Coupled with labor market control, these two factors continued to shape authority in the workplace. The push for real subordination occurred late in the century and was in many ways constrained by the tenacity of extant forms of control and resistance. Workers maintained substantial autonomy in the workplace, in part through forms of patriarchal subcontracting and craft control, and local informal conflict was the way in which both sides tested and policed the boundaries of control.[19]

For larger employers particularly, the key problem of labor discipline was production per se and what they viewed as the lack of social discipline among a disorderly working class, as opposed to intensifying productivity. Working within the limits of formal subordination they pursued at least two strategies. The first, paternalism, was an attempt to constrain male workers' independence using traditional hegemonic forms of hierarchy and obedience, given patriarchal autonomy in many trades. Capitalists focused on building compliance through structures of perceived reciprocity and mutuality, both in an attempt to legitimate their sovereignty. Workers did not internalize its vision of hierarchy, but saw it as part of the frontier of control for negotiation.[20]

A second major strategy was recourse to the law, which "was deeply implicated in the dynamic of industrial relations and, as such, it served to mediate the duties and obligation of the groups within the social hierarchy" (1986, 39). Price does not draw a division between production politics and state politics, and finds law implicated in control efforts in industrial discipline starting back into the eighteenth century and moving into the late nineteenth century.[21] Capitalists relied on a range of both statutory (especially master and servant law) and common law as tools to inhibit or prevent collective action, and punish or intimidate unruly workers to conform to their standards of workplace order and production.[22]

Contrary to Marx's famous dictum that the traditions of past generations weigh like a nightmare on the living, Price offers a narrative on nineteenth-century labor control in which continuities in the social relations of production provided both workers and capitalists with the understandings, forms of organization, and resources to engage in new bargains and struggles. Our task is to focus on how local contingencies in the everyday workplace and the communities they inhabited shaped both bargains and battles at the frontiers of control.

Both Burawoy and Price highlight the ways in which patriarchal hierarchies served as the basis for labor control. However neither systematically pursued the gendering of the workplace or the gendered organization of the reproduction of labor (Davies 1990; Warde 1989). Feminist scholars of the Industrial Revolution have refashioned the Marxian legacy to illuminate the ways gender shaped workplace organization and control, skill and the labor process, and state intervention. As Janet Greenlees asserts in her analysis of women in cotton manufacturing, "industrialization was not only a gender process, gender helped to define and interpret the process" (2007, 6). Feminists conceptualize gender as a cultural process through which economic institutions are constructed, and examine how gender difference configured household and workplace organization and how gender categories changed over the course of the eighteenth and nineteenth centuries.

Conceptions of masculinity and femininity were embedded in the notions of skill and autonomy.[23] As we will discuss in later chapters, worker independence and respectability were framed through dominant Victorian constructions of masculinity, and they served as the basis for workplace bargaining and conflict (McClelland 1996, 286–91). Conversely, state intervention on behalf of women workers from the first factory acts onwards was pursued because of their perceived essential dependence and vulnerability (Malone 2003; Rose 1992, 1996).[24]

Throughout the nineteenth century male artisans fought battles to exclude women from the workplace (Clark 1995). The movement from outwork to factory often involved the reconstruction of gender for specific occupations, and sometimes spurred conflicts between men and women (Rose 1992, chaps. 5–6).[25] If women entered a trade, the first impact of gender was generally segregation, with women restricted to ancillary positions with lower wages and subject to different forms of labor control (as we will see when we examine the pottery industry of Northern Staffordshire). Gender, however, was not a simple, uniform process for organizing the labor market or workplace. As Carol E. Morgan (2001) emphasizes, gendered divisions were a contingent outcome of the industrial development, and affected by the shape of labor markets and male workers' organization in addition to other factors. A number of industries, such as the small metal trades, coal mining, and powerloom weaving, demonstrate the breadth of variation and women's possibilities for greater parity (Morgan 2001; Osterud 1986; Rose 1992).

Burawoy, Price, and feminist theorists both build on and surpass Marx's insights into the labor process. All illuminate a politics in and of production that moves beyond the deterministic tendencies of Marx (and Braverman) to a more expansive understanding of labor control. They clarify the broader foundations of this control and workers' struggles against it, and explore the ways in which both are realized through specific historical configurations of coercion and consent. In so doing each contributes to a larger institutional analysis of how labor control is inevitably mediated by forces outside the immediate social relations in production. In the next chapter I elaborate an institutional perspective on the role of law in labor control. Here I lay out some problems that remain in the above advances.

While Michael Burawoy recognizes the relative autonomy of the law and its independent effects in production regimes, his discussion of its place in processes of exploitation tends to rely on two problematic dichotomies, that is, a distinction between the structural and superstructural, and one between an internal (production) and external (state) politics. Through the first dichotomy law is understood as part of the "expressive totality" that functions to ideologically legitimate the structural forms of capitalist domination (1985, 60). As we saw above, it operates to mystify and conceal through its classifications. However, as I argue more fully in the next chapter, there is an alternative reading of Marx's materialism and the place of law that resists this dichotomy. As Ellen Meiksins Wood argues, "Relations of production themselves take the form of particular juridical and political relations—modes of domination and coercion, forms of property and social organization—which are not mere secondary reflexes, not even just external supports, but constituents of these productive relations" (1995, 27). The legal and the economic are coupled dimensions of concrete forms of the social relations of production. In this reading law is more than an ideological form; it is an institutional process through which domination is realized.

Second, and following, there can be no neat division between production politics and state politics. Since there is always a legal dimension to the economic relations that are set in motion in the social relations of production, we cannot imagine that the law (or the state) lurks outside the boundaries of the factory walls under some regimes and intrudes under others. Drawing on the previous metaphor, Burawoy realizes the problem of the factory wall, but has not scaled it. Part of our larger analytical task is to advance an institutional analysis to understand the ways in which law always partly configures the capitalist employment relationship. As Charles Tilly (1998) powerfully argued, scripting and the generation of local knowledge are part of the dynamics through which routine interactions are organized as durable forms of exploitation in social structures. In the next chapter I will pursue how the law was often front and center in such practices, providing institutional mechanisms that routinized subjugation and channeled resistance.

Richard Price's emphases on "chains of connection" between forms of systems and authority and the importance of workplace traditions offer formative insights on these institutional forms. Likewise, his focus on the law as a key mediator of industrial relations provides an essential opening to a more protracted analysis. What I hope to add in subsequent chapters is greater clarity on how particular configurations of workplace organization, the structure of labor markets and the local institutional structure of power, among a set of factors, were important conditions for when and how capitalists deployed the law as a routine form of labor control. Law mattered, but it did not matter equally in all regions and industries, or in the same ways. Part of my task is to provide a more systematic account of the how and when through a more explicit institutional analysis.

Finally, feminist perspectives have gendered analyses of exploitation and provided accounts of how protective labor laws both were founded in gender difference and served to reinforced such distinctions. They lay a path for further explorations of how gender difference in the paid workplace was organized through law, and how this was intertwined with political institutions. However, as gender theorists are quick to note, gender distinctions are situational and variable. In the analyses I raise the possibility that capitalists and the courts at times might have disregarded distinctions of gendered difference in the pursuing and upholding labor subjugation.

Materialist theories of the labor process lack sufficient bases for explaining variations in how and why law mattered in labor control and resistance. And in some ways those who pursued such analyses have done so without sufficient attention to institutional dynamics of the processes they study. My intent in succeeding chapters is to integrate an institutional analysis with a historical materialism and illuminate how this meshing provides insights for both, theoretically and empirically. In the next chapter I address some important theoretical lacuna and offer an integration of historical materialism and institutionalism. This is not an exercise in grand theory, but a means to an end. That end is providing a perspective on how law was entwined in labor control regimes in mid-Victorian England, and to consider its ramifications on both the local and national levels. In the second half of the chapter we will make a foray into the history of the law and labor control regimes as we take a more detailed historical overview of the legal institutions that structured labor relations.

CHAPTER THREE

Law, Institutions, and Labor Control: Theory and History

In the last chapter we reviewed theories of the labor control that in many respects offer a bottom-up focus on power. Labor process theories start at the micro level, the point of production, and then cast their analytic vision upward and outward to explore external factors that contour capitalist labor relations. As we saw in surveying the work of Michael Burawoy, Richard Price, and feminist historians, their perspectives provide critical insights into the institutional structures that determine how labor control strategies are maintained and contested. In this chapter I add a top-down approach, melding a historical materialist perspective on labor control with historical institutionalism to analyze the place of the law in labor control regimes. The aim is to develop a macro framework for the analysis of capitalist institutions that fits with the bottom-up perspective of labor process theory. As Tilly (1998) observed, both bottom-up and top-down perspectives are necessary for a complete analysis of the workings of power.

To this end the chapter has three parts. The first argues that law is part and parcel of the social relations in and of production. All such relations have an economic, a technical, and a juridic form of practice. Law certainly ideologically casts these relations in particular ways, but it does more than ideological work and is never just external to the workplace. Second, I make the case that institutional analysis is both compatible with and necessary for class analyses of the labor control. I turn to a now-significant corpus of work within what is generally termed historical institutionalism to expand this framework. In their emphases on historical conjunctures, embeddedness, and path development, historical institutionalists offer important insights into how law became central in labor control regimes. Finally, I provide an overview of the English labor law that examines the institutional context in which capitalist labor relations developed in the nineteenth century. I chart how, over the course of the mid-eighteenth century and first half of the nineteenth, master and servant law was consolidated into a generalized contract of service that left most workers substantively "unfree" in the employment relationship. This survey also highlights how the development of other statutory and common law and the judicial system converged with the rise of master and servant law to produce legal institutions through which employers could exercise routine authority over the labor market and workplace.

THE MATERIALITY OF LAW

In the last chapter we noted that Marx's theoretical and empirical discussions of law and the labor process specifically, and capitalist development more generally, were sometimes contradictory and often cursory and incomplete. This has opened a wide swath of territory for competing explanations of the place of law. Perhaps the most widely recognized interpretation has fallen under a reading of Marx that differentiates between the base and superstructure, the metaphor he famously offered in the preface to his *Critique of Political Economy.* From this perspective, prominently advocated by G. A. Cohen (1978, 1988) among many others, a sharp distinction is drawn between the material realities of the base, which are the motor forces of history, and the ideological systems of legitimation, which hover above them in the superstructure. The superstructure obscures the real dynamics of the base and offers a distorted understanding of it, but does not play a determining role in social and economic life. Law, as part of the superstructure, serves to mystify material reality (see, for example, Collins 1982; Cotterell 1981; Sumner 1979). In the capitalist mode of production it creates illusions of free and equal relationships between independent people, obscures the true nature of private property, and disguises the fundamentally exploitative nature of the labor contract.[1] In Cohen's terms property and other social relations are determined by productive relations, though the latter "require legal expression for stability" (1978, 231). The legal superstructure is necessary to give power the illusion of rights, but it is a handmaiden.

Alternative readings of Marx's theory, however, centrally locate law within productive forces. Capitalism has "essential legal relations" that are "part and parcel of the basic economic structure" such as property and contract (Stone 1985, 65). Ellen Meiksins Wood argues that "relations of production themselves take the form of particular juridical and political relations—modes of domination and coercion, forms of property and social organization—which are not mere secondary reflexes, nor even just external supports, but *constituents* of these productive relations" (1995, 27).[2] She and others maintain that productive and market forces must be understood as socially embedded, institutionalized practices that are no less "material" than the commodities produced through them.[3]

In this sense productive relations should be analyzed simultaneously through their economic and juridic forms or dimensions.[4] Employer and worker, much as capital and commodities, are abstract forms defined at once through both economic and legal systems, made concrete in routinized social practices.[5] "It is an everyday fact of life," notes Richard Marsden, "that when workers sell their capacity to work, by the same act, they sell the rights attached to it. In transferring these rights from the worker to the corporation, the contract of employment effectively reduces workers of the capitalist firm to the legal status of things ('hands')" (1999, 134).[6] In Marx's terms that we encountered in the last chapter, the subsumption of labor inseparably intertwines economic and juridic, the latter being social forces that are just as "real" as the former. Capitalist social relations of production take a specific juridic form through the labor contract. Labor power is transformed into a commodity through a market exchange between legal "equals," and thus subjected to the subsumption process.[7] The labor contract gives the capitalist authority over the labor power of the worker, which is realized through specific practices of coercion and consent in the production process. It also provides the set of institutionalized practices that connect the labor market to the labor process, providing the means for creating a broader labor control regime. Put more simply, labor control and exploitation are rooted no less in law than they are in a particular division of labor or form of technology.

My choice of "rooted" as a metaphor is deliberate, because the ways in which practices of control grow, spread, and sometimes die off in part depend on the specific historical elaboration of legal rules through which the social relations in and of production are organized and implemented. As Duncan Kennedy maintains, "The legal system does not come to bear on the working economy of capitalism through general principles, but through particular rules applied in particular cases. . . . The legal component of the mode of production is, in so much as it actually functions in the world, the collection of particular rules, not the general principles" (1985, 998).[8] Contract and commodity exchange are abstractions that are incomplete bases for the organization of production. They gain social life and force through historically produced legal codes and the practices through which they are realized.[9] The labor contract is a set of "particular rules" establishing an ongoing relationship between capitalist and worker at the point of production, and this the point at which institutional analysis provides further important insights.

HISTORICAL MATERIALISM + HISTORICAL INSTITUTIONALISM

As noted in the introduction, a key tenet of this volume is that we can bring historical materialism and historical institutionalism into a working relationship to offer a more encompassing analysis of the role of law in labor control regimes.[10] The alternative framework pursued here is an eclectic fusion. Social scientists such as Jeffrey Haydu and Jonas Pontusson, and historians such as Dave Lyddon, have pursued an accord between class and institutional analysis to bolster both.[11] While some scholars stress the incompatibility between the two, in their most analytically insightful forms both focus on concrete historical processes, the construction and maintenance of asymmetries of power and the ways in which political and economic institutions conjoin to structure the exercise of this power.[12]

I draw on several orienting concepts within the broad sweep of historical institutionalism that fortify and extend Marxist analyses of labor control and the law. First is the concept of embeddedness. Specific historical nexuses of institutions provide the social and political structures through which power and resources are routinely mobilized. They create the durable hierarchies within which interests are organized and the paths along which they are pursued (Campbell 2004; Coates 2005).[13] Relations in and of production, markets, and other aspects of the circuit of capital are embedded in state policies and legal systems that critically contour capitalist dynamics.[14] Some sociologists, such as Fred Block and Margaret Somers, find the theoretical foundations of the institutional embeddedness of the economy in Karl Polyani's work, and argue that state policies provide the frameworks for capitalist-worker relations generally and labor markets and managerial authority more particularly (Block 1994; Block and Somers 2003, 2005, 2014). (We will return to Polanyi's perspective and his account of the "Great Transformation" of the Industrial Revolution in chapter 7.) Other historical institutionalists, such as Kathleen Thelen (2004), argue that state policies produced enduring effects in ordering the structure and dynamics of labor markets over the last century and a half, even when the original intent of these policies has long receded. Social scientists and historians have examined the ways in which state policy generally and legal systems specifically influenced the course of union development and labor relations from the nineteenth century onward.[15] Speaking more directly to the concerns of this study, the legal scholar Simon Deakin argues that contracts of employment in Western Europe emerged through specific national legal configurations that shaped trajectories of labor commodification.[16] These and other studies demonstrate that labor markets and capitalist-worker relations did not emerge in determined form from the chrysalis of historical capitalism, but that state policy and legal systems significantly influenced their development (and transformation) in a variety of Western countries. The concept of embeddedness provides the basis for both systematizing and moving beyond the contributions of Burawoy and Price.

From within this basic conception of embeddedness is the orienting assumption that while actors strategically pursue material interests, they do so within institutional frameworks that bound conceptions of the reasonable and practical. Institutional rules and the formal structures through which they are implemented constrain actors' assessments of feasible strategies and the horizons of the imaginable and the possible.[17] In Jeffrey Haydu's terms institutions are "problem-solving regimes" through which actors define recurrent challenges and opportunities and calibrate their responses (2010, 32). "Every work contract," Chris and Charles Tilly observe, "is embedded in a broader set of social relations, including both production and nonproduction relations. Each of those relations brings its own contribution of accumulated, shared understandings, rights and obligations to bear on the contract's execution" (1998, 89–90). In the analyses ahead I examine the ways in which employers structured workplace governance and labor control not only considering labor and product markets, the technical relations of production, and skill and worker organization, but also by assessing pragmatically how local institutional configurations of political power and the dispensation of law offered solutions to recurrent issues of labor control.

A third key orienting concept is path dependence. John L. Campbell broadly defines it as "a process whereby contingent events or decisions result in the establishment of institutions that persist over long periods of time and constrain the range of actors' future options, including those that might be more efficient or effective in the long run" (2004, 65). The origins of enduring institutional arrangements are found in specific historical conjunctures that create turning points for change. The timing and sequencing of events and actions set in motion a causal chain producing these new arrangements, though the later manifestations of these institutions can be far removed from their original development. As Paul Pierson states the matter, "when a particular issue or conflict emerges in a society becomes critical for two reasons. First, the resources available to actors at that moment in time help determine the repertoire of possible responses. Second, once a response is adopted, it may generate self-reinforcing dynamics" (2004, 75). These reinforcing dynamics include positive feedback loops in which investment in new institutional forms bring both increasing returns and impediments to alternatives. Complementarities are created with other institutions by which increasingly settled practices and arrangements are fortified. Binding commitments develop, especially among powerful actors, that steer the actions of their successors, and pragmatic adaptation occurs in which actors continually return to established rules and practices to solve both continuing and novel problems. These dynamics create the "stickiness" of embeddedness leading to institutional endurance, even as the initial purposes of their development are transformed over time through adaptation and reconfiguration. Pierson (2004, 157–59) offers the juridicalization of conflict as exemplary of these processes.[18]

"Hard" versions of path dependency emphasize distinctive and delimited event conjunctures and sequencing that produce determinative paths. Once-established institutions attain equilibrium and are characterized by considerable inertia. In many such versions, outside forces in the form of "exogenous shocks" propel change through new specific conjunctures, producing a "punctuated equilibrium" cycle of eventful transformation and extended periods of settled institutional orders. Alternatively "soft" versions argue that even settled institutional arrangements provide room for maneuver, points of continuing conflict, and systemic contradiction and incoherence; they frequently characterize change as more gradual, patchwork, and endogenous as actors confront new problems within existing regimes.[19] Some historical institutionalists argue that contradictions created in uneven institutional development, both within an institution and in relation to others, create pressures for change.[20]

To refine these critical orienting concepts I add considering the importance of space and place. Much of the work done by historical institutionalists takes the nation-state as a unit of analysis, often in comparative analyses of distinct state trajectories of political development and transformation. However, institutional path dependence, at least in the case of labor control regimes, is spatially uneven and place-dependent because production is always rooted in specific geographies (Jonas 1996).[21] And labor control more generally is always first a distinctly local challenge based on the immediate social relations in and of production and the organization of labor markets and structures of worker solidarity.[22] As Rainnie, McGrath-Champ, and Herod observe, "local labour control regimes and how work is organized are shaped significantly by the manner in which workers and capitalists are differentially embedded in the economic landscape. This is important, because when capital and workers are relatively fixed in particular places within the landscape, it is likely that certain traditions of work and ways of organizing the labour process will become congealed in those places" (2010, 303; Jonas 1996, 328–29). Geographers such as Herod and Peck demonstrate that the regulation of labor markets, the development and organization of unions, and other aspects of the employment relationship, because of their place-bound nature, are organized as distinctly locally embedded institutions.[23] Law, too, as I argued above, is as much local institutional practice as national code or judicial dictate (Blomley 1994). Bottom-up examination of the use of the law in labor control regimes therefore necessarily complements the top-down focus of much institutionalism.

Combining an understanding of the law's materiality with these institutionalist-orienting concepts we gain further insights into the development, endurance, and transformation of Burawoy's production regimes and Price's chains of connection and frontiers of control. As Burawoy maintains, capitalists and workers engage one another in the social relations in production simultaneously through both the labor process and the political apparatuses of production. However, the "state" or law is never simply "external" to this engagement. The labor contract and other legal codes provide the juridic forms and practices through which labor is commodified and expropriated, and consent and coercion are organized. The law is not a set of general principles, and it offers more than a legitimating function for the production process. The selling and consumption of "free labor" are practiced through specific rules, authoritative knowledges, and practices that organize and bound the use of labor power. Law is "deeply implicated," to use Price's phrase, because the social relations of production take shape through its specific material practices organizing not only the exchange of labor power but also the production process.

These specific practices are embedded in political and legal institutions outside the workshop door and factory gate. Labor control regimes depend on legal practices that operate through courts, councils, and other regulatory bodies. Access to and opportunity in these formal institutions shape the routine exercise of power and resistance in the workplace. This access and opportunity are in turn structured by historically specific development, maintenance, and control of these formal institutions and their relations to each other. The historical development of courts and other legal systems along specific paths influences the ways in which capitalists and workers engage these formal institutions as part of their routine repertoire of coercion and consent. The "chains of connection" that Price urges us to investigate emerge and solidify because of the intersection of the organization of the labor process and this institutional development in specific historical contexts. As discussed below, capitalists' routine recourse to master and servant law for labor control in specific regions and industries was partly determined by how the development of their industries intersected with the transformation and development of local courts. As we will see, in Victorian England the effective power of local courts for capitalist labor control depended on the relative autonomy of these courts from central state supervision, the selection processes for the magistrates who ran them, and the ways in which in some towns capitalists ascended to power in local government allowing them control of this selection.

In the English Industrial Revolution the conjoining of the labor process and legal practice were relevant especially for labor control regimes characterized by formal subsumption. As many historians have documented, significant portions of the English industrial base advanced on the basis of hand rather than steam power. These industries were organized through systems of craft labor, or more notoriously "sweated trades" in workshops. The system of real subsumption in the dark satanic mills, in which the labor process and control were organized through steam-powered machinery, remained exceptional throughout much of the nineteenth century.[24] Lacking the capacity to organize the labor process through mechanization (incomplete as that was), even owners of large manufactories (such as the pottery manufacturers in Hanley, examined below) for a variety of reasons could turn to the law to construct durable labor control regimes. The law was not only a means of defining the authority of the employer in the workplace, but also a nexus of struggle over tradition that Price notes was part of the frontier of control.

Path dependence figures into the subsequent analyses in two ways. From the top down, I focus on how master and servant law, a specific legislative solution to conflict in one industry and place in the mid-eighteenth century, became generalized over succeeding decades as other employers increasingly turned to it for their problem-solving regimes of workplace and labor control. In chapter 7, in which we revisit Polanyi's narrative of the "double movement," we will examine how class conflict over the legal order governing labor control regimes led to working-class political action to change the law. In this analysis I opt for a "soft" version of path dependence. The "law" is a contingent product of parliamentary acts and court decisions, and cannot be analyzed as a single institution. Parliament and court were not always synchronized in their interpretation of the law, and the high courts themselves experienced shifts with changes on the bench. There is a clear general trend but, particularly with the courts, it has crooked periods. From the bottom up in the case studies we will explore how employers in particular industries and places, facing specific problems of securing, organizing, and controlling labor, turned to the law for solutions at important junctures. They developed labor control regimes embedded in local political and judicial institutions that offered reliable access for exercising legal authority. Legal recourse became a routine process of securing domination in the workplace. In some of these cases, these paths affected the possibilities for later growth and innovation and, in some respects, the continued vitality of these industries. We will pursue these themes in the case studies, but first I examine the development and diffusion of master and servant law.

THE DEVELOPMENT AND TRANSFORMATION OF THE LAW

Master and servant law was part of a much larger thicket of statutory and common law developed over the eighteenth and nineteenth centuries governing labor relations. In addition to the poor laws and factory acts, which often receive pride of place in many analyses, Parliament and the superior courts proliferated regulations and rulings concerning the scope of service and the nature of the employment contract, the legality and operation of unions, apprenticeship, theft, and the function and operation of arbitration systems.[25] However, no law figured more prominently in the organization of power in the workplace. We can follow the rise of master and servant law in labor control regimes in a complex interplay of statutory law, judicial rulings, and the development and transformation of local courts and policing. Over the course of the nineteenth century all three combined on a path of increasing prominence in workplace control, though always in the context of specific regional and local institutions and industrial and trade differences that created uneven institutionalization.

While it is possible through a standard metanarrative of modernization to see master and servant law as a relic of a feudal past, the statutory and case law that emerged from the mid-eighteenth century onward marked a major departure.[26] This body of statutory law contained "significant new language" regarding the employment relationship that progressively redefined power in the workplace and labor market (Hay 2004, 83; Steinfeld 2001, 42): "The master and servant legislation was not an attempt to maintain in place a pre-industrial model of household employment. Instead, it aimed to impose a more rigorous system of work discipline upon the growing numbers of labourers, artisans and outworkers employed in manufacturing, as well as maintaining control of the agricultural labour market at a time of considerable upheaval" (Deakin and Wilkinson 2005, 65).[27]

In a period in which political economy emerged to establish the virtues of the free market, master and servant law cast the employment as a hybrid of service and contract, unlike any other form of market relationship.[28] Adult male workers were free to sell their labor in the market, but once bound in an exclusive employment relationship (a point to which I return below) they were obligated to serve their employers' dictates within legally recognized custom or formal contract. Once contractually tied workers were compelled to labor under a duty of continual service. Critically, the failure to do so under master and servant law was a criminal offense. Employers were also legally bound to remunerate workers and treat them properly, but their transgressions were codified as civil. As Robert Steinfeld maintains, "The traditional account of the rise of free labor is backwards. The advent of freer markets in England during the late eighteenth and early nineteenth centuries did not produce 'free labor,' but rather, by modern standards, a form of 'coerced' contractual labor" (2001, 234).[29] This institutional system of "unfree labor" was born of eighteenth-century capitalists' search for new forms of labor market and workplace control. The law evolved over successive decades into a system of legal coercion that affected large swaths of English labor.[30]

Over a span of about 120 years Parliament passed a series of master and servant acts that regulated the employment relationship, a number of which were industry specific, and most of this legislation was prompted by employers' requests. Looking back on the accumulation of these acts the legal commentator Alexander MacDonald observed, "It cannot fail to strike even the cursory observer that it exhibits a manifest leaning to masters. It bears the unmistakable impress of class legislation" (1868, 134). In the eighteenth century Parliament enacted twenty-six laws regarding the rights and responsibilities of employers and workers, and in the nineteenth some twenty-seven more, until the repeal of all of this legislation in 1875.[31] More than a half dozen acts concerned criminal sanctions for breaching a contract of service (Hay 2004, 66, 83; Steinfeld 2001, 42–43).

The precursors to more general acts were trade-specific, beginning with tailoring (1720), and including shoemaking (1722), the woolen trades (1725), hatmaking (1731), and the leather trades (1740). These acts were passed by Parliament to respond to collective organization and demands by journeyman concerning wages and conditions of hire. The government's concerns were less about economic equity than the social instability that trade disputes wrought. Several of these acts provided for magisterial intervention in wage determinations (though by the last quarter of the century this was a rare event) as well as limits on apprentices and mechanisms for wage recovery. The politics of this legislation, as Douglas Hay notes, involved Parliament's responsiveness both to wary masters in search of additional authority and periodically restive journeymen who the government perceived as fonts of significant disorder. Parliament continued to pass trade-specific acts through the eighteenth century, though it is likely that most prosecutions were pursued under the more encompassing acts (Hay 2004, 82–84; Napier 1975, 74; Steinfeld 2001, 43).

The first significant acts covering a wide variety of workers were 20 Geo. II, c. 19 (1747) and 6 Geo. III, c. 25 (1766). The first authorized a single magistrate in local courts (petty sessions), based on the sworn testimony of the master, to issue a warrant against a servant for breach of contract including "any misdemeanor, miscarriage, or ill behavior." Conviction under the act was punishable by abatement of part of the servant's wages, up to one month imprisonment at hard labor, or discharge.[32] The second, which did not replace the first statute, provided for sentences of one to three months imprisonment. The acts presumed that all contracts of service, oral or written, were a year's duration, unless otherwise specified by custom or in writing, and subject to three months' notice by either party. As with all such legislation, civil remedies were provided for servants in the case of wage disputes and ill treatment.[33] A 1777 act (17 Geo. III, 3 c. 36) largely focused on theft and embezzlement in the outwork trades reiterating the range of prison sentences for eight successive days of neglect of work.[34]

It was an act of 1823, 4 Geo. III, c. 23, which likely served as the bulwark for labor market and workplace control for much of the nineteenth century until its repeal in 1875. As Justice Blackburn of Queen's Bench was to note in a later landmark ruling regarding the duty to serve, "it is clear that the statute 4. Geo. 4 had for its object the protection of masters." The intent of 4 Geo. III, c. 23 was to consolidate and generalize the preceding acts, though it did not repeal them.[35] Under the act servants were subject to prosecution for shoddy work, misbehavior, absenteeism, and failure to enter into a contractual obligation. The interpretations of this range of offenses often gave masters considerable breadth for bringing charges, and the act extended the capacity of complaints to managers and stewards. A single justice was given discretion to commit a servant for up to three months in prison at hard labor (providing greater flexibility for shorter sentences) and to abate the whole of wages due a worker. The act also gave servants the capacity to seek wages from masters' agents and for summary judgments for wages up to £10, but its overall affect was to reinforce the law's inequities. The only rights of appeal to workers were writs of certiorari or habeas corpus, which spoke to errors of legal process but not the substance of the case.[36]

For the next several decades Parliament enacted no additional legislation substantively amending master and servant statutes.[37] However, under increasing pressure starting in the mid-1860s they passed one final piece of legislation, 30 & 31 Vict., c. 141, which remained the law of the land until reforms in 1875.[38] Reacting to pressure by union activists Parliament acceded to several changes. Conviction required the presence of two or more justices and for the first time workers were recognized as witnesses in their defense.[39] Warrants against workers could only be issued for "aggravated cases," and summonses were therefore the default for bringing workers to court.[40] Imprisonment was restricted to "aggravated offenses" or when workers failed to adhere to the court's other determinations.[41] The law also provided justices with a larger array of penalties, including for the first time the imposition of fines and the ordering of completion of contract and to find security for performance. These new possibilities might well have provided employers with additional weapons to insure labor workplace discipline. Overall, as Willibald Steinmetz remarks, "The reformed Master and Servant Act of 1867 did little to change the substance of the law."[42]

From the passage of the early new legislation in the mid-eighteenth century Parliament followed a path in which statutory master and servant law was broadened and consolidated. For the country gentlemen who controlled Parliament in the eighteenth century (particularly before the ascendancy of political economy) the legislation was seen as a way of insuring stability in places that could erupt in troubling disorder. Initially for masters it was a means of solidifying authority over their journeyman as proletarianization displaced other forms of influence. As the eighteenth century tapered into the nineteenth, however, capitalists in a number of industries turned to the law to assert their control in the labor market and the workplace. The successive addition of acts up through the Act of 1823 institutionalized a ready option for such control that had become commonplace juridical activity in a number of parts of the country. Master and servant law in a sense grew up with industrialization (Deakin and Wilkinson 2005, 62). However, this developmental path was entwined with superior court rulings that added a layer of complexity to its interpretation and use.

The path taken by these courts was more crooked, demonstrating that the composition of the court and its ideological shifts do not fit neatly into a hard version of path dependence. However, by mid-century it conjoined with that of the statutory law to offer a unified conception of authority that empowered employers. High court rulings addressed the nature of the contract of service and the magistrates' administration of justice that bore directly on the application of master and servant law.[43] One key issue with which the superior courts wrestled over the first half of the century was exactly which workers were included under the acts, in terms of trades and who was covered within prevailing understandings of a contract of service. The high courts, especially the King's and Queen's benches, tackled the question of who qualified as a servant at a number of points during the first half of the century. In a ruling in the first decade, focusing on a case involving the eighteenth-century statutory law, the King's Bench ruled broadly that the term "labourer" in the 1747 act applied to all workers who were "employed for any certain time, or in any other manner" and included day and piece-rate workers (Steinfeld 2001, 126). However, starting in the 1820s with ruling on cases brought under the 1823 act, the high courts narrowed this interpretation. Over the next two decades the courts ruled that piece workers who had not explicitly been engaged in an exclusive contract of service were exempt from prosecution under the act.[44] By the 1850s the courts shifted again, and produced a series of rulings in which an exclusive arrangement was recognized as any in which a worker was bound to an employer for the completion of a particular task. These court decisions brought the vast majority of wage workers back within the purview of the acts.[45]

A second issue that bore on the range of authority of the employer concerned the degree of mutual obligation implicit in the employment relationship. From the 1820s through the late 1840s high courts ruled that workers under contract for task or piece work were due a reasonable amount of work to keep the contracts binding. The service relationship was held unenforceable when employers failed to demonstrate that they provided workers with a minimum amount of work tying their workers to them. From the late 1840s onward the courts reversed course. They held that contracts that did not guarantee specifically minimum amounts of work or wages were nonetheless valid until the end of their term, obliging the worker to remain in a service relationship. Moreover, in a series of rulings in the 1850s through the mid-1870s the high courts determined that imprisonment of a worker under master and servant law did not absolve him from fulfilling the duration of his service under the contract. Conviction did not sever the authority of the master over the servant once he was released.[46]

A final issue affecting the power offered through the law was the workers' right to appeal convictions. The ability of employers to receive swift rulings in local courts provided them with substantial leverage in the workplace. Under the 1823 act workers' right to appeal was limited to writs of certiorari or habeas corpus that focused on the procedural validity of warrants of commitment. The various statutes and common law rulings that governed such issues, however, were complex and vexatious for the vast majority of magistrates who had no legal background. In the second quarter of the century the high court enforced strict terms of process on them, voiding convictions that involved shoddy procedure. Radical solicitors such as William P. Roberts, who as a high-profile advocate of colliers during these years was dubbed the "Miners' Attorney General," successfully pursued a number of widely followed cases in which warrants of commitment and conviction were overturned on such grounds. However, the high court, in combination with Parliament's response to this state of affairs, effectively ended such recourse starting in the late 1840s. In 1846–48 Parliament passed the Jervis Acts, a series of bills that simplified local court summary proceedings and made challenges far less likely, and they continued to pass additional laws in the 1850s. As Parliament provided magistrates with surer ground so too did the Queen's Bench in a series of rulings that protected magistrates from such entanglements. By the end of the decade the potential for appeal was essentially eviscerated and the summary powers of justices were secured. And as the magistrates' unalloyed authority was affirmed, employers were provided with greater certainty of their exercise of authority through the law (Frank 2010, chaps. 3 and 6; Steinfeld 2001, 153–59).

The authority of the magistracy was so vital to master and servant law because in practical terms the authority of the law was exercised through them (Hay 2000, 230).[47] As the Victorian solicitor, social critic, and union supporter Frederic Harrison observed in critiquing unreformed labor laws, "It must, however, never be forgotten that the administration of the law is almost more important than the laws themselves" (*Bee-Hive*, Jan. 25, 1873). By the nineteenth century, the foundations of legal administration were in a set of inferior courts that comprised the justice system for most working people. Local courts, or petty sessions, were held regularly by unpaid county justices and borough commissions of the peace, and in some areas by paid stipendiary magistrates, all of whom on a practical level had substantial autonomy from regular central state supervision. County justices were the centuries' old cornerstone of the legal apparatus and were appointments of the counties' Lords Lieutenant (Skyrme 1994, 614–15; Manchester 1980, 160–64). They ran the quarter sessions that tried indictable offenses and also sat on local petty sessions that dealt with a variety of matters of administrative and summary jurisdiction as well as criminal indictments. Throughout much of the nineteenth century the landed elite remained dominant in these positions.[48] County justices were sometimes criticized for their legal ignorance, but also noted for exercising a traditional paternalism in dispensing justice. For this reason some workers' representatives considered them to be more impartial arbiters then their alternatives.[49]

For workers in urban areas, however, the face of justice in Victorian England was the borough magistrate. Industrialists and their allies had already begun to populate some borough courts by the 1820s, but with the passage of municipal reform acts authorizing the establishment of borough courts this process accelerated in the 1830s and 1840s. Coupled with the expansion of local police forces as well as legislation expanding their powers of summary jurisdiction over these decades, these petty sessions became known as "police courts" and were increasing feared by working people (Hay 2004, 107). Borough magistrates were appointed by municipal government, which also frequently was controlled by industrial and commercial elites, creating what D. C. Wood characterizes in the Black Country as "self-perpetuating oligarchies who were able to dominate both borough government and borough law enforcement" (1979, 102).[50] As a witness advocating reform of the master and servant laws testifying in front a parliamentary select committee noted simply, "the justices of the peace are of the master class."[51]

Hay emphasizes that the master and servant law was administered through "local, often highly specific legal cultures" (2000, 231).[52] By the Victorian period industrial and commercial elites in some areas had succeeded in constructing interlocking economic and legal institutions under their control, which effectively had criminalized workplace disputes.[53] As their power became embedded in these institutions they became legal arbiters of trade custom and standards of misconduct and neglect (Steinmetz 2000b, 275–80). Though magistrates were to recuse themselves in cases where there was an apparent conflict of interest, manufacturers regularly adjudicated cases in their trades, often involving their friends or acquaintances. Working-class advocates and activists throughout the period complained, sometimes bitterly, of the partiality of borough courts.[54]

To address issues of partiality and competence Parliament in the 1830s passed legislation authorizing the appointment of stipendiary magistrates. Developed as an outgrowth of professionalizing the London Metropolitan judiciary, the stipendiary was to be a barrister of at least five years' experience. This legal background plus the salaried nature of the position were to add professionalism to the local court system. They were appointed at the request of the borough or region, or by the special authority of a local law that authorized their appointment. Despite the legal machinery for their installation only ten stipendiaries had been appointed by the early 1860s.[55] Nonetheless, where they were installed, the stipendiary magistrate could have a significant presence in the local justice system. Despite this supposed impartiality some stipendiaries, steeped in political economy and having well-established ties to local economic elites, were clearly hostile to working-class interests. The stipendiary for the Potteries district from 1839 to 1850, T. B. Rose was a lightning rod for unionist consternation. His successor in the 1860s, Isaac Spooner, was derided by workers as "Cruel Isaac" for his dispensation of justice.[56]

There are indications that over the decades the application of the law shifted along with the above developments. Hay suggests that in the late eighteenth and early nineteenth centuries justices were as likely to hear complaints from workers as from employers, and that both groups of plaintiffs fared fairly well, but by the 1860s masters brought at least 80 percent of the complaints (Hay 1998, 36–37; 2000, 258; Frank 2010, 83).[57] In industrial towns workers often faced mounting skepticism concerning their claims, and they sometimes feared employer retribution if successful.[58]

Because national statistics on criminal prosecutions were only published starting in 1858 it is impossible to demonstrate any trends over the course of the century. Table 3.1 shows the annual numbers of prosecutions under master and servant and other violations of summary jurisdiction most common in the policing of the working class.[59] As the table shows, both in raw numbers and percentage terms, master and servant convictions were within the range of petty larceny, breaches of the peace, various misdemeanors, and begging, and consistently higher than those for neglecting the family. Hay calculates that during this period master and servant prosecutions varied between 12 to 32 percent of all theft prosecutions (summary and trial by jury) during these years, and hit considerably higher percentages in some industrial districts (2004, 108–9). For many working people in the mid-Victorian era an experience with criminal justice, outside of one concerning drinking, fighting, or theft, was about as likely to concern work as any other sphere of life.

The parliamentary reports show that rates of imprisonment from 1858 to 1867 (when the law was modified) varied between 14 and 16 percent of the accused and 25 to 33 percent of the convicted (Hay 2004, 109). For those employers who regularly relied on the law the goal was not incarceration or even pecuniary retribution but creating a disciplinary environment.[60] As the prominent stipendiary and legal writer James E. Davis reported to one select committee, "I have always found that employers care little about the money, about getting actual compensation, and that they wanted labour." As the manager of a forge that employed about 1,000 observed before the same commission, "when a man is stubborn and self-willed he will not listen to reason, and it is the very fact of his not listening to reason that

TABLE 3.1. Number of prosecutions in England and Wales for master and servant law violations and other selected offenses of summary jurisdiction, 1864–1874

Offense	1864	1865	1866	1867	1868	1869	1870	1871	1872	1873	1874
Assault, common	77,726 (18)	81,842 (19)	77,640 (19)	74,980 (16)	77,119 (19)	77,864 (15)	74,985 (14)	77,224 (14)	80,650 (14)	79,788 (14)	83,679 (13)
Breaches of the peace	10,645 (2)	10,696 (2)	11,346 (2)	12,597 (3)	13,831 (3)	14,157 (3)	16,696 (3)	18,050 (3)	19,869 (4)	17,945 (3)	20,876 (3)
Drunkenness	100,067 (23)	103,310 (24)	104,368 (22)	100,357 (21)	111,465 (28)	122,310 (24)	131,870 (25)	142,343 (26)	151,084 (27)	183,341 (31)	185,730 (30)
Larceny under 5s	14,020 (3)	13,378 (3)	14,159 (3)	16,585 (3)	17,482 (4)	17,675 (3)	16,088 (3)	15,487 (3)	14,502 (3)	13,982 (2)	13,768 (2)
Master and servant law	10,246 (2)	10,412 (2)	12,345 (2)	9,953 (2)	8,024 (2)	7,365 (1)	8,670 (2)	10,810 (2)	17,082 (3)	16,230 (3)	13,544 (2)
Police acts/ misdemeanors	7,514 (2)	8,210 (2)	9,074 (2)	7,778 (2)	7,553 (2)	13,420 (3)	8,761 (2)	11,617 (2)	11,631 (2)	11,789 (2)	11,483 (2)
Poor law/neglect family	3,739 (1)	3,714 (1)	3,942 (1)	4,588 (1)	4,973 (1)	5,033 (1)	4,887 (1)	4,827 (1)	5,073 (1)	5,677 (1)	6,046 (1)
Vagrancy/begging	9,545 (2)	9,124 (2)	8,424 (2)	11,343 (2)	13,536 (3)	17,541 (3)	15,954 (3)	13,603 (2)	11,279 (2)	10,225 (2)	9,328 (2)

Note: Numbers in parentheses are percentage of the total number of prosecutions.

Source: England and Wales, Police–Criminal Proceedings–Prisons, Judicial Statistics, Returns, BPP.

renders it necessary you should have a force at the back of the man which will compel him to do what his reason will not induce him to do."[61] Prosecutions could be used as exemplary acts to instill discipline in the rest of the workforce. Testifying before an 1874 commission for labor law reform, the secretary to the Mining Association of Great Britain (himself a solicitor) agreed that the law was used "In terrorem."[62] As we will examine in more detail in chapter 7, in the 1860s and 1870s many employers' association representatives testifying during the parliamentary select committees and commissions on the law strongly advocated for the retention of imprisonment as a necessary ultimate cudgel.[63]

Longer contracts facilitated the use of master and servant law for labor control, and length of service varied significantly by trade and region. The customary length for servants in husbandry was a year, though as the century progressed some agricultural districts turned to more seasonal relationships. Once yearly annual bonding was a practice of a number of industrial labor markets. Bonding of miners, for instance, was a common feature in northern coal pits until the abolition of master and servant laws in 1875 (Frank 2010, 44–47; Jaffe 1991, 101–4; Simon 1954, 172).[64] As we will see in chapter 4, pottery workers were hired by bonding for many decades. As the century progressed capitalists in some industries (such as the pottery) turned to formal contracts that specified rules of employment, eliminating the possibility of disputes over trade custom, as well as the length of service. Employers sought to tie valued craftworkers to multiyear contracts, which were common for millworking and glassblowing through the first half of the century for example (Hay 2004, 101–4; Jacoby 1982, 95–96). Bonding and contracts had some advantages for workers in terms of employment security (though, as we saw, this was weakened by high court decisions) and some agreements contained dispute resolution mechanisms (Jaffe 2003). However, such extended terms of service gave employers more leverage to use master and servant law as effective labor market and workplace discipline.

The annual statistics reinforce anecdotal evidence that there were significant variations in the use of the law across the face of England. As I noted, the Black Country (encompassing parts of Worcestershire, Warwickshire, and Staffordshire) had high annual numbers, as generally did the metal trades towns of Birmingham, Sheffield, and Wolverhampton in this region. The Potteries district, which I analyze in the next chapter, also had a consistently higher record of prosecutions. The Durham coalfields had significant yearly numbers. Leeds, in the Yorkshire woolen district, showed moderate but steady numbers, distinctly higher than the other wool manufacturing towns. Within the cotton-manufacturing district encompassing Cheshire and Lancashire there were differences between towns, with Stockport and Preston showing somewhat higher rates of prosecution than other towns and Manchester low to moderate, but quite steady numbers. What distinguishes this area from others is the wide swings taken by some towns from year to year. For example, the numbers prosecuted for Preston, Lancashire, in 1863–66 respectively were 38, 90, 285, and 498. In the cotton districts these undulations might well reflect the use of master and servant law as a strike-breaking strategy. Dutton and King have documented how cotton manufacturers controlled the Preston bench in the 1850s and used the law to break strikes, and other historians have argued that it was one of the most effective tactics to do so.[65]

Master and servant laws were gender-neutral, although they did not apply to domestic servants who by the mid-Victorian period might have composed at least 10 percent of the labor market (Craven and Hay 2004, 36; Hay 2004, 66–67). For all those who were covered under the law's scope the annual statistics suggest that the burden of prosecutions fell heavily on men. In the decade and a half before reform males generally constituted well over 90 percent of all cases, though the rates of conviction for each gender were roughly equal at around 60 percent. The case studies that follow conform to this pattern, and only in the final case of Redditch will we see rates of female prosecution reaching 10 percent. As I discuss in the introduction to the case studies, reading gender dynamics from court records and newspaper accounts is a difficult task.[66]

Looking over the first half of the nineteenth century from the top down we can see three converging paths of legislation and legal administration. First, from the mid-eighteenth century, Parliament passed successive and broader statutes, layered one atop the other to use a metaphor of historical institutionalists, gradually solidifying a national institutional infrastructure that strengthened the hand of capital. Though not readily apparent in its eighteenth-century origins, master and servant law in the following decades developed along a path to become the legal infrastructure through which most employers could exercise authority over the labor market and workplace. This generalized hybrid of status and contract left workers under its purview substantively "unfree" in service. Second, the superior courts, following a more uneven path, established a holistic understanding of the law's range and power by mid-century. In their rulings on the breadth of the law's coverage and the certainty of its summary convictions, high courts foregrounded the law as a regular tool by which employers could exercise power over a labor force. Thus by mid-century both state institutions had converged on a unified account of the scope and use of master and servant law.

Third, looking from the bottom up, the developmental path of local courts of summary jurisdiction reinforced this confluence of national state institutions. It was in petty sessions that local justices gave specific substance to master and servant law, translating statutory and common law into everyday practices. The transformation and proliferation of these courts in many urban areas made them reliable venues through which employers could wield master and servant law for labor market and workplace discipline. This development was accelerated in the 1830s when new legislation led to transformed borough governance and the spread of borough courts. In many urban areas capitalists succeeded in dominating borough government, insuring their ascendance to the bench. Additional legislation and high court decisions during this period provided borough courts with an increasing secure range of summary powers, and constabularies by which they could exercise them, making the "police court" a more effective arena of class control. There was a developmental path to power by which industrial and commercial elites, creating an interlocking set of economic, political, and legal institutions, could exercise increasing control over both place and working people. Where they existed, stipendiary courts generally became equally reliable venues of enforcement.

Thus, by mid-century, a legal system had solidified, offering capitalists a dependable means to exert substantial control over the labor market and the workplace. However, as I have noted, the adoption of this legal control was quite uneven over the English landscape. In the following case studies I argue that employers in specific industries and places embedded their labor control regimes in the law and its formal institutions because of conjunctures of circumstances that created a type of path dependence. The organization of local labor markets, consolidation of borough power and strategic alliances among local elites, and access to friendly courts, conjoined with the particular dilemmas of exerting control in the social relations of production in the workplace to lead employers to turn to the law as a regular mechanism of labor discipline. This was particularly the case in struggles of formal subordination in which capitalists could not wrest control of the production process through the technical relations in production. Once the prominence of master and servant law was established as a routine power for labor discipline employers settled into these regimes, even though in some cases it created problems for the long-term vitality and dominance of their industries.

In turning to the case studies I offer three examples of these developmental paths, each distinct, but all demonstrating the centrality of master and servant law in labor control regimes. Through these analyses I demonstrate the materiality of the law as suggested at the beginning of this chapter. We will examine how the contract of service was a central facet of several labor control regimes. In addition, by drawing eclectically on key institutionalist concepts we will examine how prosecutions became embedded features of these regimes as capitalists pragmatically reached for solutions to labor discipline and, in the felicitous conjoining of legal and economic institutions, found stable answers in the law.

PART II

Introduction to the Case Studies

The previous chapter combined a top-down analysis of the national development of master and servant law with a bottom-up examination of the growth of local legal institutions to explain how the law became a plausible option for labor control regimes by the mid-nineteenth century. The three case studies that follow are decidedly bottom up. Each investigates a path-dependent process by which employers in specific industries and places came to rely on the law as a reliable and significant vehicle for exerting control in the labor market and workplace. The focus will be on a period roughly from the early 1860s to the repeal of master and servant law in 1875, a time that several historians suggest was the most active era for prosecutions. In some respects the case studies prima facie have little in common. Hanley was in the northern part of Staffordshire and at the heart of England's great pottery industry. Redditch was on the southern end of the Black Country in Worcestershire and the home of the nation's needle industry as well as a regional center for dairy and livestock farming. Hull lay on the northeast seaboard in East Riding, Yorkshire. It was a major shipping port for Black Sea trade and a significant base for England's burgeoning fish-trawling industry. What unites all of these cases is that the annual parliamentary reports show that on a percentage basis of all prosecutions for summary offenses their master and servant prosecutions were multiple times the national average. In these terms Hanley, Hull, and Redditch stand out for their zealous prosecution of workers, and the question to be pursued is why.

In each place the answer can be found in a series of factors that were conjoined by mid-century for employers in each industry to find routine recourse to the law for labor market and workplace discipline. The availability of workers and structure of labor markets, the organization of the workplace and labor process, and the reliability of local courts all combined to lead employers in each industry down a path to master and servant law in developing labor control regimes. In each case during this period these employers incorporated master and servant law in their routines of labor control, though the specific configurations of the local legal institutions differed. Hanley had a local bench dominated by pottery manufacturers and their industrial and commercial allies and a sympathetic stipendiary magistrate in the region. In Hull fishing trawler owners depended likewise on both the borough magistrates and the local stipendiary. And in Redditch local landowners and needle manufacturers forged an alliance to initiate and then control a borough court during this period.

However, it was not just the ready nature of these local courts that led these employers to master and servant law: it was also in some ways the lack of alternatives for developing labor control regimes. In each industry, for different reasons, reorganization of the social relations in production was not readily feasible, and there were no technological means to embed domination in the production process. Given these contexts pragmatic employers forged viable labor control regimes with the means accessible to them. They turned to the law because they could make it work for them. In at least one of these cases there is some evidence that in the longer term this path had negative consequences. Settled reliance on the law, as we will see, might have stunted the adoption of technology in the pottery industry both during this period and beyond. As historical institutionalists note, path dependence occurs because of increasing returns in the near term, but it does not always bring long-term advantage.

Several words of caution are necessary before we pursue these cases. First, this is not a comparative analysis in the formal sense. I have not selected these cases so that I can analyze carefully cross-case variations to isolate the specific contributions of each factor. In fact, in a very real sense I did not select the cases at all; the vagaries of time did. Readers who have done archival research know how we are at the mercy of what remains. This was certainly true in my case. My goal was to locate court records for the last decade of prosecutions under master and servant law, before its reform in 1875. Starting with the parliamentary annual reports I selected a number of places that had high numbers of prosecutions. Both through extensive correspondence and liberal use of the English rails I found that most of these town or regional archives had no court records for this period. Partly this was due to the law of the times. It was not until later in the century that towns were required to retain their court records. Partly this was also due to the passage of time and events. Old records were lost or possibly simply discarded; they fell prey to the elements or even the destruction of World

War II. Some archives contained court records for a few years within this roughly ten-year span. Hanley, Hull, and Redditch are the cases I consider because they remained. Such are the pragmatic choices under institutional constraints that the historical researcher faces.[1]

The court records (minute books and registries kept by court clerks) in each case provide continuous documentation for the period, and on the whole they are reliable sources. Reliable, but not perfect. Matching tallies from these records to numbers given for each place in the annual parliamentary reports sometimes produced an undercount. Moreover, the records of the cases in the minute books, in which clerks labored to document the proceedings, were uneven and often sketchy. Sometimes I would find pages of material on one case and in the next simply a listing of the prosecutor, defendant, and judgment rendered. To supplement these archival sources I turned to local newspapers, which were weekly publications in each town or region. A standard feature of many papers by this time was the "Police Reports," a section that offered readers accounts of a review of local bench cases during the previous week. The papers presented only a fraction of all cases, and the selection biases of the editors are inscrutable. Nonetheless, the reports do provide more details than are sometimes available in the court records, and at times offer cases that do not appear in the archival sources at all.[2] For each town I reviewed all of the local and regional papers that had continuous coverage for the period and reported on the town in their police reports, and selected the paper with the most extensive coverage.[3] The master and servant case data for each study thus are a composite derived from both court records and newspaper reports.

One more word of caution concerning the data, this having to do with their use in terms of a gendered analysis. In the last chapter I noted that the workers subject to prosecution were heavily disproportionately male. These cases provide no exception, and only in the case of Redditch are more than a handful of females represented. However, as we are well aware by now, gender analysis is about the construction of masculinity and femininity through gendered discourses and practices. We also know that in mid-Victorian England dominant representations of masculinity informed how the working man should act, not only in the public and family spheres, but also in the workplace.[4] However, the archival and newspaper sources rarely offer such gendered discourse. It is a rare event in these records when prosecuted male workers are accused of or chided for unruly masculinity by their employers, or told to conform to an accepted gender standard by magistrates. In the small number of female cases, women's and girls' work behaviors were rarely verbally measured against an expected set of feminine virtues and behaviors. The case that opens this volume, that of the unfortunate fishing apprentice Charles Taylor, is highly unusual for his reference to the need to support his wife and child.

The discourse of these court cases focuses on work and its neglect, misconduct, and malfeasance, but usually not in gendered terms. There are at least three ways of reading this absence. The first is to suggest that the acceptable gendered performances at work were so self-evident to those involved (particularly employers and magistrates) that they did not require articulation. Hegemonic gender prescriptions and proscriptions were so ingrained in judging misconduct that they usually were left unstated. Potters who were prosecuted for showing up late to work and drunk, for example, well knew that they were failing at performing a workman's respectable masculinity.

A second possible reading focuses on the context of the proceedings, the local bench, and the extent to which the routine theater of the courts foregrounded violations of statutes while de-emphasizing its gendered dimensions. From this perspective employers and magistrates might have concentrated on establishing the "facts" of the claimed transgressions, with the gendered dimensions of the violations being ancillary to the outcomes of the proceedings in their minds. Certainly gender and sexuality were routine aspects of many prosecutions concerning public and domestic misconduct adjudicated by local justices, but these cases often prominently involved the public policing of respectable gendered behaviors.[5] In this court context, perhaps, in the minds of the empowered and the powerful what mattered most was demonstrating willful violation of the law, gender transgressions being less immediately germane. That a male needle stamper absented himself from work one day did speak to his masculine respectability, but that was not the primary concern of the court.

Finally, to paraphrase the magistrate and legal writer James E. Davis quoted in the last chapter, perhaps it was often the case that the only thing capitalists really wanted was labor. They were less concerned with policing the gendered respectability of their workers than they were with insuring control over delivery of labor power under the conditions of service. As we will see in the case of Hull trawler owners, they were desperate for any form of labor available to them, and they were not at all particular about the origins of their fishing apprentices.[6]

With these cautions in mind we can now turn to the three cases, beginning with Hanley, where pottery was royalty if not king among trades, and the manufacturers of the industry in many ways princes of the political and judicial system of the borough.

CHAPTER FOUR

Hanley and the Pottery Industry

The earthenware industry (including pottery and porcelain) of northern Staffordshire grew up with the Industrial Revolution.[1] It had taken root in the district in the early seventeenth century because of accessible local supplies of both coal and clay. Throughout the 1600s and into the next century the number of master potters gradually proliferated. The increasing concentration of the trade led to the development of a skilled workforce drawn from the ranks of former agricultural workers, which reinforced the advantages of the area. Master potters established themselves by setting up potbanks and a firing oven, which was the self-limiting standard of the trade until the mid-eighteenth century. During that period a few entrepreneurial potters expanded the productive capacity and began to establish what would become the factory system of the Potteries. "The master potter," noted Josiah Wedgwood, "became a capitalist" (Wedgwood and Ormsbee 1947, 35). His famous predecessor and namesake opened up the renowned Eutria works in 1769 and by that time a cluster of potters had established manufactories in the six-town area. Technical advances in the materials and improvements in the production process abetted this growth. From the early 1760s to the end of the decade the workforce grew by 40 percent and then by another 50 percent in the 1770s to 15,000. So dominant was the region becoming that master potters were transplanting themselves to the area by the turn of the century to participate in its advantages (Whipp 1990, 18).

The pottery industry marked the geography of the district in ways that defined it to outsiders as well as its inhabitants. In the early 1840s one popular periodical described the district as

> a portion of the county about ten miles in length and two or three in breadth . . . and occupying an area of perhaps twenty thousand acres. It

> may be characterised as one long street from end to end, for the successive towns and villages are so near each other, and gradually have been so connected by rows of houses, that the eye glances from one to another with scarcely an appreciable interruption . . . and if we pass through these towns on the high road, we shall find on either side a continued string of potteries and porcelain works, so large and so numerous that one may wonder where a market can be found for the immense mass of articles produced there.[2]

By 1841 there were 522 separate earthenware firms in its five major towns. They employed over 14,000 workers, including about one-third of the entire male workforce and thousands of women and children, in twenty-eight distinct occupational categories (Botham 1982, 166; Dupree 1995, 56; Moyes 1979, 42–43). At mid-century almost half of all its males and close to two-thirds of all females worked in the pottery trade as well as upwards of 11,000 children. By 1861 there were some 27,000 pottery workers in the district producing over £2 million worth of goods a year (Gatley 1989, 11; Whipp 1990, 18). As the trade grew during these decades most labor recruitment was largely local or relied on short-distance migrants, a substantial percentage coming from within a thirty-mile radius of the district (Dupree 1995, 89). With so much of the national industry concentrated in this corridor, and other smaller centers not within easy travel distance, the Potteries became a relatively insulated and specialized labor market.

Firms varied widely in size depending, in part depending on their niche. By mid-century there were about two dozen firms that employed more than 500 (including some such as Mintons and Copeland and Garrett that tipped 1,000 workers), though most concentrated in either enterprises of a few hundred or small shops of well under 100.[3] The estimate for that the average workforce for firms in the region was 167, though 60 percent had fewer than twenty employees. Hanley was the largest manufacturing center of the six towns that composed the pottery district, and the industry dominated the local economy (Moyes 1979, 40). Hanley, which listed 195 manufacturing premises in its rate books in 1862, contained some of the largest and best-known companies in the business, such as Brown-Westhead, which employed 1,500 at its two factories (one in neighboring Burslem); George L. Ashworth Brothers, whose four-acre establishment gave work to some 500 hands; and of course the Wedgwoods' firm located in nearby Etruria.[4] In this sense, following Burawoy, there was a high level of intra-industry competition.

The industry as a whole produced a dizzying array of household, decorative, and sanitary ware. Companies tended to have a dominant product line in a few of these wares, but large firms produced a variety of goods for both the home and export markets. Small firms specialized in a particular niche. Overall 40–50 percent of earthenware was produced for the export market, and the industry faced increasing international competition in the latter nineteenth century (Jewitt 1878, 316, 319, 325, 334; Whipp 1990, 25, 34). While the labor market was decidedly local, the industry was well ensconced in a global product market that fed commodity chains to many places around the globe, particularly continental Europe and the Americas. Apart from periodic trade depressions, such as that which occurred during the US Civil War, trade grew from the 1840s through the mid-1870s, with profits peaking in 1873. Few records remain to calculate profit margins, but the Wedgwoods managed a 12–15 percent average return on net worth throughout the period (Dupree 1995, 53, 191; Moyes 1979, 42, 45–47).

Marx highlighted these potteries as exemplary of the capitalist exploitation in the Industrial Revolution, though the social relations in and of production were quite distinct from the dark satanic mills of the cotton industry (1968, 243–46). The dominant form of organization of production, given sufficient size, was vertical integration. Large companies produced their own "slip" (the clay mixtures for production to start the process) and employed separate departments for decorating at the end (Moyes 1979, 42, 48). However, mass manufacturing did not mean standardization. Production was often highly specialized, and manufacturers often produced for orders by wholesalers and overseas merchants, creating fairly tight time constraints and sometimes demanding very irregular working hours.[5] Mass production and the huge variety of ware necessitated a very refined division of labor. This task specialization, decomposition of craft, and installation of disciplinary rules were pioneered by the Wedgwoods in the later eighteenth century in an effort to control the workforce, and became a signature of earthenware production.[6] Nonetheless, many of the production processes, especially in the formation and firing of wares, involved a fair degree of accumulated knowledge and skill.

Adult males dominated the high-skilled and highest-paying occupations in the initial production and firing, while women were mostly found in the decorating departments and warehousing.[7] There were some thirty craft specializations in the potbanks and each developed elaborated work processes. As Richard Whipp notes, "Each occupation generated its own commonly accepted work methods and rules. Potters consciously decided how they were to organize their work and legitimated their behavior by reference to notions of accepted practice with nineteenth-century antecedents."[8]

Skilled males dominated in the major production departments of production, including throwing, pressing, casting, and firing. Throwers produced small household and decorative items such as teacups, jugs, and vases. Pressers were divided into the flat- and hollow-ware divisions, the former making simple single-mold items such as plates, and the latter components for more complex, larger multipiece hollow-ware, such as large jugs, servers, ornamental goods, and sanitary ware. Casting often was reserved for large and complicated pieces, and involved producing successive coats of dried slip (liquefied clay) within plaster casts. Skilled throwers and pressers could have prodigious output. Throwers could average more than a teacup a minute, while flat pressers could produce 60–70 dozen plates a day. One or two children or women assisted the throwers by preparing clay and keeping the throwing wheels in motion. Women assisted turners and pressers by sponging and fetting ware. They were also employed in painting departments under female supervision, though the finer painting work and gilding remained the ken of males. As the century progressed the printing department, in which machinery was used to transfer patterns to ware, became a female area, as did the production of the stilts and thimbles used to stack ware for firing in the large biscuit ovens. After the Factory Act of 1864, which extended the original law concerning the working conditions and hours of children to the pottery industry, the number of females employed in the area rose by roughly 50 percent.[9]

The organization of these workshops was highly patriarchal. Family hiring was an important foundation of this unit, and many potters brought their sons into the trade through such apprenticeships. In this way employment relations resemble Burawoy's ideal type of patriarchal despotism although, as we shall see, the use of master and servant law complicates such classification. Employers readily acquiesced to such subemployment schemes since it both saved considerable time and helped maintain the loyalty of the skilled male workers.[10] Family hiring, subcontracting, and immediate control over production in the potbank affirmed claims to a working-class masculinity centered on freedom and independence, but it might also have rubbed up against the respectable masculinity of employers who legitimized their manliness through control of their factories discipline (McClelland 1991, 82–83; 2000, 101; Tosh 1994, 193).

As Sabel and Zeitlin (1985) argue, craft-based production reliant on subcontracting has substantial advantages for capitalists in industries responsive to varied product markets needing uneven batch production. Pottery was such an industry, and many of its subdivisions were organized through patriarchal subcontracting. While this system contained advantages, it posed persistent problems for employers concerning workplace control. Until well into the 1870s the substantial majority of their work was done without the advantages of steam power.[11] Factories were generally an accretion of workshops and these workspaces were rarely amenable to retrofitting the machinery necessary for mechanized power. Ultimately the adult male worker, particularly in subdivisions defined as skilled, had substantial immediate control over the pace of production.[12] The highly defined division of labor was not accompanied by real subordination through machinery, and thus work discipline thus could not be imposed by mechanization. As one inhabitant of the area recalled, "Machinery means discipline in industrial operations. In the Potteries there was no such discipline, and very little of any other . . . Owing, as I believe, to the absence of machinery, there was no effective economical management of the potworks."[13] As I suggest later, the institutionalized dependence on the law for workplace discipline might well have both resulted from this dilemma earlier in the century, and contributed to a slow turn to mechanization in later decades.

While normal factory hours were usually 6:30 a.m.–6:30 p.m. on weekdays, actual hours varied by the specific orders, and there was no standard workday. In part, this suited manufacturers who needed the flexibility to respond quickly to changes in market demand and orders from their distributors. There were no clocks in the potbanks and no official timekeepers (Whipp 1987, 226). Responding to one of the initial surveys of the factory inspectors in the 1830s, a number of manufacturers stated that they basically ceded the issue of time to their workers. Responding to a question on irregular working hours a manufacturer in Stoke-on-Trent stated that this occurred "when the men have been at the new beer-shops, Monday, Tuesday, and perhaps Wednesday," adding a bit later on that night work happened because "sometimes the men contrive to work all night after drinking one or two days, but quite without or against our knowledge." A representative of a Burslem firm noted, "If a man has the occasion to work one night in the week, if he wanted to make arrangements to play the following day, we should have no objection." By the 1860s a factory inspector reported that, "It is still too frequent a practice among the flatpressers as well as with other potters to waste the first days of the week in idleness or the beerhouse, and then work themselves and their boys until 8 or 9 o'clock on Thursday and Friday in order to recover their lost time."[14] But what was unobjectionable in the 1830s was a flashpoint of labor control conflict by this time, because of the transformation of the industry in the intervening years (discussed below).

Specialized production made it cost effective for manufacturers leave each workshop to organize and supervise itself (Whipp 1990, 66). As Shaw recalled, "There was only the loosest daily or weekly supervision of the workpeople, in their separate 'shops,' and working by 'piece-work,' they could work or play very much as they pleased. The weekly production of each worker was not scanned as it was in a cotton mill" (1970 [1903], 185). This independence also characterized the work of the saggar makers, the placers, the ovenmen and their assistants, who arranged and fired the ware in large "biscuit" ovens.

Critical to the potbank was the rule of custom, and divisions between workers and manufacturers concerning its assumptions marked battles over what Price terms the "frontiers of control" (Whipp 1990, 23, 57). Workshop rules were developed to allow for irregular production flows and the specifics of the piece work. As with many other industries, what passed for custom was as much a process of contemporary contention as enduring practice and, following Price, the politics of custom was often at the frontiers of control. This conflict sometimes made its way to the local bench. Small-scale pay disputes could frequently arise over specific patterns and items, and union locals often sent representatives to press claims (Botham 1982, 272; Whipp 1990, 147–49). Major confrontations occurred in the 1830s and again in the 1860s and 1870s concerning both piece rates for potters and wages for ovenmen (Thomas 1971, 194–95). Unions were involved in these disputes but, divided along craft lines and even by towns, they often lacked the power of numbers, particularly throughout the 1850s and into the 1860s (Warburton 1931, 168–73; Warrilow 1960, 254; Whipp 1990, 88–89). When trade was brisk, as in the early 1870s, skilled workers were able to exact significant wage increases.[15] With labor accounting for between a third and a half of all production costs, wages were a flash point for conflict.

One final area of considerable periodic contention from at least early in the century was the wage payment practice employed by manufacturers known as "good from oven," an enduring frontier of control. Potters were credited for their work after its firing and inspection for imperfections, for which discounts were exacted. The practice incensed the potters, who argued that most bad work was the product of inferior clay and poor firing rather than their own hands. Potters also accused manufacturers of using such discounts to compensate for wage increases, and of selling this ware and not remunerating the potters for their work. Periodically from at least the 1830s through the end of the period the potters agitated on this issue. In a major conflict in the mid-1830s (discussed next), manufacturers defended the good-from-oven system, claiming the need to "adhere to this principle of custom."[16]

A series of conflicts in the 1830s set manufacturers on a path of a labor control regime that they would follow into the last quarter of the century. Through the first quarter of the nineteenth century adult male pottery workers were organized in craft-based organizations that periodically engaged manufacturers over piece rates, though there is no evidence of more formal unions. With the repeal of the Combination Laws in 1825, partially legalizing union activity to bargain for wages, two unions were formed and struck for increases in piece rates and the abolition of the truck system (the payment of wages in goods). They met with some success with the latter goal, but with the commercial downturn of that year the strike and the unions collapsed (Thomas 1971, 188–90; Warburton 1931, 29–31).

In 1830 delegates from the National Association for the Protection of Labour, a national union of all trades established by cotton spinners in Lancashire, made recruiting visits to the Potteries, and in August of the following year the National Union of Operative Potters was established. This was the first attempt at a general union, and at its height the organization contained fifty-four craft-based lodges, claiming 6,000 members in the district. In 1833, when trade was brisk, the union successfully used selective strikes and negotiations with a manufacturers' committee to establish a uniform list of piece rates in an effort to raise wages at many firms. Emboldened by this achievement, the union engaged in strikes against manufacturers in Burslem and Tunstall the following year, winning piece-rate increases of 30–35 percent after a fifteen-week confrontation.[17]

While the 1833 actions had been met with conciliation among some manufacturers, who saw it as an opportunity to create stability, the 1834 strikes shifted them toward open hostility, laying the groundwork for the bitter struggle of 1836–37. The prelude to this confrontation occurred in August 1835 when potters at several firms struck. Under trade custom all workers were hired under an annual bond system every year at Martinmas (in November). The contracts bound workers to a manufacturer for an entire year and prohibited them from making arrangements with other employers over the duration of the contract. In signing such agreements, under master and servant law, potters effectively undermined their collective bargaining positions vis-à-vis manufacturers. It is not clear how regularly manufacturers regularly resorted to prosecutions for violations of service against workers in the previous strikes, but in these cases the employers had the strike leaders convicted for neglect of work, and in one case for intimidation of strike breakers under the new Combination Laws (Warburton 1931, 87–88).

In mid-March of 1836 three-fourths of the manufacturers inaugurated a Chamber of Commerce to combat the "tyranny" of the union, with a "determination to endure no longer the continual and progressive annoyances imposed on them, and to defend and support each other unitedly in all sacrifices for the maintenance of their rights" (Chamber of Commerce n.d., 4, 8). In August the N.U.O.P. engaged in strikes against thirteen manufacturers in Tunstall and Burslem. Critically, the union sought redress not on wages and piece rates, but on issues of "principle." They sought to modify the annual bond, proposing that with a month's notice they should be able to opt out of their contracts, changes in the apprentice system, good from oven, and other work-control issues. From the manufacturers' perspective, the union "framed a new form of hiring, and announced their intention of forcing it on the Masters. They next avowed their intention of regulating the mode of work, the hours of labour, and the number of apprentices and terms on which they could be employed: thus assailing the rights and usurping the authority of the Masters, while themselves were complaining of injustice, demanding liberty, and denouncing oppression!!" (Chamber of Commerce n.d., 9).[18] The Chamber responded with a refusal to negotiate with the union and, after consulting both with local magistrates and legal counsel, announced its intention to add a suspension clause in the upcoming annual bond under which factories could be shut down for six weeks when deemed necessary by the manufacturer. The union interpreted this not only as a strike-breaking strategy, but also as an attempt to exert more complete authority over the workplace generally whenever a dispute over conditions or control arose (Chamber of Commerce n.d., 10; Owen 1970, 34).[19]

At Martinmas the Chamber went on the offensive and half of all firms in the district, employing about 7/9ths of all labor commenced a lock out. The N.U.O.P. drew support from other trade unions from outside the district, and soldiered on until the end of January. At the point of collapse it accepted a guaranteed sixteen days work per month under the annual bond and a modification of the good-from-oven system. However, the Chamber had won an uncompromising victory, these clauses were soon violated, and the union sank into demise under the weight of considerable debt (Boyle 1838, 43–44; Chamber of Commerce n.d., 20–23; Warburton 1931, 98–105).

In the summer of 1838 forty petitioners, among them some of the largest pottery manufacturers and coal-mine owners, petitioned the government to appoint Thomas Bailey Rose as a stipendiary magistrate for the district. Rose, a staunch Anglican and Tory (who blamed Liberals "for encouraging the working classes in their subversive ideas"), joined the bar in 1827 (Stuart 1985, 185–86). He assumed this position in 1839 and apparently engaged it with considerable zeal. Through 1850 his clerk estimated that Rose heard on average 800 cases a year, a significant number involving labor disputes.

As Christopher Frank (2010, 205–8) details. Rose rapidly became a detested presence among working people. In the Chartist riots, led by colliers, that swept the region in mid-August of 1842 Rose's house was attacked and burned. In the wake of two days of rioting, after which over 700 were arrested and 276 prosecuted, Rose sat with other area magistrates to mete out justice, including over some who participated in the assault on his house.

The following year Rose created a cause célèbre in the prosecution of cases involving a strike at a pottery firm over the lack of reciprocity in the annual bond. In the second case, the defendant argued that he had not returned to work for fear of retribution by the union, but he refused to cooperate with Rose in naming his supposed persecutors. Rose sentenced the defendant to three months in prison at hard labor and then, according to the *Potters' Examiner and Workman's Advocate*, pronounced, "There is a set of idle vagabonds about, I know, trying to induce both colliers and potters to absent themselves from work, by threats and promises. Let but one of them be brought before me, and I'll commit him—I'll send him to the House of corrections for three calendar months, to hard labour or commit for a trial at the assizes."[20] As Frank (2010, 210) notes in his detailed analysis of workers' legal battle with Rose, this became a rallying cry for workers in the district. Commenting on Rose's decision the *Potter's Examiner* poured out enmity: "He, as we have before stated, who would administer the law from vindictive, or class-regulated feelings, is a villain, and ought to be subject to some heavy, penal enactment. The judge who would act from passion, prejudice, or class interest, and not from the letter of the law, is a blot on jurisprudence of a country,—a moral pestilence in the very heart of social existence, that threatens the security of life, liberty, and property; and ought, consequently, to be removed, as the greatest possible evil of civilized society."[21]

With the annual bond firmly in place and reigning as the arbiters of trade customs at work, pottery manufacturers established a labor control regime through which they could exercise significant authority in the workplace. They influenced the pace and intensity of the production process not by direct supervision, but through the power invested in them through the annual bond. One means by which they accomplished this is through the "allowance system." Under it workers were forced to accept a drawback of anywhere between 5 and 20 percent of their piece rates so that they would be hired. Also in the annual hire the actual number of items in a dozen, on which piece rates were based, was set considerably beyond twelve, and could reach as high as thirty-six.[22] Through such schemes employers could determine the intensity of work. Larger employers also turned to printed contracts in these years. Exactly when they became standard practice is difficult to say, but they appear in Wedgwood's hiring books in the early 1840s. In a printed contract used from 1853 to 1870 workers agree to work "faithfully diligently and honestly" ' during the year of the agreement and "agree to do and perform their work in a good skilful and workmanlike manner and to attend to the business of their said employer during the regular and usual working hours to execute h[is] lawful commands and in all respects to behave as honest and faithful servants and the said Workmen agree to be satisfied with such work as the Potter can fairly and reasonably provide for them during the said term and to be subject to the Rules of his Manufactory."[23]

Such general language gave manufacturers substantial authority in setting the conditions of work. The annual agreement left manufacturers with the upper hand as arbiters of "custom," a currency of legitimation in arguments before the bench. "Reasonable standards" became the contractual terrain of the employer. Most important, the annual hiring allowed the manufacturers to use the full weight of master and servant law as a disciplinary tool in the absence of other mechanisms, as the union leader William Owen argued before a parliamentary committee.[24] Workers complained bitterly about the annual hiring from its inception in the late 1830s throughout the next several decades. As one potter remarked in a letter to the *Potteries Examiner*, "It is a veritable chain which binds its victims to a state of serfdom. The man that signs it is the bond servant of his employer. It takes away from all his discretionary powers as to the course he shall use in relation to the disposal of his labour during the term of the agreement, and the labour so performed under such an agreement , is no longer free, but at once becomes, to all intent and purposes, slave labour" (Oct. 21, 1871, 8).

As contractual arrangements in other industries changed to shorter periods the annual hire became a more blatant marker of servitude for the potters. In 1864 they began to mount a campaign for its abolition, and by 1866 finally extracted an agreement from manufacturers to abolish the practice, though the latter continued to prefer to sign their most skilled workers to annual agreements.[25]

From 1864 onward manufacturers faced the additional impediment to control in the Factory Extension Act of 1864. Pottery factories had escaped state regulation of child labor and hours under the original acts, but by the 1860s reformers led by health professionals, clergy, educators, and even twenty-six manufacturers petitioned for their extension to cover the industry. Besides humanitarian goals to protect young children, large manufacturers probably saw an advantage in it since they were more likely to adapt than their smaller counterparts (Dupree 1995, 223–30). In Hanley six firms, including those of E. J. Ridgway, J. W. Parkhurst, and Joseph Clementson (all borough magistrates) supported the initial petition. As the final legislation approached in 1864, however, most masters seemed to have turned against the idea. Prominent manufacturers such as Edwin Powell (also a borough magistrate), William Moore, and William Stubbs all strenuously objected to any limitations.[26] As the data below illustrate, all were among the most prominent users of the master and servant law.

While annual hiring ended, the accretion of disciplinary practices through the law remained. In the absence of any other ready mechanisms for labor control, work discipline had been institutionalized as part of the culture and practice of the local courts. The manufacturers' reliance on this mode of control increased during the 1860s and 1870s for two reasons. First, the 1864 Factory Extension Act created less flexible production hours, given the reliance of adult male workers on child and female assistants. Second, the end to annual hiring coincided with both this increased state supervision and the resolution of the US Civil War. The United States had accounted for 45 percent of the export market prior to the war, and peace brought with it an expansion in orders. With the price of labor high, and critical raw materials at a premium, profit margins continued to be squeezed for many firms.[27]

As Burawoy, Price, and the feminists all note, capitalists sometimes turned to paternalism as a control strategy. With production highly localized, and workers tied to community as much as craft, manufacturers attempted to cultivate a paternalistic despotism in many pottery towns. Some of the larger manufacturers conducted annual teas and picnics and sat on the boards of public institutions and made donations to a wide variety of improvement associations and other similar organizations. And there were some reciprocal acts by workers, who collectively honored factory owners for their exertions in maintaining employment levels during lean years.[28] These manufacturers seemed to engage in more paternalistic practices in an effort to exert authority, though neither in Hanley nor any other of the Potteries communities was such paternalism very successful.

Overall, then, most pottery manufacturers did not rely on paternalistic despotism. At the point of production, following both Burawoy and the feminists, we find a form of patriarchal despotism in which many parts of the social relations in production were organized under the supervision of adult male workers. Yet the politics of production did not leave the state external to the workplace. Rather, manufacturers incorporated master and servant law into their labor control regimes to exercise domination. Struggles over control over work centered on formal subordination, with steam-power technology being limited to a few areas of the production process and mostly in the largest firms. As Price suggests, manufacturers turned to the law to cement their authority.

In the Potteries it appears that a particular turning point for this process was the strike of 1836. Certainly manufacturers had turned to the law prior to this point and Hanley's rates of prosecution were probably higher than the national average, but in earlier decades the balance between master and worker cases was more even, and some of the larger firms rarely engaged in prosecutions (Hay 2000, 2004). However, with the great strike many manufacturers coalesced, particularly the largest, in a united front to combat unionism and maintain their control through the annual agreement and over definitions of custom. Legal domination became an even more reliable strategy with the establishment of the stipendiary magistrate soon after. These factors conjoined to establish a path that pottery manufacturers took for many decades.[29] This path was further augmented in Hanley in the late 1850s with the establishment of the borough court. Added to the stipendiary magistrate these formal institutions and their control reinforced the established labor control regime. The organization of justice in Hanley became even more hospitable to putting the power of legal coercion to use.

GOVERNANCE AND JUSTICE HANLEY

Hanley was controlled by an oligarchy fostered by its industrial and commercial growth. In 1857 Hanley was given borough status, and in 1859 the borough received a commission of the peace, authorizing a borough magistracy. Petitioners argued that they did not have enough easy or ready access to courts of summary jurisdiction (Crapper 1882, 33–36; Greenslade 1963, 159; Warrilow 1960, 205–7).[30] The town borough court added another venue for the prosecution of master and servant offenses, and, as we will see was a realm of the pottery manufacturers.

Throughout the 1860–75 period Hanley continues to be controlled by a relatively close-knit oligarchy of manufacturers, petty-bourgeoisie, and professionals who had links not only with each other but also with their peers in the other boroughs of the Potteries. Pottery manufacturers were well-ensconced leading figures in many of the town's institutions, and in a metaphorical sense were institutions themselves. Joseph Clementson, a leader among manufacturers, was president of the Borough Association for the Prosecution of Felons for twenty-one years, held several offices in the Methodist New Connexion conference, was on the old Hanley market trust, the Board of Health, and the Commission for watching and lighting, and served as chief bailiff and borough magistrate.[31] A partner of another large firm, William Brownfield, was an exemplar of Victorian individualism who, as a memorialist recounted, ascended from the ranks of common potters "into the governing class." Brownfield was president of the Hanley School of Art, the Hanley subscription newsroom, and the Working Men's reading room (to which he donated £500), vice-president of the Mechanics' Institute, a leading member of the auxiliary Religious Tract Society and the Liberation of Religion from State Patronage and Control Association, a market trustee, chief bailiff, a director of the Staffordshire Potteries Waterworks Co., alderman, mayor, and, of course, a borough magistrate.[32] Others, including the Wedgwoods, were local churchwardens and trustees, prominent position holders in the local temperance societies, and were a significant proportion of the local school board. Many, of course, were also members of the North Staffordshire Chamber of Commerce.[33]

It was from within this oligarchy that the approximately two dozen borough magistrates that served during the period were chosen. Among the group about half were in the pottery industry, though only a few, such as Joseph Clementson, Edwin Powell, and George Ridgway, were among the stalwarts who served as the backbone of the bench. The borough court was aided in these years by the stipendiary magistrates James E. Davis from 1864 to 1870, and J. Balguy through the end of the period. Davis was of mind with the oligarchy in many respects, and their affection for him was shown by a testimonial given in his honor shortly after he left to take up his new post at Sheffield. At that celebration he noted that the master and servant acts "operated beneficially both to the employers and employed of North Staffordshire in regulating and terminating their differences."[34] He also provided testimony for two parliamentary commissions on master and servant law, arguing in the first instance that workers had an advantage over capitalists because of their mobility, that the breach of contract by workers was a "public wrong," and that some form of imprisonment must remain a necessary possibility to compel a worker to fulfill his contractual obligations.[35]

Hanley's borough magistrates saw their task at the twice-weekly court sessions as maintaining an appropriate level of civility and morality in their town, and that goal kept them well occupied. In the administrative year ending in September 1871, for example, the borough court alone (exclusive of the hearings before the stipendiary) tried 1,782 cases, and it dipped modestly to 1,638 the following administrative year. Throughout the period respectable folk fretted that working-class culture was becoming a spawning ground for immorality. Correspondents to the *Advertiser* complained the town was "infested with beggars, cadgers and impostors."[36] As table 4.1 shows, the constabulary and magistrates particularly targeted

TABLE 4.1. Number of prosecutions in Hanley for master and servant violations and other selected offenses of summary jurisdiction, 1871–1875

Offenses	1871	1872	1873	1874	1875
Assault, common	299 (17)	372 (23)	141 (10)	164 (8)	151 (8)
Breaches of the peace	50 (3)	43 (3)	38 (3)	48 (2)	39 (2)
Drunkenness	648 (36)	287 (18)	370 (26)	369 (18)	444 (24)
Factory acts	. . .	5 (.3)	. . .	2 (.1)	. . .
Larceny under 5s	43 (2)	37 (2)	42 (3)	45 (2)	42 (2)
Local acts, bye-laws	149 (8)	287 (18)	272 (19)	676 (34)	567 (30)
Master and servant	131 (7)	237 (14)	58 (4)	55 (3)	39 (2)
Poor law, deserting or neglecting family	. . .	6 (.4)	17 (1)	34 (2)	41 (2)
Vagrancy acts, all offenses (including begging and prostitution)	98 (5)	44 (3)	77 (5)	80 (4)	65 (3)
Total	1,782	1,638	1,416	2,005	1863

Note: Numbers in parentheses are percentage of the total number of prosecutions.
Source: England and Wales, Police–Criminal Proceedings–Prisons, Judicial Statistics, Returns, BPP.

the inebriated. Prosecutions for drunkenness in Hanley were three times that for surrounding rural areas and twice as high than neighboring mining districts (Warrilow 1960, 401). However, the governing class deployed far more than magisterial discipline. As with many manufacturing and commercial elites during the period, they sought to create a hegemonic culture that fostered the kind of public order in which they themselves truly believed. They helped underwrite a Mechanics' Institute (albeit one with anemic and declining numbers), reading rooms, the local Ragged and Sunday schools, and in the early 1870s founded a British Workmen's public house, an alcohol-free establishment for conviviality.[37] However most paternalism was personally exercised by a few larger manufacturers and never cohered into a more general hegemonic civic culture.

Despite this largesse of the governing class, many working people continued to view the local courts as a thinly veiled exercise in class control when it came to issues of work and employment, as they had the stipendiary in the previous decades. The local working-class paper, the *Potteries Examiner*, summarized such frustrations over prosecutions in these courts in a comment on master and servant law and its revision in 1867: "The sum of these cases is a great national injustice that mocks at our boasted freedom, and it rankles the minds of the class that suffers most. . . . The matter is the great sore of the English legal system, corrupt in principle, nothing but corruption flows from it, but unquestionably the greatest victim of the rottenness of our administration are working men" (Sept. 14, 1872, 4). And the paper opined that "Justice is represented to be blind, but when attempted to be administered by employers of labour, it generally has its eyes open, though it does not see straight, but looks obliquely, on the side of capital" (June 8, 1872, 4). Thus, in Hanley an institutional infrastructure existed by which pottery manufacturers and other capitalists readily could bring problems of formal subordination to a court system in which they had a heavy hand, and that became a source of considerable antagonism between capitalists and workers.

HANLEY MASTER AND SERVANT PROSECUTIONS

Testifying before a select committee on master and servant law in 1866 the long-time union activist and editor of the *Potteries Examiner*, William Evans, suggested that prosecutions were occurring almost every week in the Potteries district, and that they were on the increase. In part, he argued, the number rose with trade prosperity, with manufacturers resorting to the law as a means of labor discipline.[38] The motto for the Hanley court was "Fiat justitia ruat cœlum"—roughly "Let justice be done, though the heavens fall"—and there was certainly plenty of justice meted out.[39] The local bench was a mechanism through which pottery manufacturers enacted their labor control regime. Beyond the issues of control posed for these manufacturers, however, we might also expect that the court itself developed as an institutional mechanism for such discipline available to all of the town's capitalists, regardless of trade or industry. The record of prosecutions for the period is suggestive in this regard. Table 4.2 gives a preliminary indication,

TABLE 4.2. Number of prosecutions under the Master and Servant (1871–1881) and the Employers and Workmen Act (1875–1881) and total number of prosecutions in Hanley Borough Magistrates' Court as reported in annual parliamentary reports, 1871–81

Year	1871	1872	1873	1874	1875	1876	1877	1878	1879	1880	1881
Master and Servant/Employers and Workmen	131	237	58	55	39	n.a.	n.a.	8	7	21	19
Total prosecutions in Hanley Borough Magistrates' Court	1,782	1,638	1,476	2,055	1,836	n.a.	n.a.	1,533	1,521	1,454	1,381

Source: England and Wales, Police–Criminal Proceedings–Prisons, Judicial Statistics, Returns, BPP.

showing the relative prominence of prosecutions under master and servant law for the period.[40]

Data

I have been able to collect data on the Hanley borough and stipendiary courts from two of sources. First, magistrates' clerks maintained minute books for Hanley's court from 1864 through the end of the period.[41] The descriptions of cases heard before the bench vary considerably in length, and there is no particular logic to the extent of the details provided for a given case. In addition, the entry books are clearly not a comprehensive record. Several comparisons highlight these deficiencies. In 1872, for example, about 1,260 cases are recorded in the minute books. However, as reported by the borough Watch Committee to Parliament for the administrative year September 1871–September 1872 the borough bench heard 1,638 cases (*Staffordshire Advertiser*, Oct. 12, 1872, 5). Given that this was only slightly less than the previous administrative year, and assuming a rough distribution of cases by month, this represents a difference of almost one-quarter. Of more particular concern is the underrepresentation of master and servant cases. Table 4.2 provides the number of prosecutions recorded for Hanley borough in the annual parliamentary reports starting in 1871.[42] As can be seen by comparing tables 4.1 and 4.2 there are significant discrepancies, with the combined court minutes and newspaper reports yielding only about 20 and 25 percent of all master and servant convictions reported to Parliament in 1871 and 1872 respectively. This seriously understates the percentage of all court cases that involved master and servant prosecutions, which in 1872 climbed to a substantial 14 percent, or nearly *five times* the national percentage for that year. This suggests that the magistrates' minute books significantly underrepresent master and servant cases in the years of heavy prosecution.

To expand the coverage of cases found in the court records I have extracted reports of master and servant prosecutions from the *Staffordshire Advertiser* from 1864–75 and the *Potteries Examiner* from 1871–75.[43] These newspapers provided weekly "Police Report" columns on local court activity, reviewing selected cases. They too are clearly not nearly comprehensive. To take 1871 again as an example, the two newspapers combined provide information on seventeen master and servant cases that do not appear in the minute books. In 1872 these combined sources yield fifty-nine master and servant cases, 23 percent of which are reported only in the magistrates' minute books and 36 percent of which are recorded there and in at least one newspaper source. Thus, taken together, all of the above sources do not provide even close to a comprehensive record, and it is impossible to know the selectivity biases of each source. Nonetheless, used cautiously, the composite data from the court records and newspapers provide a telling picture of court activity for the period 1864–75.

Prosecutions 1864–1875

The data for the period are suggestive in a number of respects. As noted, table 4.2 provides the total number of prosecutions by employers for the borough as a whole, and table 4.3 by industry as well as the percentage of successful prosecutions.[44] For almost all of the period the pottery industry prosecutions are a strong plurality or a majority of those recorded. The remainder of prosecutions come from the iron trades and smaller trades that run the gamut of the local economy, from crate-making and color manufacture to beer-selling and butchery. The vast majority of all cases were prosecutions of single workers, though in some cases employers used master and servant law to quash strikes and disputes.[45]

Assuming the data are roughly representative of the total number of prosecutions they tend affirm several suppositions about the use of master and servant law. First, as table 4.3 demonstrates, the number of prosecutions rose with industrial demand. The year 1866 was one of significant expansion of overseas trade, which had languished until the end of the US Civil War. Moreover, a monthly accounting of prosecutions shows a clear increase from June on when workers mobilized against the anticipated annual hiring process. The years 1871–73, boom years in the trade (the last

TABLE 4.3. Number of master and servant prosecutions by year for pottery and all other industries and as a percentage of yearly master and servant prosecutions by industry, from court records and newspapers

Industry	1864	1865	1866	1867	1868	1869	1870	1871	1872	1873	1874	1875	1864–75
Pottery	8 (67)	9 (64)	39 (81)	8 (89)	5 (80)	13 (76)	5 (42)	12 (43)	35 (59)	33 (54)	18 (49)	10 (37)	185 (59)
Other	4 (33)	5 (36)	9 (19)	1 (11)	1 (20)	4 (24)	7 (58)	16 (57)	24 (31)	28 (46)	19 (51)	17 (63)	134 (41)
Total	12	14	48	9	6	17	12	28	59	61	37	27	329

Note: Percentages in parentheses.
Sources: 1864–65, 1867–70: Hanley Magistrates' Court Draft Minute Books, *Staffordshire Advertiser*; 1866: Hanley Magistrates' Court Draft Minute Books (Jan.–March only), *Staffordshire Advertiser*; 1871–75: Hanley Magistrates' Court Draft Minute Books, *Staffordshire Advertiser*, *Potteries Examiner*.

TABLE 4.4. Number of successful master and servant prosecutions by year for pottery and other industries and as a percentage of yearly master and servant prosecutions by industry

Industry	1864	1865	1866	1867	1868	1869	1870	1871	1872	1873	1874	1875	1864–75
Pottery	7	7	34	4	3	10	4	9	29	28	12	10	157
	(88)	(88)	(89)	(50)	(60)	(77)	(80)	(75)	(83)	(85)	(67)	(100)	(86)
Other	2	2	8	1	1	2	6	15	22	22	12	12	105
	(50)	(40)	(80)	(100)	(50)	(50)	(86)	(94)	(92)	(79)	(63)	(71)	(79)
Total	9	9	42	5	4	12	10	24	51	50	24	22	262
	(75)	(64)	(88)	(56)	(67)	(71)	(83)	(85)	(86)	(82)	(65)	(81)	(85)

Note: Percentages in parentheses.

Sources: 1864–65, 1867–70: Hanley Magistrates' Court Draft Minute Books, *Staffordshire Advertiser*; 1866: Hanley Magistrates' Court Draft Minute Books (Jan.–March only), *Staffordshire Advertiser*; 1871–75: Hanley Magistrates' Court Draft Minute Books, *Staffordshire Advertiser, Potteries Examiner*.

being the tail end) when exports peaked and home demand was strongest, show significant increases in the number of prosecutions.[46] Given the tightness of the labor market and the waning of the annual hire, it seems reasonable to assume that company owners and managers took legal recourse to keep relatively scarce labor both productive and bound to the firm.

Second, as table 4.3 shows, the vast majority of all prosecutions for which a conclusion could be determined were successful. Overall 86 percent of all pottery cases for the period resulted in favorable outcomes for employers, with employers in other industries experiencing a slightly lower rate of success. Prosecution was thus a highly credible threat, and if these numbers are representative, pottery workers throughout Hanley might well have known peers who experienced such discipline each year. Certainly, the local courts were generally seen by potters as odious and class-biased.

Table 4.4 indicates that for master and servant prosecutions in which occupation can be identified, skilled occupations clearly dominate the distribution in the pottery industry, in some contrast to all other trades.[47] Almost four-fifths of the adult workers in these occupations were skilled by the industry's standards, which was twice as high as that for other industries. When the percentage of apprentices is added it is apparent that virtually all workers with listed occupations had claim to some skilled work. The prosecutions among pottery workers encompass well over two dozen distinct occupation lines, with no branch being outstanding. Among some of the more prominent transgressors were potters, ovenmen, and placers, the last two occupations being critical in the extent to which product was spoiled in the production process. In most years, pressers, potters, and placers are the most frequently prosecuted, but workers from virtually all stations found themselves before the bench over the period.[48]

The breakdown of judgments in table 4.5 also illustrates a tendency to use the law as a means of discipline, rather than simple retribution. As noted in the last chapter, magistrates had a variety of sanctioning options available, both in the 1823 act and amended law of 1867, from a lenient order to return to work, to fines and damage awards, and on the severe end up to three months' imprisonment. As the tables show, in virtually all years the magistrates took the middle road, using a somewhat fluctuating mix of fines, payments, and sureties in sentencing. Over the course of the period a simple court mandate to return to work was handed down to about 20–30 percent of pottery workers and to about a third of workers in other industries. Prison sentences were rare for all workers, and some mix of pecuniary sanctions, particularly damage payments and sureties, dominated the sentencing. There was a shift in court sentencing during the period from fines to employer compensation or insured work performance, probably due to the partial reforms of 1867. Perhaps in this sense the stipendiary magistrates James E. Davis was quite correct: what employers wanted, and what the executors of justice delivered, was not a pound of flesh but, more vital for the capitalist, the full weight of the workers' labor power.

Though the use of master and servant law has been thought of as the disciplinary tool of the small master, large companies frequently sought the court's authority. The most frequent prosecutors are listed in table 4.6. As the table shows eight of the ten top prosecutors were pottery manufacturers, and they include some of the standards of the industry (though this of course is likely a function of their size). I have already noted the size and importance of the firms Bishop & Powell and Brown-Westhead. J. & G. Meakin, which ran the Eagle Works in Hanley, had two branch factories in nearby Cobridge and Burslem, were large producers of white granite earthenware for the American market, and also leaders in the introduction of steam-powered jiggers (Hollowood 1951). J. &. H. Davis ran the Trent Pottery Works (originally established as Livesley & Davis) and were substantial producers of white granite ware for the US market (Jewitt 1878, 336, 340). While company employment data are lacking, it would not be surprising if the number of prosecutions a firm conducted were roughly proportionate to the size of its workforce.

Finally, table 4.7 shows the gender breakdown of prosecutions for the entire period. For pottery in particular it is quite clear that manufacturers targeted their male workers, often skilled adults, for prosecution. Given the

TABLE 4.5. Judgments rendered for successful prosecutions by year for pottery and other industries and as a percentage of yearly total successes by industry

Judgments	1864	1865	1866	1867	1868	1869	1870	1871	1872	1873	1874	1875	Total
Fines	6 (67)	7 (78)	36 (86)	2 (40)	2 (50)	2 (17)	2 (20)	7 (30)	12 (24)	6 (13)	5 (21)	3 (14)	90 (34)
Pottery	6 (86)	6 (86)	31 (91)	1 (25)	0	1 (10)	1 (25)	1 (11)	8 (28)	3 (11)	2 (17)	1 (10)	61 (39)
Other	0	1 (50)	5 (63)	1 (100)	1 (100)	1 (50)	1 (17)	6 (40)	4 (18)	3 (14)	3 (25)	2 (17)	28 (27)
Sureties	. . .	. . .	. . .	0	1 (25)	4 (33)	5 (50)	14 (61)	15 (29)	12 (25)	8 (33)	10 (45)	69 (26)
Pottery	. . .	. . .	. . .	0	1 (33)	4 (40)	1 (25)	5 (56)	9 (32)	6 (21)	4 (33)	2 (20)	32 (20)
Other	. . .	. . .	. . .	0	0	0	4 (67)	9 (60)	6 (27)	6 (27)	4 (33)	8 (75)	37 (35)
Damage payment	. . .	. . .	. . .	0	1 (25)	4 (33)	0	2 (9)	11 (22)	16 (33)	4 (17)	10 (45)	48 (18)
Pottery	. . .	. . .	. . .	0	1 (33)	4 (40)	0	2 (22)	6 (21)	12 (43)	3 (25)	4 (40)	32 (20)
Other	. . .	. . .	. . .	0	0	0	0	0	5 (23)	4 (18)	1 (8)	6 (50)	16 (15)
Prison sentence	2 (22)	0	5 (12)	1 (20)	0	0	2 (20)	1 (4)	2 (4)	6 (12)	0	0	19 (7)
Pottery	1 (14)	0	3 (9)	1 (25)	0	0	1 (25)	1 (11)	0	5 (18)	0	0	12 (8)
Other	1 (50)	0	2 (25)	0	0	0	1 (17)	0	2 (9)	1 (5)	0	0	7 (7)

Note: Percentages in parentheses.

Sources: 1864–65, 1867–70: Hanley Magistrates' Court Draft Minute Books, *Staffordshire Advertiser*; 1866: Hanley Magistrates' Court Draft Minute Books (Jan.–March only), *Staffordshire Advertiser*; 1871–75: Hanley Magistrates' Court Draft Minute Books, *Staffordshire Advertiser, Potteries Examiner*.

TABLE 4.6. Firms by number of master and servant laws prosecutions in Hanley, 1864–1874

Company	Trade	Number of Prosecutions
J. & G. Meakin	Pottery manufacture	21
J. & H. Davis and Co.	Pottery manufacture	20
Bishop & Powell	Pottery manufacture	19
Messrs. Wedgwood	Pottery manufacture	17
J. Clementson & Co.	Pottery manufacture	14
George Jones	Crate manufacture	11
Brown-Westhead & Co.	Pottery manufacture	10
Livesley and Davis	Pottery manufacture	8
William Stubbs	Pottery manufacture	6
John Warner	Engineering and iron foundry	6

Sources: Borough of Hanley Magistrates' Court Draft Minute Books, *Staffordshire Advertiser, Potteries Examiner.*

TABLE 4.7. Gender distribution (percentages) of master and servant prosecutions in Hanley by pottery, iron, and all other industries, 1864–1875

Gender	Pottery	Iron	Other	Total
Male	91	91	94	92
Female	7	3	3	6
Unknown	2	6	3	2

Sources: Borough of Hanley Magistrates' Court Draft Minute Books, *Staffordshire Advertiser, Potteries Examiner.*

town elite's concern with inebriety and other rowdiness, pursued both in court and through sponsorship of civic institutions, this might suggest an attempt to tame a certain form of working-class masculinity that defied labor discipline. As noted in the introduction to the case studies, this cannot be demonstrated easily from the court minute books or newspaper reports.

Throughout the years under review several typical kinds of workplace conflicts seen through the lens of legality became master and servant prosecutions. Most frequently workers were prosecuted for not showing up, for tardiness, or early exits. Sometimes absence was simply a matter of avoidance of work, though often it was related to a dispute over work conditions or pay. Many prosecutions concerned lack of time discipline, absence, and irregular work habits of the potters and other skilled male workers. At the extreme end of punishment in such instances was the case of the saggar maker James Pedley who missed parts of three days' work at Messrs. Ford in early September 1872. The foreman complained that the establishment had suffered £3 in damages for this neglect and Pedley was sentenced to a month in prison.[49] At times it was the threat of imprisonment that settled matters. In March of 1864 the thrower Thomas Hughes, disputing with his employers, Messrs. Harding, over the exact nature of his agreement, left work. Hughes's lawyer argued that this was a civil matter between the parties, but the court saw otherwise and offered Hughes the option of returning to work or two months' imprisonment (*Staffordshire Advertiser*, March 5, 1864). Generally fines, damage awards, surety bonds, or some combination of these were meted out by the court. Stephen Pope, a hollow-ware presser, appeared before the court on a neglect of work charge by Brown-Westhead and Co. in mid-October 1873. Pope had walked out of work after a dispute with a manager over a change to a new type of pattern jug that the firm decided to produce after his first several months at work. Pope argued that this was a change in the conditions of his work and pay, but the court ordered him to return to work.[50]

In many potbanks "good from oven" or other conflicts over the quality of work could lead to a court summons. John Bradbury, a flatpresser, was summoned by the manufacturers E. T. and R. Moore for walking out of work in late March of 1869. Bradbury was angered that the firm not only had not given him full employment, but that they had glazed and sold some of his work that had been discounted or condemned as damaged. Appearing for the firm Moore confirmed Bradbury's account, but the court ordered the latter back to work and to find a surety bond to insure the completion of his contract (*Staffordshire Advertiser*, May 8, 1869).

Drinking, often associated with an unruly independence and spotty work behavior, was another target of prosecution. Two saggar makers of Messrs. J. & G. Meakin, William Leek and Alfred Kelsall, felt the sting of the law in the fall of 1875, when they were accused of neglecting their duties and absences due to spates of inebriation that the manager argued cost the firm at least £50. Leek was ordered to find two bonds of £10 and pay £5 damages, Kelsall to also find two bonds and pay £10 damages and both were ordered back to work.[51]

Extant records also provide evidence that manufacturers turned to the courts to suppress small-scale work stoppages by fractious workshops. Messrs. Davis summoned six workers for neglect in early September 1871. Five apologized and agreed to return to duty but Thomas Colcough remained

TABLE 4.8. Number of wage claims by industry in Hanley, 1864–1875

Industry	Number of Cases	Percentage of All Court Actions	Percentage of Successful Claims
Pottery	13	7	62
Other industries	47	26	66
Total	60	15	65

Sources: Hanley Magistrates' Court Draft Minute Books, *Staffordshire Advertiser*, *Potteries Examiner*.

obstinate. The manufacturers finally consented to a court arrangement in which Colcough was ordered to return to work, post a surety bond, and pay court expenses "in the hope that the defendant would behave better in the future" (*Staffordshire Advertiser*, Sept. 9, 1871).

Complaints by workers concerning wages or related contract violations never amount to more than one-third of all cases in any one year of the sample, and were likely a smaller percentage of the borough court total.[52] Though small in number, what is significant is that in many years a substantial majority of these complaints were settled in favor of the workers (see table 4.8). In pressing claims where there was a clear violation of contract workers could expect their due. Additionally, employers' complaints generally were dismissed because of their inability to substantiate their claims with sound proof of a contractual agreement. These worker victories, while small in number, could have been significant in buttressing the legal hegemony exercised by local capitalists. They established a moral consistency *within* the letter of the law, a consistency that also legitimized the legal process by which employers pressed their considerably greater number of prosecutions. In this sense the courts might have had some importance in legitimizing the asymmetrical reciprocity that Burawoy and Wright note is a feature of consent, although given the workers' dim view of courts this patina was probably limited.

There is one final piece of evidence to suggest that legality was a commonplace of the labor control regime. Minutes of the executive committee of the Hollow-ware Pressers' Union for the 1860s and 1870s show that, particularly in the early years of the period, the union routinely authorized funds to pay for legal counsel on behalf of their members to defend them against such prosecutions. These minutes and newspaper accounts of the hearings suggest that the pressers and other workers regularly hired local solicitors to represent them, underwriting at least ten cases in 1864, for example.[53] Pottery workers well understood that their battles over control of the workplace were partly exercised outside its confines in the venue of the court.

1875 AND AFTER

The demise of the Master and Servant Act and advent of the Employers and Workmen Act in 1875 offers further evidence for the argument that pottery manufacturers' labor control regimes were embedded in legal institutions. The slow transformation of the industry in the last several decades of the century, noted by many contemporaries and historians, resulted from many factors, but one that has not been considered is the path dependent nature of labor control.

The Employers and Workmen Act became law in 1875 and superseded all previous legislation. It decriminalized all employment offenses, and left workers subject only to damage claims for the transgressions defined by previous laws. Workers could either pay these damages or provide a surety and continue working in order to pay off the claims. In the event a worker refused either, an employer would have to take civil action against him in another court to collect damages. Labor historians have argued that decriminalization and the additional proceedings for collection took the teeth out of the law and, as we will further investigate in chapter 7, many employers lobbied against its passage precisely for this reason. Nationally prosecutions reported under the new act dropped by more than half, and Hanley was no exception. The parliamentary annual reports of judicial statistics for summary prosecutions report that for the years 1878–81 prosecutions under the Employers and Workmen Act of 1875 numbered, eight, seven, twenty-one, and nineteen respectively (see table 4.2 above).[54] These numbers should be interpreted with caution, since production also declined as Britain slipped into the depression of the 1880s. Nonetheless, the trend does suggest that once the law became a less effective coercive instrument its use waned substantially. The number of prosecutions increases slightly in 1880–81, years in which strikes occurred. The annual tally suggests that the law was no longer a routine vehicle for workplace coercion.

The history of the industry in these final decades suggests that manufacturers increasingly relied on a mix of strategies to replace labor discipline that they had exercised through the law. One such strategy was feminizing the workforce. Manufacturers increasingly used machinery such as the jigger, a molding device that facilitated the pressing of flatware, and the jolley, a machine that made it easier to fashion small hollowware such as teacups. There had been a shift toward adult female labor after the inclusion of the industry under the factory acts in 1864, which made the widespread use of child labor more difficult. Machines such as jiggers and jolleys had been introduced during these years, but their proliferation seems to have accelerated in the 1870s and 1880s. Whipp observes that once such technology was introduced and women were employed extensively in these branches, the positions ceased to be viewed as skilled. Women workers became direct employees of the firm and subcontracting was reduced. Internal labor markets became more dominant, as men were confined to the remaining "skilled" positions and treated differently than "staff." By the early 1890s the secretary of the United Firemen's, Dippers' and Placers Association testified before a royal commission that female labor "has been introduced so very largely in the last few years that I could not give you anything like a fair estimate of it."[55]

To a certain extent larger firms also engaged in increased supervision and managerial rationalization, though this made slow headway. Control was attempted through other strategies, such as an arbitration and conciliation board, which met sporadically but finally collapsed in 1881. A few larger manufacturers sought to create paternalistic regimes by informal benevolence, provision of housing, and social activities, but this was never general within the region.[56] Over these decades manufacturers thus revisited old strategies and adopted forms of labor control, a process that was to continue into the next century. While craft- or industry-wide strikes remained infrequent because of sectional and weak unions, workplace conflicts over the production process, conditions, and piece rates remained a commonplace of the potbanks.[57] What is reasonably clear, however, is that the law was no longer a centerpiece of their control efforts.

The increasing use of machinery introduced gradual changes in the potbanks. As Whipp observes, "In spite of the low level of mechanisation, the isolated changes in ceramic technology were particularly important since they concerned strategic points in the production process" (1990, 47). New factories built from the mid-1860s onward were more likely to have some steam-driven machinery, again in response to the factory acts (Lamb 1977, 55).[58] Yet most of this horsepower remained devoted to the preparation of materials for claymaking and the process of making the clay or slip itself, not ware production. In 1870 perhaps a third of the Potteries had steam engines of any sort (Lamb 1977, 58). Commenting on the introduction of new machinery in several firms at the end of this decade the *Pottery and Glass Trades' Journal* cautiously observed, "And from the progress thus made, it will be easily seen that the application of power to the manufacture of pottery has as yet in comparison with its future attained a very limited rank"

(March 1878, 38). In the 1880s steam-powered jiggers, the devices by which flatpressers molded clay, become increasingly common as well as batting machines, which prepared the clay for pressing. In some instances the introduction of new machinery, such as plate- and cup-making machines used by Limoges china makers, came soon after strikes. Technological histories of the industry suggest that many of these innovations were deployed more widely in the "outer" potteries such those in Glasgow and Lambeth (London) prior to their spread in the Potteries (Harris 1905–6, 58–63).[59] Smaller producers lagged behind in this transition, and craft production still remained a significant feature of the potbanks through the end of the century. At the turn of the century a catalog of one of the most prominent machinery manufacturers contained a variety of devices that could be powered by either steam or hand.[60]

We have already noted a few of the reasons that analysts of the industry have given for its laggardness in mechanization: The construction and physical layout of older plants, the reliance on patriarchal subcontracting, the need to respond to changing markets in batch production and the limitations of machinery itself for producing much of the finer ware. However, no attention has been paid to the way the industry's reliance on legal means of domination in its labor control regime might have also contributed to the slow pace of technological change. From the start of the Victorian era onward manufacturers in Hanley (and other Potteries towns) embraced a path in which master and servant law was a critical means of labor discipline. Having established this course many firms continued to expand production on a labor control regime that relied significantly on master and servant prosecutions. In Hanley discipline became embedded in local legal institutions that provided a ready and reasonably sure system of control. The courts delivered, and manufacturers were not pushed to look elsewhere for ways of controlling their adult male workers in the workplace. When the law was changed in 1875 they were well ensconced along this path, and almost of the attributes that had dampened the introduction of steam-driven machinery remained. By the turn of the century American and German producers were biting into England's once-secure export markets, and technological advantage was one of the reasons (Whipp 1990, 39–41).

CONCLUSION

Over the course of the nineteenth century pottery manufacturers tackled the problem of the subordination of labor. Unlike other industries (most famously cotton manufacture, which Burawoy addresses), the technical and social organization of pottery production imposed a number of boundaries on the possibilities for labor subordination. While the labor process had been successfully and highly subdivided into a series of discrete operations, manufacturers remained unable to fully engage in the real subsumption of labor. The production process remained largely manual, and relied on craft knowledge of materials and techniques. Manufacturers were neither able nor necessarily willing to fully wrest control of the labor process, given both the barriers posed by the production process and the advantages conferred by patriarchal subcontracting. In addition, as Price suggests, struggles at the frontiers of control often involved the control over custom.

Hanley's pottery manufacturers pragmatically constructed a labor control regime in response to these conditions by partly embedding labor discipline in local legal institutions. Through the labor contract of service, both in the annual bond and as it developed standardized printed contracts, manufacturers developed a regime that relied significantly on the power to exert control through master and servant law. The strike of 1836 marked a turning point in the industry when many manufacturers coalesced in a united front to soundly defeat the general union, reinforce their supremacy through the annual bond, and reassert their control over customs such as "good from oven." The fulfillment of their request (along with other local elites) for a regional stipendiary soon after the strike marked the back end of this conjuncture, and provided them with a ready means of pursuing labor discipline through the local court. Ascending to power over borough governance and adding the borough magistracy in the late 1850s further reinforced the path that embedded their labor control regime in local legal institutions. This particular embeddedness of labor control in local legal institutions explains both how struggles over the frontiers of control frequently took a legal turn and how the politics of production, even in the absence of central state intervention, was nonetheless tied securely to state authority. Through master and servant law, manufacturers exercised control both in the labor market and in the workplace where they had little or no direct supervision.

Extant data from the 1860s and early 1870s demonstrate that master and servant law was comparatively a common form of criminal prosecution for Hanley's working population, only regularly bested in its frequency by prosecutions for inebriety and assault. These data demonstrate how manufacturers tied workers to the workplace and disciplined them for actions that created problems in the flow of the production process. The overwhelming prosecution of men—many involving issues of drunkenness, erratic performance, and periodic absences—hints that partly this discipline involved the policing of a working-class masculinity discordant with capitalist dictates of production, though court records provide little direct evidence for this claim. Through prosecution or—perhaps just as important—its threat, manufacturers exercised formal subordination in the potbanks though they did little direct supervision.

The post-1875 history of the Potteries industry suggests possible negative consequences of this path dependence. There are a number of reasons why the North Staffordshire pottery industry was a relative latecomer to mechanization. However, it seems credible to argue that the manufacturers' labor control regime, predicated significantly on legal domination, was a "problem-solving regime" that made a turn to steam power and real subordination less pressing. For four decades manufacturers followed a path that provided reliable returns. With the law changed in 1875 the North Staffordshire trade lagged behind other parts of Britain and Europe, and the last quarter of the century was the start of a slow but steady erosion of its supremacy.

Potters described their position under the annual bond as no better than an African slave trade. However, had they turned their eyes eastward, they might have taken pause. By comparison their situation was one of relative freedom compared to that of the Hull fishing trawlers apprentices.

CHAPTER FIVE

Hull and the Fishing Trade

Both geographically and economically Kingston-upon-Hull looked out to the sea. Situated on the northwest bank on a bend of the River Hull, the town looked out to the widening mouth of Humber estuary, which emptied into the North Sea.[1] And the river and the sea in many respects were the lifeblood of Hull's economy. In 1871 about one-third of the labor force was directly tied to waterfront commerce in some fashion and other significant manufacturing and processing industries depended on the port for raw materials (Bellamy 1952, 38). However, it was one industry, fishing, employing a little less than 3 percent of the male workforce that dominated master and servant prosecutions in the local court and, as we will see, tough justice was focused on the apprentices in the trade, or fisherlads as they were called. The structure of its labor market, the economics of the trade itself, and apprenticeship as a particular form of labor contract along local judicial institutions led fishing trawler owners to turn to the court with great frequency as a means of controlling their apprentices. The status of these apprentices in the division of labor left them exposed to a despotism that cannot be characterized as either market or paternalistic, but rather a form of bondage that defined their position as unfree. Custom played only a perfunctory role in their labor, and the diktats of trawler owners and ship captains and hands, sanctified by the law, substantively ruled their lives.

By 1872 this town of about 125,000 people was the third-largest port in England, shipping about 9 percent of all its exports (amounting to £23 million) and receiving almost 5 percent of all imports (or £16.5 million), and employing close to 1,800 dock workers. It specialized in cxporting manufactured goods such as textiles and machinery from the industrial North, as well as coal and cattle. Imports were largely raw materials, such as timber and cotton, and foodstuffs such as wheat and oilseeds. Trade was anchored in the Baltic region, but there was also a substantial global network of shipping ties. This trade fostered a substantial seed-crushing industry of thirty-seven mills, several extensive cotton hemp and flax manufactories (the largest employing 1,500 hands), perhaps the largest concentration of furniture makers in the country, several large paint and coatings manufacturers, and of course a major shipbuilding industry for both steam and sailing ships, with the largest yard employing about 2,000 workers. It also fostered substantial inland water transport of goods and products.[2]

In 1871 transport employed almost a quarter of the male workforce, metal trades and engineering 14 percent, the building trades 10 percent, followed by other industries in the single digits.[3] No other English port had a higher concentration of workers tied to these industries. In that year Hull's shipyards ranked sixth in the total tonnage of vessels produced, well below their rivals to the north in Scotland, but equivalent to London in its now-sunset years. In transport the years of its most rapid growth were 1864–74, and shipping tonnage of its firms tipped sooner to modern iron vessels sooner than other ports.[4]

Compared to other port towns during these years Hull had a relatively quiescent labor force both in terms of the skilled and unskilled waterside workers. Why this was the case is not entirely clear, though several factors might have contributed. One might be the significant expansion of shipbuilding and shipping in these years, which was addressed by migrant labor from other parts of the country (Brown 1972, 10). There is little information on the organization of the Hull shipyards, but in general iron shipbuilding in England was based on a craft division of labor with engineers and metal workers organized in hierarchical work groups with substantial autonomy. Because ships were constructed on order according to the varying specifications of their future owners, little capital investment was made in machinery and, coupled with the cyclical nature of the industry, this craft division was the most pragmatic and flexible organization of labor. The division of labor was relatively new and arose with the transformation of iron shipbuilding from about midcentury, combining new skilled groups such as boilermakers and other engineers, platers, and angle iron workers with older trades such as joiners and caulkers. Within each work group skilled workers supervised a number of assistants and helpers.[5] This organization into semi-autonomous skilled work groups might have been the basis for successful labor discipline in the shipyards.

It appears that the boilermakers, joiners, and engineers were in some form of union organizations by the mid-1860s, though the extent to which these unions had organized the shipyards is not clear.[6] A substantial influx of skilled labor during the period from outside into this newer craft-based system might have dampened worker solidarity, particularly across skill groups.

In addition, given the importance of the shipping trade, Hull had a higher proportion of unskilled to skilled labor than many other large English towns, and as a port had a substantial transient workforce (Brown 1972, 10–11). While there was a recognized division of labor among dockers, this does not seem to have led to sectional labor organization, and there is little record of any union activity until the early 1870s. It is not clear how permanent the dockers' organizations were. Raymond Brown suggests that both the casual and seasonal nature of this work, coupled with the large growth of the workforce by migrants in the 1860s and 1870s created a difficult environment for union development, though dock workers had some form of continuous organization during these years (1972, 10).

It is also possible that the relative dominance of a few firms in both shipbuilding and shipping, particularly by the 1870s, created a balance of power in these industries that tipped the advantages further to capital. In shipbuilding firms such as Messrs. Martin Samuelson & Co. (later the Humber Ironworks Co.), Humphrys and Pearson and Messrs. Charles and William Earle employed upwards of 2,000 workers at peak periods, well more than twice the size of the average firms in the more important shipbuilding ports on the northeast coast or in Scotland (Bellamy 1963, 29; Sheahan 1864, 584–86). Growing concentration was similarly found in the shipping lines. By the later 1870s three out of the forty-one firms controlled about 46 percent of the registered vessels, and Thomas Wilson & Co. which had rapidly expanded over the previous decade, controlled about one-quarter of all ships and 30 percent of the total tonnage.[7]

Neither in cases of skilled or unskilled waterfront work are there many recorded disputes regarding labor discipline and control in the workplace. There was sporadic conflict among the skilled trades and the major shipbuilders over wages, which became a little more frequent in the prosperous early 1870s. The sparse record of these conflicts suggests that unions had a difficult time gaining victories against tenacious employers who on at least several occasions resorted to importing strikebreakers. In 1864 shipyard laborers at two of the largest firms, Messrs. Samuelson's and Messrs. Earle's lost a strike over piece rates and the former permanently replaced a number of the strikers (*Hull and Easter Counties Herald*, May 12, 1864). Engineers and molders successfully struck for wage increases in 1866 but the following year Earle's rescinded these increases and these groups appear to have engaged in an unsuccessful strike to maintain them. In 1868 Earle's responded to a strike by bringing substitutes from London.[8] In 1874 a strike by joiners at Earle's in May was quickly followed by engineers at all shipyards. The engineers endured for three months and obtained few if any concessions; while Earle's joiners persevered two months and received modest concessions, though by the end of the strike many had sought employment elsewhere.[9] The largely unskilled dock laborers had formed a union by 1872 and also pressed for improvements in wages and hours. Employers deployed ordinary seamen as replacement workers and at the end of three weeks the strike collapsed and union activists were blacklisted (Brown 1972, 19; *Beehive* March 30, 1872).

The largest shipbuilding and shipping lines did on occasion turn to the court in their efforts to combat strikes.[10] They used prosecution as part of a repertoire of tactics to intimidate workers and cow strike leaders. In an 1863 ruling that was eventually upheld on appeal by the Queen's Bench, the president of the Hull boilermakers' union was sentenced to three months' imprisonment for making threats to a society member. The union had voted to cease work in a yard where angle-iron bending work was being given to blacksmiths in violation of trade rules. The president was to warn his fellow member that he would be "despised" and "put to all sort of unpleasantness" if he persisted in working at the yard. The case hints at the ways in which some shipbuilders might have been shifting the customs of work in the yard, and the case might have had some impact of securing the authority of yard owners over the division of labor and their power vis-à-vis craft unions (Curthoys 2004, 41). However, firms employing waterside labor, whatever form of labor control regime they used, generally did not rely on the local court to enforce labor discipline. Rather, as we will see shortly, the use of the law was highly concentrated in the much smaller fish trawling trade.

THE JUDICIAL ORDER IN HULL

Raymond Brown has noted that "the Town Council of Hull up to the latter part of the 1890s was not, on the whole distinguished" (1972, 5). Local magnates did not participate in local politics and town government was populated by lesser businessmen and merchants.[11] Local politics was organized around networks of "Blues" (Liberals) and "Oranges," though Liberals generally held advantage in town elections. By midcentury elections were characterized by vote buying, and the town suffered through an embarrassing parliamentary investigation of this corruption in the early 1850s (Gillett and MacMahon 1989, 338–39). Through a Commission of the Peace the council appointed alderman and the mayor to a borough court, and about a dozen and a half council members were members of the bench in the 1860s and 1870s.[12] While they met in local petty sessions they do not seem to have been the guiding force in the local justice system. Rather, its backbone appears to have been the stipendiary magistrate Thomas H. Travis, aided by his deputy stipendiary, Walter Wrangham.

Travis was first appointed as stipendiary magistrate in 1854. Along with his deputy he appears to have presided over a substantial number of the borough cases (*Hull and Easter Counties Herald*, March 16, 1865). In reference to a dispute over increasing his salary the *Hull and Eastern Counties Herald* observed that "of all the unpopular men in Hull, it may truly be affirmed that Mr. Travis enjoyed the least amount of public favor," though he clearly had a group of supporters in borough government (June 21, 1866).[13] In addition, there are indications that he was integrated with the local commercial elite through charitable institutions. In civic life Travis appeared as a stern moralist, speaking out against the scourges of criminality and drunkenness (Jan. 1, 1864; Aug. 2 and Oct. 21, 1869). Speaking at an annual meeting for a training ship for convicted youth, Travis spoke of the efforts of youth reformation as part of a larger war on crime; "It was confessed that criminals were a class, as much as the army, or navy, or any other class, habitually warring against society, and bringing up their children as habitual haters of what is right. The Legislature now said 'such being the case we will make exceptional rules for you criminals. We will take such steps against you as to bring war into your own territories and disperse you.' If that were done what might they not hope" (Sept. 2, 1869).

Travis envisioned himself as a strict and impartial defender of the law and, so far as that benefited working people, a champion of their interests. From his perspective this impartiality was exercised by upholding the contract of service and the laws regulating it. As he noted in a master and servant case concerning a group of striking platers at one of the larger shipbuilders in town, Humphrys and Pearson's, "He would stand on the side of the men whenever and by whomsoever they were tyrannised over; and on the other hand, he would stand on the side of the masters whenever an attempt was made to do them wrong" (Feb. 8, 1871). Standing on the side of the masters meant enforcing any legally extant agreement. In a case concerning three strikebreakers hired by the local shipping magnates Messrs. Wilson, Sons & Co., he dismissed their defense that they had stayed away from work because of intimidation by the strikers and insisted that the strike was none of their business. He admonished the men to return to Messrs. Wilson: "Well go and make the best bargain you can with them.

You had better show them [the men on strike], by your good work how foolish they are. Messrs. Wilson, I am sure, will prove good masters. If you do not carry out your agreement you will find yourselves in very great trouble" (April 4, 1872). In a master and servant prosecution of three other strikebreakers who pleaded intimidation by strikers for not showing up at work, Travis in rendering his decision delivered a stern warning about how labor relations were conducted in Hull,

> He would give fair warning, that such audacious conduct could not be tolerated. With respect to the defence of intimidation, it was simply nonsense, because one man had actually passed through the wonderful danger without injury. However much they might talk at their unions and clubs, he would tell them that in this country there was a desire to uphold law and order, which was stronger than any wish of theirs, and the law had abundant strength to protect those who relied upon it. His Worship then, after a few more remarks upon the law, which he said was the same for rich and poor, ordered each of the prisoners to pay £3 compensation, or in default of payment distress would be levied; or in default of that he ordered each of them imprisoned for three months.[14]

If in Travis's mind the law was the same for the rich and poor, his strict enforcement of master and servant law, as we shall see, provided little succor for Hull's fishing apprentices. Before turning to their case we first turn to the court's rulings on wage claims under the master and servant act and prosecution of seamen under the Merchant Shipping Act.

To analyze the use of summary prosecutions for labor control regimes I have compiled data on all labor cases heard before the court from 1864–75 using the Hull magistrates' clerk's minute books.[15] I have supplemented this data set by collecting all labor cases mentioned in the weekly "Police Reports" section of the *Hull and Eastern Counties Herald*, which provides summaries of many of the cases heard before the borough court over the previous week.

Given the size of Hull's workforce the court did not adjudicate a great many wage disputes. When it did, though, the strict application of master and servant law produced largely favorable outcomes for workers bringing claims for unpaid wages. As table 5.1 demonstrates, in these civil cases workers were successful in winning claims for unpaid wages between half and two-thirds of the time, with the bench arbitrating a settlement in roughly 10 percent of the cases. Where nonpayment of wages was clear, Travis and other magistrates could maintain their stance as impartial and strict upholders of the law.

TABLE 5.1. Outcomes of workers' wage claims before Hull Borough Court, 1864–1875

Year	Total Cases	Judgment for Workers	Dismissed	Settled	Other
1864	105	75 (71)	24 (23)	1 (1)	5 (4)
1865	83	43 (52)	37 (45)	2 (2)	1 (1)
1866	81	57 (70)	21 (26)	3 (4)	0
1867	60	40 (67)	15 (27)	5 (6)	0
1868	21	13 (62)	6 (18)	2 (10)	0
1869	23	13 (56)	5 (22)	5 (22)	0
1870	72	54 (75)	12 (17)	6 (8)	0
1871	61	38 (62)	16 (26)	6 (10)	1 (2)
1872	41	21 (51)	10 (24)	8 (20)	2 (5)
1873	46	26 (57)	14 (30)	5 (11)	3 (7)
1874	75	47 (63)	20 (26)	8 (11)	0
1875	52	37 (71)	7 (13)	0	8 (16)

Note: 1868 and 1869 are January–June and December only. Numbers in parentheses are percentage of total annual cases.

Sources: Hull City Archives, Hull Magistrates' Court Minute Books, DPM/1/76–83, 85, 87–102, *Hull and Eastern Counties Herald*.

In upholding the contractual obligations of workers this strict reading produced decidedly favorable results for employers. We can see this in the bench's rulings in prosecutions of seaman under the Merchant Shipping Act. The act, passed in 1854 and amended in 1862, was intended to protect what Parliament deemed among the most vulnerable population of workers to unfair dealing and abuse. Much of the act was written to protect seamen from lost ages, abandonment, ill treatment, and other abuses in its expanding aqueous Empire. Under the acts marine boards were established in ports and agreements between captain or ship owner and crew had to be signed in the presence of the board. The board also served as a station for reporting complaints (Maude and Pollock 1861, 124–56; Greenhow 1863, 24–33). The act gave seamen rights even if they were far removed from Britain. However, section 244 of the act also provided for stiff penalties for desertion of insubordination that mirror the criminal sanctions found in master and servant law. It imposed up to 10 weeks' imprisonment for unauthorized leave and 12 weeks and a forfeiture of all wages for desertion. The act empowered magistrates to order the forced return of the seaman to the ship to continue duty, and to permit the transfer of a seaman on board a vessel in the middle

TABLE 5.2. Outcome of prosecutions of seamen under Merchant Shipping Act, 1864–1875

Judgment	1864	1865	1866	1867	1868	1869	1870	1871	1872	1873	1874	1875	Total
Prison	23 (56)	22 (48)	25 (58)	16 (53)	8 (58)	3 (25)	8 (24)	25 (37)	16 (50)	8 (27)	14 (28)	16 (30)	184 (41)
Sent on board	11 (27)	12 (26)	9 (21)	8 (27)	3 (21)	5 (42)	16 (47)	29 (43)	8 (25)	9 (30)	23 (46)	31 (58)	164 (36)
Judgment respited	1 (2)	6 (13)	0	0	2 (14)	1 (8)	7 (20)	5 (7)	6 (19)	7 (23)	5 (10)	1 (2)	41 (9)
Discharged	2 (5)	1 (2)	0	2 (7)	0	2 (17)	3 (9)	5 (7)	2 (6)	4 (13)	1 (2)	0	22 (5)
Other	4 (10)	5 (11)	9 (21)	4	1 (7)	1 (8)		4 (6)	0	2 (7)	7 (14)	5 (10)	42 (9)
Annual case total	41	46	43	30	14	12	34	68	32	30	50	53	453

Note: 1868 and 1869 are January–June and December only. Numbers in parentheses are percentage of total annual cases.
Sources: Hull City Archives, Hull Magistrates' Court Minute Books, DPM/1/76–83, 85, 87–102, *Hull and Eastern Counties Herald*.

of serving a sentence should his labor be required by his master. Further, the act provided for the master or ship owner to seize a seaman without warrant and hold him on board for 24 hours prior to a hearing, voiding basic civil liberties. This law remained in force until a clamor for revision in 1880 (Maude and Pollock 1861, 117–20; Rule 1976, 401).

It is not clear that captains or vessel owners used the law with much frequency in Hull, given the volume of traffic in the port. In 1871, for example, 2,551 vessels sailed from the port (1,417 of which were steam) and 3,236 entered (1,368 steam) while the court heard a total of sixty-eight prosecutions under section 244 (Kelly 1872, 386). Nonetheless, as table 5.2 demonstrates, judgments rarely went in favor of the seamen. A plurality of the time over the period they received prison sentences, and in over three-quarters of the cases they either served time or were sent back to finish their agreements regardless of the reasons they presented to the court. When violating a contract of service seamen rarely received a sympathetic hearing from the bench. The results of prosecutions under the Merchant Shipping Act demonstrate the bench's exercise of justice and more particularly Travis's vision of standing "on the side of the masters whenever an attempt was made to do them wrong." The local institutions of justice, as well as the dispositions of those such as Travis who passed judgment on defendants, provided a welcome venue for employers seeking to exercise control over their workforce. The fishing apprentices of Hull experienced the full weight of this justice as we will see shortly.

APPRENTICESHIP AND YOUTH LABOR

Before turning to the prosecutions of the fisherlads we should first consider the role of youth labor generally and apprenticeship more specifically in the Industrial Revolution. Jane Humphries argues that child labor remains an underemphasized facet of eighteenth- and nineteenth-century English economic development. Far from just being an important factor in the early advancement of textile factories "it contributed actively to the developing divisions of labour and organizational readjustments that sustained traditional units of production and maintained their competitiveness" (2010, 366).[16] There was, she finds, an upsurge in child labor in the 1780–1850 period and it was a mainstay in a wide variety of industries.

One form of child labor was apprenticeship, a specific legal form of unfree labor, which mostly remains in the shadows in studies of nineteenth-century English capitalist development. Though K. D. M. Snell has termed the debate over the decline of apprenticeship as one of the most "chaotic" in English social history, many economic historians offer a Whiggish view of the institution, suggesting that it was largely a relic of an early economic system (Snell 1985, 230). The neoclassical economist Clark Nardinelli, for example, straightforwardly asserts that "the industrial revolution ended apprenticeship. The early factory masters employed an apprentice workforce because no other was available. Free children, however, rapidly replaced apprentices in the textile industries in the early nineteenth century. Furthermore, as modern industry replaced handicraft industry, the institution of apprenticeship began to disappear throughout the economy" (1988, 259). With a few exceptions (such as Humphries) child labor in general, and pauper apprenticeship in particular, are seen as artifacts of the early nineteenth century, a phenomenon caused by a need for industrial labor and eventually obviated by technological advances.[17] As Snell observes, the traditional system of apprenticeship was unmoored from its institutional roots to craft, parish, and family, and mutated into a number of skill-training variants. To the extent that apprenticeship extended into the latter part of the nineteenth century, it has been depicted as a self-enforcing system by which youths (largely though not entirely males) were able to gain entrance into a trade in exchange for service (Snell 1996, 315–17; see also Humphries 2003).

Certainly with the textile industries, mining, many workshop industries, and agricultural labor increasingly regulated by parliamentary acts, the use of apprentice and youth labor became more problematic. However, during the mid-Victorian period there was a substantial increase in the number of male children under fifteen employed in navigation, dockwork, and on the railways. Moreover, as some historians note, despite the ill-repute of pauper apprenticeships, they remained a potentially important means for parishes to reduce their fiscal burdens. The case of the fishing industry illustrates how youth labor in general, and a degraded form of apprenticeship in particular, could still be vital to the process of industrial expansion. This was particularly the case when apprentice labor could be disciplined and controlled through the law.

THE CASE OF THE HULL TRAWLING INDUSTRY

The fishing trade was a relatively recent development in Hull's economic history, a product of the discovery of extensive fishing grounds in the deep waters off the Yorkshire coast in the 1830s and 1840s and the extension of the railroads. The industry developed rapidly in Hull, Grimsby, and other ports in the 1860s, at first through the migration of trawler owners from other regions of the country. In the early 1850s there were only a few dozen fishing trawlers (or "smacks" as they were generally called) in Hull; by 1863 they numbered about 270 and by 1873 there were some 330 smacks. Between 1864 and 1874 the number of trawler voyages had increased 86 percent to 4,785 (Brown and McLaren 1969, 225). The *Hull and Eastern Counties Herald* reported that in 1867 the industry employed some 1,500 hands (Jan. 3, 1867). Where in the early 1850s smacks were recording about 8,000 baskets caught annually, by the mid-1860s this had risen to around 170,000 baskets. By the early 1870s their catch was annually worth about £400,000 (Dec. 28, 1865, Dec. 27, 1866, Nov. 13, 1873). Hull was in keen competition throughout the period with nearby Grimsby on the southern tip of the Humber, and by the early 1870s the latter port had outstripped Hull both in terms of smacks (360) and men and boys employed in the trade (3,300) (Feb. 23, 1871).

A new fully equipped smack sold for at least £1,000, though used trawlers were perhaps half to two-thirds that price. The self-made masters of Hull's fishing trade often heavily mortgaged their vessels, working off the payments with each catch. The proportion of fixed to variable capital was actually higher in fishing than cotton manufacturing and from the start many ship owners found themselves in highly leveraged positions.[18] Newspaper accounts for the period point to at least fifteen smack owners filing for bankruptcy.[19]

It is difficult to reconstruct the finances of these smack owners, but a rough indication can be gleaned from the Registry of Ships for the port of Hull during the period. All smacks were registered with the port, which also held a record of their financing (including their mortgages) and sale.[20] Reconstructing the record of Thomas Halfyard, the smack owner responsible for the most convictions of fishing apprentices during the period (see table 5.3), shows a dynamic web of financial entanglements. Between 1860 and 1875 Halfyard was involved in eighteen sales of smacks and underwrote twenty-three mortgages for these and other vessels. On the other side of the ledger he took out thirteen mortgages himself, about two-thirds of them from a London fish factor. Overall, Halfyard appears to have maintained a positive balance sheet of several hundred pounds over much of the period between his own mortgage payments and the income from his borrowers. However, in the early 1870s, with a series of mortgage payments due on vessels, the balance might have tipped the other way. Halfyard's mortgages for vessels he purchased were generally £4–500, at 5 percent while those he underwrote when selling vessels were generally in the £6–700 range. His loans were usually paid back within a three-year time span, though those of his

TABLE 5.3. Most frequent prosecutors of apprentices by number of convictions, 1864–1875

Name	Trade	Convicted Apprentices	Number of Trawlers
Beeton, J. W.	Basketmaking	38	. . .
Halfyard, Thomas	Trawling	31	n.a.
Rogers, George	Trawling	25	n.a
Rouse, John	Trawling	24	5
Loram, Richard	Trawling	22	6
Shepherd, H. C. W.	Trawling	22	n.a.
Bates, Peter	Trawling	21	n.a.
Anderson, George	Trawling	20	2
Evans, James	Trawling	19	7
Exon, William	Trawling	19	n.a.
Harding, James	Trawling	19	5
Ansell, Alfred	Trawling	17	11
Drew, Walter	Trawling	17	n.a.
Maddock, Henry	Trawling	17	4
Apter, Thomas	Trawling	16	n.a.
Pollard, J. C.	Trawling	16	n.a.
Vinton, Charles	Trawling	16	n.a
Palmer, David	Trawling	15	n.a.
Webb, John	Trawling	15	3
Blanchard, Henry	Trawling	13	5

Sources: Hull City Archives, Hull Magistrates' Court Minute Books, DPM/1/76–83, 85, 87–102, *Hull and Eastern Counties Herald*.

buyers were often over four to five years. It is not possible to determine the percentage of his total income that Halfyard generally received through the selling and underwriting of his older smacks.

The ship registers do suggest a very active market in smacks and one in which larger fleet owners were cogs in a chain of a growing port fleet. They depict a trade in which credit sources were largely internal, with loans mostly provided by smack owners selling vessels or by fish merchants.[21] The sheer volume of this trade, which increases over the course of the period, hints at a growing speculative market with the expansion of the industry. However, exactly how much capital was represented by a port's fleet in this period is open to question. A Grimsby smack owner, testifying before the

Commissioners of Sea Fisheries in 1866, noted that because of highly speculative loans £300,000 invested in smacks had only procured about £100,000 worth of vessels.[22] A major Hull smack owner, Alfred Ansell, reported in 1869 that 242 Hull smacks were worth about £149,000.[23]

The rate of return on investment is also unclear. William Markchow, a Hull smack owner testifying in 1866, claimed that 5 percent could be achieved with careful management. In a latter report the Inspectors for the Commissioners suggested that for the trade as a whole a smack could net £70–80 a year, though testifying before a parliamentary committee in the early 1880s a Grimsby smack owner maintained that his average profit rate over the previous five years was at best 2 percent.[24] While rates of return might vary, however, mortgage payments were a constant. Many smack owners depended on regular runs to stay afloat.

As a contemporary commercial review noted, "There is little romance with the history of this trade" (*Trade and Commerce* [1878], 133). The work was considered some of the least desirable in the port and, despite its rapid growth, smack owners had difficulties recruiting reliable crews. These crews were small, labor-intensive units, consisting of only five, including the skipper. Between solo voyages in the winter generally lasting one and a half to three weeks, to fleet voyages of thirty or more smacks in the spring and summer going from eight to as many as fifteen weeks, smacks were at sea at least forty weeks a year regardless of the weather. The crew was housed in a single small cabin in often miserable conditions, and remained in their work clothes throughout the voyage in order to respond quickly to orders. The cabins themselves were frequently flooded, and hands complained of inadequate maintenance of the vessels. Such small vessels were not subject to port regulation or inspection. A full day at work frequently involved at least two trawls, one during the day and one at night, which in bad weather could take two to three hours, and left little time for anything besides navigation, maintenance, meals, and sleep. The historian John Rule quotes one observer of the trade describing the routine at sea as "suffering—monotonous ceaseless suffering" (1976, 385). Moreover, given the small size of the boats and periodic transference of boxed catch by small boats to cutters for shipping, the work was extremely dangerous, ten times more so than mining.[25] From 1876 to 1882, for example, 304 men and boys sailing on Grimsby fishing smacks perished (Robinson 1996, 56).[26] In 1867 alone nationally 188 fishing smacks were lost at sea and 2,325 suffered wreck or casualty (*Hull and Easter Counties Herald*, Oct. 1, 1868).

Adult crew members, generally the skipper, the second, and sometimes the third hands, received shares of the gross from the catch (net of deductions for provisions), with the smack owner receiving the remainder. This assured their interests were aligned with the smack owner. However, casual adult labor for the lower positions was considered too unreliable, and smack owners generally could not compete with the shipping industry's going wages for able seamen. Needing a cheap and secure labor force to fill out the crews, smack owners turned to the apprenticeship system.[27] As Rule comments, "The smackowners solved the problem of labour supply in a way which strikingly recalls the methods of the factory masters of the early Industrial Revolution: they relied on poor-law apprentices."[28] Apprenticeship in merchant shipping had been common in the first half of the century until the passage of the Merchant Shipping Act in 1850, which made it significantly less attractive and viable (Burton 1999a). While there was an institutional history on which the trawling industry could pattern itself, apprenticeship for fisherlads assumed a different form and substance.

By the 1860s there were two forms of apprenticeship, indoor and outdoor. The former group was housed with their master (generally a lesser smack owner), who in addition to room and board was responsible for all other basic provisions such as clothing for both sea and shore. Outdoor apprentices received wages of 7–16 shillings per week in lieu of having their room and board provided. Typically they were bound to fleet owners, though indoor apprentices after the age of seventeen or eighteen might request a change to this status. Apprentices of either type were the fourth hands and cooks (and sometimes served the position of third hand as well). The former was responsible for watch, handling the smack in good weather, steering the small boat, taking soundings, gutting fish, and other tasks. The apprentice cook was the lowest hand and newest member who assisted the fourth hand, cleaned the deck, performed basic maintenance, and coiled the warp net when it was retrieved. Under the apprenticeship system smack owners were not obliged to pay their apprentices any wages, but it was customary that they were to receive a portion of the stockerbait, or money received at port for the sale of inferior fish. While not required, a modest amount of weekly pocket money was also traditional, especially for older apprentices.[29]

As a labor source they were frequently as capable as a grown man, though training did take several years and the return on the initial sunk investment was largely during the second half of the apprentice's term. Binding a young person (generally male) into service apprenticeship systems in the nineteenth century was never free labor, and the trawling industry was no exception. Estimates vary, but at least half of all apprentices were bound by their parents and were generally locals. However, as the trade rapidly expanded in the 1870s it increasingly came to rely on poor law unions, reformatories, and other institutions as a labor source, and was indiscriminate in its recruitment. The lack of experience at sea made many such apprentices only a liability to themselves once at sea.[30] Pamela Horn suggests that pauper apprentices were more valued because they were more easily subject to coercion. The historian of the industry, Robb Robinson, observes that "many apprentices were treated by the smackowners as their personal property."[31]

With some hyperbole a contemporary London paper pronounced the apprentice system in the trawling industry as "a system of slavery as infamous as any system of slavery every devised" (Horn 1996, 187).[32] Complaints about maltreatment by crew members were common, and many fisherlads preferred to commit crimes or refuse to obey orders so that they would be sent to jail rather than to sea. Increasingly many absconded completely or ran away as the smacks embarked.[33] Those disposed toward the industry argued that charges of cruelty were often inventions of apprentices to break their binding, and that troublesome and confrontational fisherlads often drove the crew to administer tough discipline. "I quite believe," noted Baldwyn Fleming in his report on the Grimsby pauper apprentices, "that many punishments which look serious when the subject of magisterial investigation have been inflicted with a rough and ready hand—perhaps with undue severity—but with no thought or intention of malicious cruelty." And he maintained that all the apprentices he interviewed stated that they "were fully aware that if ill-treated they would have no difficulty in obtaining redress."[34] Hull apprentices frequently claimed abuse as a reason for absconding.

On occasion an adult hand would be prosecuted by an apprentice for abuse as an assault, since the more severe cases generally involved beatings (often with a rope and termed "rope-ending"). During the years reported here there were at least a dozen such prosecutions, all involving assaults of some form.[35] Most commonly these adult hands were ordered to find sureties of £20–100 to keep the peace, though sometimes they were released on their own recognizance. In two cases fines of 20–50s were exacted, the latter for a stabbing and pitching overboard of a fisherlad by a captain. The most severe punishment was meted out to a smack hand who hit an apprentice over the head with a poker, cut a piece of flesh out of his arm with a belt, rubbing saltpeter in the wound and eventually throwing the boy into the sea. Apologizing and admitting drunkenness, he was given two months at hard labor, a sentence that as we shall see was commonly administered to the fishing apprentices themselves for absconding. When a smack owner fired a skipper or other adult hand for mistreating an apprentice, the abuser was readily hired by another owner given the constant need for experienced labor.[36]

In addition to the rough conditions and often poor treatment, older apprentices, such as Charles Taylor with whose case I started this book, came to resent their comparatively paltry compensation. Smack hands and able seamen who were often not much older earned substantially more. During the back years of their terms, when they became most valuable to their masters, apprentices fully realized the extent of their exploitation. Absconding was seen by many apprentices as a means of rectifying this injustice as well as escaping their demeaning circumstances. As the number of apprentices increased, so too did the problems of keeping them compliant and bound for their full service. One smack owner reported that a deserting apprentice could cost him £30–50 a week in replacement wages and lost revenue, a considerable sum for a small capitalist.[37]

While smack owners may not have been able to compete with the shipbuilders and shipping fleet owners in terms of wealth or prominence, they were not without political voice. Their industry was recognized as central to the town, and from their stronghold in the South Myton ward they sent some of the more prominent of their peers to represent them on the borough council.[38] To maintain this system of cheap labor, it is not surprising that smack owners felt comfortable in turning to the borough court, particularly given their economic contributions to the town and a bench headed by stipendiary Travis.

An analysis of all labor cases before the court from 1864 to 1875, and of the fishing trade cases in particular, reveals the extent to which the latter industry relied on the court as a means of labor control. To start, a review of summary prosecutions for the period across a variety of offenses shows that, in general, beyond assault or drunkenness, the working people of Hull were as or more likely to be convicted summarily of a violation of master and servant law as of any other single criminal offense most often connected with their class. As table 5.4 shows, proportionately master and servant convictions for these years hovered between 4 and 7 percent of the town court's total summary convictions, which was between two and three times higher than the national percentage.

Table 5.5 shows the percentage of cases all master and servant prosecutions that involved disorderly apprentices, and the percentage of these cases in turn that were of fisherlads. The numbers are bluntly telling. Virtually all prosecutions during these years were of disorderly apprentices and roughly three-quarters were of fisherlads, despite the fact that they constituted no

TABLE 5.4. Number of summary criminal prosecutions by type reported to Parliament for Hull, 1864–1875

Type of Conviction	1864	1865	1866	1867	1868	1869	1870	1871	1872	1873	1874	1875
Assault on peace officer	158 (5.6)	168 (6.2)	140 (5.6)	114 (4.6)	126 (4.8)	140 (5.6)	142 (5.2)	166 (4.5)	181 (4.3)	118 (2.7)	132 (3)	89
Assault, common	234 (8.3)	267 (10)	190 (7.7)	166 (6.7)	166 (6.3)	146 (5.8)	146 (5.3)	379 (10.2)	485 (11.6)	503 (11.4)	510 (11.6)	424
Drunk and disorderly	966 (34)	895 (32)	834 (37)	779 (31.2)	963 (37)	927 (37)	794 (29)	1,018 (27.3)	1,100 (26)	1,484 (32)	1,467 (33)	1,172
Poor law/ neglecting family	18 (.6)	7 (.2)	4 (.2)	5 (.2)	16 (.6)	10 (.4)	12 (.4)	15 (.4)	9 (.2)	21 (.5)	12 (.3)	15
Master and servant	77 (2.7)	177 (6.6)	144 (5.8)	165 (6.7)	157 (6)	90 (3.6)	126 (4.6)	140 (3.8)	183 (4.4)	192 (4.4)	205 (4.6)	230
Larceny under 5s	83 (2.9)	80 (3)	76 (3)	117 (4.7)	122 (4.6)	125 (5)	107 (3.9)	140 (3.8)	113 (2.7)	119 (2.7)	101 (2.3)	132
Larceny above 5s	79 (2.8)	103 (3.)	119 (4.8)	90 (3.6)	92 (3.5)	91 (3.6)	78 (2.8)	92 (2.5)	86 (2.1)	94 (2.1)	107 (2.4)	124
Vagrancy act/ prostitution	76 (2.7)	81 (3)	107 (4.3)	72 (2.9)	64 (2.4)	55 (2.2)	66 (2.4)	141 (3.8)	95 (2.3)	99 (2.2)	112 (2.5)	n.a.
Vagrancy act/ begging	72 (2.5)	26 (1)	56 (2.3)	117 (4.7)	149 (5.7)	177 (7)	151 (4)	118 (3.2)	106 (2.5)	103 (2.3)	77 (1.7)	n.a.
Total criminal convictions	2,812	2,683	2482	2,468	2,624	2,507	2,746	3,722	4,168	4,406	4,445	n.a

Note: Percentages of total in parentheses.
Sources: Hull City Archives, Hull Magistrates' Court Minute Books, DPM/1/76–83, 85, 87–102, *Hull and Eastern Counties Herald*.

TABLE 5.5. Number of master and servant prosecutions by type, 1864–1875

Type of Prosecution	1864	1865	1866	1867	1868	1869	1870	1871	1872	1873	1874	1875	Total
All master and servant cases	112	175	171	161	89	56	131	125	152	170	199	257	1,798
All disorderly apprentices[a]	110 (98)	169 (97)	170 (99)	144 (88)	86 (97)	55 (98)	131 (100)	120 (96)	149 (98)	166 (98)	181 (91)	243 (95)	1,724 (96)
Disorderly fishing apprentices[b]	55 (50)	118 (70)	114 (67)	102 (71)	68 (79)	44 (80)	97 (74)	96 (80)	110 (67)	139 (84)	161 (89)	198 (81)	1,302 (76)

Note: 1868 and 1869 are January–June and December only.

[a] As a percentage of all master and servant cases

[b] As a percentage of all disorderly apprentice cases.

Sources: Hull City Archives, Hull Magistrates' Court Minute Books, DPM/1/76–83, 85, 87–102, *Hull and Eastern Counties Herald*.

more than 1 percent of the entire male laboring population of Hull. Moreover, assuming a contemporary estimate that there were about 750 apprentices in the later 1870s, at least 20 percent of this group was caught up in the criminal justice system for almost all of these years.[39] Given the rapid expansion of the trade in the 1870s, this percentage during 1864–74 is probably significantly higher.

Tables 5.6 (below) and 5.2 (above) can be used to compare the sentences meted out to the fisherlads and to adult seamen prosecuted under the Merchant Shipping Act, which had comparable if not more severe sentences for deserters. Once again the numbers are striking. First, the sheer number of fishing apprentices' cases is always larger, despite the fact that their representation in the maritime labor force was vastly smaller. Second, the percentage of prison sentences shows a clear imbalance. At an 82 percent average rate of incarceration the fishing apprentices were fully twice as likely to be sent to prison as seamen for similar offenses such as disobeying orders or absconding.

Tables 5.6 and 5.7 show respectively the distribution of sentences received by fisherlads and the distribution of jail sentences. With the most common sentences being twenty-one, thirty, and seventy days in prison with hard labor, convictions were highly punitive. Interestingly, notations in the minute books indicate that around 20–30 percent of these fisherlads were released to their masters prior to the completion of their sentences; and during one hearing Travis complained that "the only fault he had with some masters was that they were too anxious to take their boys out of prison before the expiration of their punishment" (*Hull and Easter Counties Herald*, March 6, 1873).

The data suggest that through both the apprenticeship and criminal justice systems smack owners fashioned a labor control regime for a portion of their labor supply that could not be maintained through a free labor market. On the one hand they needed a supply of inexpensive labor to be able to insure that their net return from each voyage allowed them to work off mortgage payments and expenses and make a profit. On the other hand this labor pool was young, often bound against their will, and became more valuable as a source of profit the greater their experience at sea. Therefore smack owners were reluctant to part with apprentices, and indeed the records show very few such annulments of indentures.

The answer was to use the criminal justice system as both a means of threat and coercion—a disciplinary tool that could be used repeatedly and reliably against obstreperous apprentices—and also as a holding pen for this labor supply.[40] Long sentences insured that apprentices could not flee

TABLE 5.5. Outcome of prosecutions of Hull fishing apprentices, 1864–1875

Judgment	1864	1865	1866	1867	1868	1869	1870	1871	1872	1873	1874	1875	Total
Prison	42 (76)	92 (78)	95 (83)	90 (88)	58 (85)	38 (86)	79 (81)	81 (85)	97 (88)	112 (81)	124 (77)	162 (81)	1,070 (82)
Sent on board	0	0	0	1 (1)	1 (4)	0	0	4 (4)	6 (5)	4 (3)	18 (12)	26 (13)	60 (5)
Judgment respited	9 (16)	22 (17)	6 (5)	1 (1)	9 (11)	3 (7)	10 (11)	6 (6)	5 (5)	19 (14)	12 (7)	9 (4.5)	111 (8)
Discharged	0	0	3 (3)	3 (3)	0	2 (5)	4 (4)	5 (5)	2 (2)	3 (2)	4 (2)	1 (.5)	27 (2)
Other	4 (8)	4 (5)	10 (9)	7 (7)	0	1 (2)	4 (4)	0	0	1 (1)	3 (2)	0	34 (3)
Annual case total	55	118	114	102	68	44	97	96	110	139	161	198	1,302

Note: 1868 and 1869 are January–June and December only. Percentages of annual total appear in parentheses.
Sources: Hull City Archives, Hull Magistrates' Court Minute Books, DPM/1/76–83, 85, 87–102, *Hull and Eastern Counties Herald*.

TABLE 5.7. Prison sentences of convicted fishing apprentices, 1864–1875

Sentence Length	1864	1865	1866	1867	1868	1869	1870	1871	1872	1873	1874	1875
1–14 days	11	31	14	4	5	1	6	5	2	7	6	10
15–28 days	14	25	32	22	22	6	14	12	17	31	35	41
29–42 days	8	9	23	37	15	17	31	38	46	43	49	63
45–56 days	0	4	3	4	1	1	4	5	3	3	8	14
57–70 days	9	23	23	23	15	13	24	21	29	28	26	31
Total	42	92	95	90	58	38	79	81	97	112	124	159

Note: 1868 and 1869 are January–June and December only.
Sources: Hull City Archives, Hull Magistrates' Court Minute Books, DPM/1/76–83, 85, 87–102, *Hull and Eastern Counties Herald*.

in between voyages. The extent to which smack owners were granted the early release of their charges also indicates that the punishment itself was secondary to secure access to this labor supply.

In Travis and the borough court the smack owners found sympathetic ears. Seen through the linked lens of bourgeois order and respectability and a belief in the "impartial" application of the law, the waywardness of the fisherlads represented a serious problem, particularly given their often pauper origins. The concern of smack owners was expressed by Alfred Ansell in 1869 at a meeting of the South Myton Reform Association—the biggest borough ward and the one with the largest concentration of smack owners—in which he noted that steps had been taken to "improve the moral condition of the fishermen," and that the decline in the number of apprentice prosecutions from the previous year was a signal of their success (*Hull and Easter Counties Herald*, Nov. 25, 1869).

These paternalistic actions were best exemplified by the room and school inaugurated for fishing apprentices at the Fish Street Chapel in the latter 1860s. Characteristic for the times, the school provided regular Sunday Bible study classes, and by 1875 it claimed to have had 1,300–1,400 participants in them. Its reading room was open several nights a week, it made available saving accounts, and had an annual tea that drew between 100–200 fisherlads each April. Some of the largest smack owners were involved in its governance, including Ansell, its secretary, who was also one of the main prosecutors of apprentices during this period. The school mirrored the larger concern of smack owners and town elite for fishermen in general, which was reflected in their founding and maintenance of a Fishermen's Institute. The institute was similar to the mechanics' institutes of the times, and sought to provide spiritual and intellectual outreach and sustenance to the growing legions of adult fishermen.[41] Given the continued resistance among many fisherlads, it seems doubtful that these institutions had the salutary impact that Ansell and others desired and imagined.

Less systematic evidence from the nearby port of Grimsby, where the trade grew even more rapidly (eventually dwarfing Hull) suggests a similar pattern. Fleming's 1873 report into the status of apprentices in that town records that for the previous administrative year (May 1, 1872–April 30, 1873) there were 251 total cases involving fishing apprentices, 208 for absconding, 33 for disobeying orders, and the remainder for other offenses.[42] Ten percent of the prosecutions represented repeat offenses. Sixty-two percent of the hearings resulted in convictions, a somewhat lower rate than in Hull, and the most common sentences were for two and three weeks' imprisonment. In Grimsby magistrates relied on the Merchant Shipping Act for prosecution, which the Hull magistrates turned to after the repeal of the Master and Servant Act in 1875. It is not clear why the latter justices chose a different legal foundation or exactly why, after the reformation of the Merchant Shipping Act in 1880, they interpreted its sections in a way that stopped them for using it for further prosecutions while their Grimsby counterparts continued to do so.[43]

It is apparent from the data that employers in the trawling industry were the only Hull capitalists to employ the law systematically as a means of labor control. As table 5.3 (above) shows, nineteen of the top twenty prosecutors were smack owners.[44] The remaining prosecutions of apprentices are from a wide variety of industries, with no one trade representing a significant percentage of the total.

These data give credence to the argument that the practice was employed by smack owners as a means of controlling their labor supply and the labor process, and satisfying their requirements for cheap labor to stay afloat. As Fleming himself noted in his report on the Grimsby apprentices, "For its ensuing continuance and development, it is absolutely necessary that the lads should be obtained as apprentices to the trade."[45] Many smack owners were heavily mortgaged. They faced a growing but also increasingly competitive trade, not only among their peers in Hull, but also from the trawlers of nearby Grimsby, Whitby, Scarborough, and other ports in the South as well. Moreover, it is probable that an increasing proportion of their labor force was also the least enthusiastic, that is, poor law union boys who were indentured to relinquish their home parishes of a burden. A number of these apprentices were shipped considerable distances, including from London parishes. As Boswell suggests, many were physically unprepared for the rigors of the sea (1973, 58).

Legal action became a lynchpin to keep this system of exploitation in motion. The Master and Servant Act, coupled with apprenticeship binding, insured that smack owners had unmitigated power over this portion of their labor supply. The borough court and police provided a ready enforcement mechanism for this power. Drawing on the authority of the criminal justice system, smack owners were not only able to create a potent disciplinary system, but they were also able to securely house recalcitrant labor at the expense of the borough until needed for use. This was certainly not a system of slavery, but in its darker dimensions there were some disconcerting parallels.

By 1880 the industry in Hull alone employed some 1,200 apprentices, and there was probably a larger number in Grimsby.[46] There were by then 420 smacks with some £500,000 invested in Hull's trade (Bellamy 1971, 49). In 1876 Hull magistrates sent 216 fisherlads to prison, probably under the Merchant Shipping Act (Robinson 1996, 60). However, changes in the act and the passage of the Payment of Wages Act in 1880 led to the abandonment of apprentice labor in Hull, though in Grimsby and perhaps other fishing ports the practices waned more slowly. This was in part because of variations in the local labor supply. As an 1894 parliamentary report noted, "if there had been at Grimsby the same supply of weekly hands as there is at Hull and Lowestoft it is probable that the apprentice system would have died out as it has done in other ports" (Chance 1985, 281). Perhaps this is why the Hull magistrates interpreted a critical section in the Merchant Shipping Act regarding willful disobedience as applying to on-board behavior only, while their Grimsby counterparts understood it to mean desertion as well.[47] Such was the nature of the local legal institutions. As a result apprentices in Grimsby continued to abscond in substantial numbers, and many fled to Hull where there labor was finally and fully freely contractual.[48] As the beam size for the trawl grew, increasing the efficiency of the labor, casual labor replaced apprentices in most other ports. Youth labor became less vital and smack owners relied on a larger transient labor pool. More important, by the 1880s the Yorkshire fleets were beginning to lose a competitive battle with a burgeoning Scottish industry, and the trade experienced a slow decline (Robinson 1987, 83–99).

CONCLUSION

Reflecting on the industry, Robinson remarks, "It remains ironic that a trade which benefited so much from laissez faire on the high seas should have relied so heavily and for so long on such a tied and ragged labor force"

(1996, 65). However, given the economics of the trade, the necessity of finding a ready supply of cheap labor for continual production, and the character of local judicial institutions, it perhaps seems less ironic. For a rapidly growing industry with an increasing need for workers to fill unskilled, low-paying, and undesirable jobs, urban parishes were all too willing to relieve themselves of unwanted pauper charges in the formed of apprenticed labor. Indeed, even after considerable unwanted public and parliamentary scrutiny in 1882, after two publicized brutal deaths of fisherlads by the hands of their skippers, the trawling industry continued to rely heavily on apprentice labor as a mainstay (Rule 1976, 395).[49]

As the fishing industry grew rapidly in the 1860s, trawler owners pragmatically responded to their circumstances by depending heavily on poor law unions and the local court to both provide them with requisite labor and to discipline this workforce. For a quarter of a century a labor control regime, increasingly dependent on child pauper apprentices, was embedded in these institutions and provided and controlled an essentially captive source of labor. The indenture system was a labor contract that assured a steady supply of unfree labor to an industry otherwise unable to recruit and retain enough workers willing to brave harsh conditions for little remuneration. Trawler owners, facing the need to have their vessels at sea almost all year to repay mortgages and get an adequate return on their investments, depended on apprentice labor for their fourth and fifth hands. Second and third hands were in essence partners in this scheme, since they received a percentage of catch rather than a set wage.

Many fisherlads, as we have seen, were unwilling participants in these ventures. Most were ill prepared for seafaring, though they became more valued labor as they gained experience. Beyond the taxing conditions of North Sea fishing, many were also subject to sometimes brutal despotism aboard ship that was more severe than a free labor market would support. While the fishing industry created a façade of paternalism with its school and periodic social events, it seems doubtful that for most fisherlads any of these efforts mitigated the stark realities of their lives. They regularly rebelled and fled in significant numbers, and trawler owners relied on the stipendiary magistrates and the local courts for control. The local justice system was not only a mainstay for discipline, it provided a means of physically containing fisherlads until they were required for another sea voyage. Stipendiary Travis and the borough magistrates were willing participants in the process. In many respects they were suspicious of and hostile to labor resistance, and in the case of the fisherlads more specifically often viewed them as ungrateful and ill-disciplined youth in need of correction. Coupled with their perceived responsibility to uphold "impartially" all labor contracts, the magistrates were a critical means for insuring discipline.

This labor control regime remained in place into the 1880s. As steam trawlers rapidly overtook their venerable sailing counterparts, the economics of the industry changed quickly. The capital requirements necessary to acquire and maintain larger steam vessels led to a consolidation of the industry into a significantly smaller group of owners. Longer voyages further afield from the traditional North Sea fishing grounds changed the nature of the trade as well (Brown and McLaren 1969, 254–55). However, it is also possible that changes in the law abetted this transformation. With the new Merchant Seamen Act in 1880, arresting and holding apprentices became much more difficult. Robb Robinson reports that by 1882 the number of apprentices fulfilling their indentures dropped by 75 percent. The apprenticeship system quickly declined and trawler owners replaced it with "weekly-paid hands over whom they had less immediate control" (1987, 64). The economics of the trade rapidly changed, but so too did the labor control regime that trawler owners had depended on for several decades.

CHAPTER SIX

Redditch, Commercial Agriculture, Needle Manufacturing, and Small-Town Justice

In the previous two case studies we examined towns that, while not the size to rival the likes of Manchester, Liverpool, or Birmingham, were nonetheless significant urban areas. Redditch by contrast was a small, though rapidly growing, town and in some respects rural in character. It was in the northeastern corner of Worcestershire, a little over a dozen miles south of Birmingham and about half that distance to the Warwickshire border. The town was the market center and the economic nexus for a cluster of small agricultural communities within a radius of several miles, including Beoley and Holt End to the north and Headless Cross, Hunt End, Webheath, Feckenham, Astwood Bank, and Studley forming an arch from the west to the south. In a visit to the town in 1852 Charles Dickens described it as sitting on the crown of a high hill overlooking "in all directions, a true English country scene of hill and dale, orchard and sloping fallow, humble church-tower and comfortable farmstead" (1852, 540). Between the 1841 and 1871 censuses Redditch experienced a doubling in its population, to a little over 6,700 inhabitants. The town became an ecclesiastical district in 1855, adopted an Improvement Commission in 1858, and added health and highway boards at the same time. The local paper commenced publication in 1859, and the same year the town acquired a rail link. A year later a nearby railway station was erected, and by the mid-1860s it was an important transference point for agricultural products. In 1862 Redditch was of sufficient importance to warrant its own weekly petty sessions, and to house its local political institutions the town erected a public office in 1863 where the petty sessions and other official business were conducted.[1]

The town and its smaller neighbors relied principally on two industries. In Redditch proper (and places such as Alcester, Studley, and Astwood) the needle trades exerted a dominating industrial presence, as I will discuss below. In the remainder of the district agriculture remained a major employer. That employers in both of these economic sectors turned to the court for their labor control regimes demonstrates how local legal institutions could respond to disparate demands for assistance with discipline through contracts of service and master and servant law.

COMMERCIAL AGRICULTURE

A plurality of all prosecutions during the period were of servants in husbandry, many of which were employed on farms short distances from Redditch. In 1871 nationally some 13 percent of all male agricultural labor was still defined as "farm servant" in the proper sense, and that percentage could be significantly higher in some regions (Dewey 2000, 813). Farm servants might conjure up images of a traditional past in which servants boarded with farm families, shared their table, and were often recognized as members of the household. Such images seem antithetical to the realm of modernized capitalist agriculture, but even in later nineteenth-century England farm service and commercial agriculture were often highly compatible in a number of regions. Recent research on farm service reveals it to have been "a resilient form of hiring, compatible with capitalist agriculture, and able to adapt to changing local conditions" (Howkins and Verdon 2008, 367). While studies on the large farmers of the capitalist southeast suggested the demise of farm service in the wake of agricultural laborers, research on northern and midlands farming demonstrates that commercial farmers relied on farm servants as a stable labor supply, especially in areas where the call of industrial employment in nearby cities made a reliable labor supply more problematic. Having farm labor bound in yearly contracts of service in such areas was part of the "development of specialized, commercial production for capitalist markets" (Gritt 2002, 50). Size of farm was not determinate in the employment of servants. For farmers specializing in provisions for urban markets, such as dairying, farm service was an important means for procuring the (largely young male) workforce necessary for regular production.[2]

Agricultural laborers, of course, were the original degraded proletariat in Marx's tale of capitalist development, and as Stephen Caunce remarks, "in the late nineteenth century most British farm servants had no option but to sell their labour to get a living, and most had no prospect of achieving any significant alteration of that status. In that sense they were proletarians" (1997, 50).[3] Whereas in previous centuries farm service represented the low rungs of a ladder by which a young male could build a life as a yeoman, by the mid-Victorian period neither they or their employers were under any such illusion. There was no commitment to train farm labor, and one contemporary commentator remarked that decline in farm apprenticeships had made discipline more problematic (Leighton 1873, 394). With annual turnover and new boarding arrangements outside of the farm household that developed during the century, farm servants became more socially as well as physically distanced from their employers. Rising prosperity of tenant farmers from midcentury onward also produced a greater social divide between farmers and their servants.[4] However, as Caunce and others have noted, the contractual relationship between farmer and a portion of the labor force remained in several regions anchored in the annual hiring. Farm servants, particularly those pledged to yearly terms, found themselves bound in formal subordination through a concept of continual service that was often implicit, locally constructed, and legitimized by expectations of rural deference and hierarchy.[5] While farmers claimed customary authority over their servants, shifting arrangements of service, including those of boarding and training, left justifications based on the weight of tradition on weakened ground. Commercialization in some respects made farmers' claims to tradition more problematic at the frontiers of control.

"Statute" or "mop" fairs, which had once nationally been the characteristic events for the annual hiring of servants in husbandry, had declined in many other areas of the country by the mid-Victorian era, but they were still common in this region. Local fairs in small agricultural towns such as Alvechurch, Evesham, Feckenham, and Inkberrow, in addition to Redditch, were common venues at which a range of farm servants sought yearly hire.[6] One agricultural historian has described these annual events in a northern county as having devolved into "labour marts" (Moss 1999, 84). The region's fairs held in the late summer or early fall appear to have this character, though they retained some of the festive aspects.[7] Agricultural historians of northern counties have argued that farm service survived in those regions because it was a way for farmers to stabilize their labor supply given the increasing lure of industrial employment (Caunce 1997; Moses 1999). There is evidence of this in some villages around Redditch, as for example in Astwood, Feckenham, Headless Cross, and Hunt End, where the growth of the needle industry (discussed below) changed both settlement patterns and the local labor market (Maynard 2005, 270–71).

Given the tighter labor markets from midcentury onward that led farmers to seek yearly contracts of service, workers had somewhat more leverage in contract bargaining. They were also more likely to change employers if they were dissatisfied and were less tied to particular villages (Kebbel 1893,

165–66; Moses 1999, 91; Newby 1987, 120). Nonetheless, the service relationship remained strongly colored by rural hierarchy and the younger males who dominated the labor market remained at a significant disadvantage in setting terms. In this sense "the hiring process and the hiring contract were one-sided agreements existing to ensure that the farmer had the services of key workers when he needed them, and defining the terms of those services" (Miller 1992, 207). As we will see below, many of the cases adjudicated by the Redditch magistrates were annual hires, but it is not clear what percentage of the local agricultural labor force worked under such agreements. Given that a substantial portion of local production was focused on livestock, which needed continual care and supervision, the percentage was likely substantial compared to farming regions in the south and east.

The politics of production thus was entwined with more general considerations of status in rural society that were being transformed. As Howard Newby suggests in his now-classic study of farm workers in East Anglia, a politics of deference on the farm was tied to a village order of authority and hierarchy that formed a local totality (1977, 45–53). This conception of rural order, even if increasingly an idyllic vision, was still drawn on as a template for master-servant relations. For example, a prize-winning essay by a servant on these relations, published in the *Farmers' Magazine*, depicted the hierarchy in the following terms:

> Masters occupy a higher step in the order of society, and they should consider it below their honor to deal unkindly towards those who are toiling for their comfort and well-being. It is a law in nature that the greater attracts the less; so they, being a greater in the world's esteem, should all as one man begin to show to the servant-class a spirit of sympathy and kindness, especially to the rising generation, and in a few years there would be fewer complaints about *and lawsuits with* their demoralized, insolent and incorrigible class of creatures [emphasis added].[8]

During the second half of the century "a network of obligations" between farmers and laborers frayed in many parts of England (Randall and Newman 1995, 206). The laborer's deference, which depended on a stable paternalism in a localized and totalizing rural order, waned with the attenuation of ties and fewer boarding farm servants. As several historians have noted, agrarian capitalism relied on constructions of service and deference to grease the wheels of production, yet in many areas older understandings and practices of paternalism were increasingly ill-suited to capitalist imperatives.[9] As paternalism faded, it was perhaps replaced by a patriarchal despotism anchored in the broader village order, of which the local justice system could be a significant buttress.

Among agricultural laborers there remained a hierarchy of positions and remuneration. Those who worked with animals had higher status due to the specialized skills required and the value of their charges. Stockmen, ploughmen, carters, and horsemen were among the most select, followed by cattlemen and shepherds. They were almost universally employed on yearly contracts, and because of their skills more mobile and thus less anchored to the area. This was also a masculine sphere. Farm servants who were yearly hires, a few whom still boarded with the farmers, were next on the pecking order, followed by the seasonal and finally ordinary day laborers. The latter two groups were disproportionately made up of women and children used during harvest periods who supplemented family incomes. Female farm servants might have been expected to engage in a variable mix of household and farm chores, though legally they were not considered domestics because of the latter duties.[10] However, as Raphael Samuel observed, occupational boundaries were complicated by the seasonal nature of work on the farm and the farmer who employed two or three servants could see these boundaries as permeable given his shifting needs (1975, 4–5). The tasks of farm servants could not be parsed out easily into a regimented labor process.

Both the seasonal and everyday practical needs of the farmer, especially those attuned to commercial markets, led to shifting demands of their servants. The need for such flexibility from labor marked the employment relationship as qualitatively different from many of the urban, industrial alternatives. As a letter addressed to the Midland Farmers' Club observed, "Many well-intentioned, but ignorant speakers and writers, put farm labour on the same platform with factory or contract labour. This is a great mistake; only a small part of it can be gauged or measured. The major part is changeable, desultory, and often wasteful, requiring personal and constant supervision" (*Farmer's Magazine* [1872], 419).

Job definitions, the intensity of work, the license to range beyond the farm's confines, and seasonal expectations were all potential flashpoints for disagreements. As Howkins notes in his examination of rural radicalism in the Norwalk countryside, "Personal conflict . . . was endemic in a work situation which was often marked by close personal contact between master and man, and whose ideology elevated this relationship to a position of prime importance" (1985, 17). As we will see, conflicts over duties and responsibilities were often the bases of prosecutions, with the authority of the farmer taking center stage.

Of course wages were also grist for conflict, particularly in such a labor-intensive industry that still relied for a number of positions (particularly those in animal husbandry) on annual service. There is general consensus that rural wages increased between 1850 and 1870 as labor markets tightened. Nonetheless, as Howkins (1990, 133) observes, "Since at least the middle of the nineteenth century the farm worker has been virtually the worst paid and worst treated of all English manual workers. At virtually no point since 1850 have agricultural wages exceeded 50 percent of the national industrial wage. . . . For women who worked the land the conditions were worse."[11]

In Eastern Worcestershire, barring a few exceptions, grazing lands figured prominently, accounting for perhaps a little more than half of the tended land, with cultivation concentrating on wheat and to a lesser extent oats, barley, and legumes. In the areas near Birmingham livestock farming was oriented to the dairy industry and to the feeding of cattle and sheep bred in other areas. The region had experienced enclosure earlier than others, and had witnessed a considerable investment in drainage. The consolidation of smaller enclosed farms and such capital investments meant that farming was geared to commercial markets but was less prone to mechanization found in the southeast of England.[12]

The northeast corner of the county was characterized by small occupiers who often took yearly tenancies, and modest landholders. Farms rarely exceed 300 acres and, as in the county as a whole, small holdings were more modest in size. Smaller farms continued to rely on labor-intensive production. In Alvechurch, a farming town a few miles north of Redditch, for example, farms averaged slightly under 100 acres in 1871. A little over a third of the farms were under 40 acres and about 55 percent were under 100 acres. The economic fortunes of these farmers varied cyclically with the economy. Prices for livestock generally rose during these years, but disease plagued the market intermittently in the 1860s and 1870s, creating heavy periodic losses for some. Wheat prices similarly experienced moderate undulations in the 1860s and the beginning of the 1870s before the gradual decline into prolonged depression in the latter decade. Rents rose throughout at least the 1860s.[13]

During the 1860s and 1870s wages for ordinary male laborers in Worcestershire ranged roughly 9–12s per week, adding a couple shillings for in-kind perquisites such as beer and cider during harvest season. Rates for harvest labor were several shillings above the ordinary rate. As with the rest of the Midlands, this was probably a shilling or two below rates in the southeast and north. Cattlemen, wagoners, and shepherds typically earned 1–2s more per week and lodging. Female labor, which was often needed to sustain the family economy, was often paid at less than half the rate of men.[14] By 1872 the National Agricultural Labourers' Union was rising in many parts of the country seeking wage increases. There was some activity on behalf of the union in the county generally, and a couple of meetings held in the Redditch area, but there seems not to have been any sustained agitation by unionists.[15]

The formal subordination of farm servants was thus predicated on a village hierarchy refashioned by the increasing commercialization of agricultural production. The politics of production had been anchored in a hegemonic deferential rural order. However, it is possible that marketization was transforming not only farm production and labor relations and markets, but also the rural hierarchy more generally, so that this hegemony became less natural and reliable as a mechanism of subordination in daily interactions between farmer and servant. To the extent that paternalism was being replaced by patriarchal despotism, farmers faced more regular challenges to their authority by farm servants less tied to place. There was little union activity in the farming area surrounding Redditch compared to other parts of the country, but that does not mean that the system of subordination was necessarily more intact. As we will see in the analysis of court data, servants chafed under the patriarchal dictates of farmers, and the latter sought to shore up their authority through the local justice system.[16]

NEEDLE MAKING

Redditch was also the center of the specialized micro-economy of needle-making, which had a global reach. As a contemporary guide observed, "It has virtually absorbed and monopolized the whole needle-making trade of the kingdom and of half of the rest of the world and more" (Burritt 1868, 338). The needle district radiated outward from Redditch with most of the factories strung along the Arrow River. "It may be said," observed a writer in the *Indicator*, "to extend about ten miles north and south, and at its widest part, from Studley to Feckenham, about five or six miles east and west" (April 13, 1860). Its origins were in the mid-1700s to turn of the century, and many of the founding firms commanded a central place in the mid-Victorian industry. A diminutive, industrially distinct relative, the fishhook trade, was also centered in the area. By the mid-1860s there were perhaps 100 large and small manufacturers in the district with 10,000 people dependent on the trade and an additional 600 employed working on fishhooks and tackles. In a town that had a total population of only about 6,700, needle-making was, as one observer suggested "the staple, the all-in-all, without which almost every house in the place would probably shut up"; Dickens concurred that "almost every man, woman and child lives by needles."[17] By far the largest manufacturer in Redditch itself was Henry Milward & Sons, which employed over 450 workers in the early 1870s, followed by William Bartleet & Sons with about 180 hands. Many of the larger firms employed 60–120 workers, though workshops that specialized in one of the many parts of the production process could employ as few as a half dozen hands.[18]

The industry was anchored by about ten major firms, though there were dozens of smaller establishments that specialized in particular products such as sewing machine needles or steps in the production process. Within this district, when busy 200 million needles were produced each week, of which about 70 percent found its way to the export market.[19] The figure is all the more impressive because, as I detail below, many aspects of the production process still relied on water power and were not technologically intensive. Expansion of the industry was particularly extensive from the mid-1850s when production and employment was only one-half of the above figures. As an observer noted in the mid-1860s, "Within the last half-a-dozen years, factories, warehouses, dwellings, and new buildings of all descriptions, have been erected, and new streets would have risen much more extensively if the land had not been chiefly leasehold."[20]

An account of the production process resonates with Adam Smith's classic discussion of the division of labor in pin-making in its highly refined division of labor and the labor process. In *Capital* Marx referenced it as an exemplar in this regard, though he saw it as part of the handicraft industry transition to the factory system proper because it lacked the real subordination of machine-controlled labor power (1976, 589). In some respects it paralleled the organization of pottery manufacturing with a large number of specific operations that involved batch processing. However, the organization of the production process in this case depended less on skilled males who subcontracted women and children at key points in the production process, and there was less independence in the organization of the stations in the factory or workshop.

There were thirty distinct steps in the labor process to create a needle and as a contemporary observed, "Labour could hardly be more minutely subdivided than in the production of the needle here. With all the introduction of machinery and improved methods, it still passes through *seventy* pairs of hands before it is fully ready for the market" (Burritt 1868, 341). Production varied between outwork and factory labor, and hand and machine processes. Occupations were also highly stratified by gender and age, with men controlling skilled positions and women and children significantly employed in preparatory and finishing processes. Approximately equal numbers of children, and adult men and women were employed in the trade, with children earning generally no more than 5s per week, women 8–15s, and men from 12–40s, depending on their skill level (Bartleet and Woodward 1967 [1866], 202).

The initial processes of wire cutting (done by both hand and machine), straightening (by annealing and rolling), and pointing were dominated by men. In the cutting shop an adult male took a coil of wire (about a mile in total length) and made cuts with large shears every few inches, producing 10,000–15,000 pieces that served the basis for production. He then placed several thousand of them inside two iron rings, which held the cut pieces at each end, and placed them in a small furnace until red hot. With the wires heated they were placed on an iron plate and iron or steel bar inserted in the interior between the rings and the wires "rubbed" back and forth until they were fully straightened.[21] Straightened wires were then taken to the pointing shop (which generally was factory work), which was among the most skilled and deadly occupations in the process.[22] Adult males grasped 50–100 needles in one hand and with the other manipulated them across a high-speed grindstone perfectly pointing each end of the wires, completing as many as 10,000 an hour.[23]

After they were washed and dried, the pointed wires were then passed to the stamping department. There, adult males or females would take a fistful and, one by one, place the wires in a stamping machine consisting of a die attached to a heavy hammer and a channel iron bed where the wire rested. The die dropped in the middle of the wire created two partially formed eyelets and a weakened division between each nascent head. (The stamping machines were operated by water or steam power.) Though the stamping was done on single wires, the stamper produced 4,000 or more per hour (or 8,000 partially formed needles). These in turn were passed to boys (often apprentices) who took about 50 and spread them fan-like on the base of small presses, and one by one punched through the eyelets. The wires were in turn passed to a filer who passed filing wires through each eye on either side of the wires and, having assembled several dozen, filed down the protuberances on each head created by the stamping. Once the wires were filed, boys "spit" them, breaking the wires in half and creating single roughly hewn needles.[24]

After these processes the partly finished needles were passed to "soft-straighteners," females either in the factory or in workshops who used a curved steel bar to roll the needles on an iron plate to insure that they were straight. They processed about 3,000 an hour and then the needles were conveyed to the hardening shop where men placed the needles on iron trays and heated them in furnaces; the needles were subsequently cooled in water or oil, and then returned to a furnace for tempering. The next department was "hammer straightening," in which females with small hammers smoothed and straightened about 500 needles an hour. This was often outwork, though it was performed in larger factories in a separate department.[25] The needles were then taken to the scouring mill which was either a separate workshop or a department in the larger factories. Up to 65,000 were bundled on to pieces of thick canvas about two feet long; a mixture of soap, emery, and oil was added, and the bundles were rolled and tied off into "setts" resembling giant sausages.[26] Up to two dozen of these at a time were rolled by water-powered mangles for between 8–14 hours under the eyes of the male scourers and the process was repeated up to five times to insure smoothness of the needle surfaces.[27] With the finishing complete the needles were washed, dried in sawdust, and separated by size.[28]

The above processes took about a week to complete. After scouring, the needles were transferred to the "bright shop." There they were inspected and sorted by girls who passed them along to drillers. These adult males blued the heads for finishing and then used triangular drills to insure the eyes were properly beveled. The needles were passed to boys or girls who used drills with thin wires to individually impart a final smoothness to the eyes; they each could finish about 150,000 per week. The needles were then passed to adult male polishers who, using small grindstones and leather buffers, and employing a similar technique as the pointers, finished the heads and polished about 1,000 needles per hour. Finally finished, the needles were passed on to women who cut pieces of paper and packaged 25 into a packet at the rate of 3,000 an hour. In another room boys placed labels on each packet, and then they bundled, packed, and sent the packets to the warehouse. The largest firms in the district, such as Messrs. Milward & Sons, coordinated the production of around 7 million needles per week.[29]

Power-assisted machinery was introduced into the labor process in the 1820s through the 1840s for tasks such as pointing, stamping, filing, and drilling. The new machines initially met with considerable resistance from handworkers (particularly the pointers in the mid-1840s), but this was generally short-lived (Rollins 1984, 63).[30] As Marx suggested, however, the labor process still relied heavily on hand labor (Allen 1929, 109). Machinery did not set the pace of production, and some of the operations performed, especially by the adult males, required skill and considerable dexterity. As Dickens noted when comparing a fish-hook machine to needle manufacture,

"In needle-making there is no such marvelous machinery: the marvel consists chiefly of the dexterity of attainable human fingers; but the monstrous numbers are simply overwhelming" (1852, 543). When new drilling machinery was finally installed after 1875, it was imported from Germany, which was providing increasingly stiff competition.[31]

It appears that the pace of production was kept up through a combination of piece rates and, in the factories, managers who attended to the departments. A contemporary debate on the introduction of half-days on Saturdays suggests that the average work week was sixty hours. Though there was often no strict time-keeping, and St. Monday (the practice of skipping work on Monday) existed in Redditch, the impression is that manufacturers had far fewer problems with irregular hours kept by their employees than their contemporaries in Hanley.[32] The generalized acceptance of half-days on Saturdays in 1865 as well as the application of the factory acts to the industry in 1866 likely added to the necessity of insuring labor productivity during factory and workshop hours.[33]

Issues of labor control were complicated by a few other factors. Up through the 1850s the traditional seat of the needle industry had been Long Credon in Buckinghamshire, and there was some production in other places. Many of Redditch's manufacturers had in fact migrated from Long Credon, and several of the significant ones maintained facilities in both towns (Allen 1929, 81–82; Shrimpton 1897). However, Redditch's advantages concerning closeness to necessary materials and its increasing infrastructure eclipsed Long Credon in economic advantage. As a result, though, manufacturers had to rely on this one local labor market. "It is very difficult to establish a needle factory out of the needle district," noted the manufacturer Michael Morrall. "As a general rule, only the worst workmen can be obtained, as the others will not leave their own district, those who do, only remain a short time" (Morrall 1866, 28). While this created some symbiosis between labor and capital, it also left the latter with a constricted labor supply and few options for outside recruitment. Manufacturers faced skilled labor shortages in robust periods and sought ways of substituting females and apprentices as the industry expanded (Jones 1980, 176, 186).[34] The labor supply was further constricted in 1870 with the passage of an act extending mandatory education of children to the industry.[35] Second, S. R. H. Jones has calculated that upwards of 80 percent of production costs in the first half of the nineteenth century were for labor, and of this only 15 percent was for skilled work (1980, 170). How much these percentages changed in succeeding decades is not possible to say, but labor certainly remained a significant (if not dominant) production cost.[36] Managing productivity by controlling the labor process was thus the principle means by which manufacturers maintained their profits.

One local historian observes that "labour relations between master and craftsmen were never very good," and cites the periodic organized reactions (including a few riots) against the initial introduction of new production techniques from the late 1820s through the mid-1840s as examples of the sometimes fraught relationship (Land 1986, 36–37). The 1850s and 1860s were a period of relative labor quietude, though the drillers successfully struck for an advance in wages in 1869.[37] In the economic boom year of 1872, in which unions across the country pressed demands, there was some stirring within the needle district. The needle scourers formed a union in March and by mid-May had persuaded most of the manufacturers to allow Saturday half-days. There were meetings of fishhook makers and machine drillers as well to form unions, but it is not clear that these nascent unions won advances, and the drillers' organization might have been stillborn. Conversely, as noted above, leading manufacturers supported the expansion of Saturday half-days as well as the extension of the Factory Act in 1866 to include needle factories.[38] Overall, however, there was no substantial union presence in the industry during the first three-quarters of the century and manufacturers were able to surmount any challengers by their workers to the introduction of new machinery.

Depending on the time period and employer, labor control was probably accomplished by attempts at paternalistic or a muted market despotism. Scattered evidence from the mid-1860s to the end of the period suggests that the larger manufacturers tried to exercise some form of factory paternalism. They treated their workers to annual rounds of dinners, lunches, teas, picnics, and excursions. Henry Milward not only held compulsory prayer services in his factory every morning, he also kept attendance records for Sunday services at the Anglican church St. Stephen's. Milward also chaired the local British and Foreign Bible Society, which distributed Bibles and New Testaments throughout the district and superintended classes for the Mission Room. Robert Bartleet was president of the Temperance Society, which held an annual festival that entertained 1,000 people. He also delivered addresses on the need for Free Schools and shorter hours for children, and he and other major millowners were active in both the National and Wesleyan schools, which taught some 700 students all told. Redditch also offered the usual array of elite-sponsored and supervised institutions, including a literary institute and reading room for working men that had been established in the 1850s (which had manufacturers as committee members), a recreation society that maintained a local field, factory sick clubs, and allotment gardens.[39]

Whether these paternalistic efforts made much of an impression on the local workforce is difficult to discern. Milward's employees presented him with piece of plate to honor his seventieth birthday during regular morning prayer session at factory, but there remains little else in the extant historical record to indicate worker appreciation (*Redditch Indicator*, May 5, 1872). Lesser manufacturers and workshop owners appear uninvolved in these civic enterprises. They received little attention in contemporary sources, and within Burawoy's scheme they might well have exercised some form of market despotism; though given the limitations posed by the localized nature of the labor market they might not have been able to exercise the full whip of the market.

Additionally, throughout the period there is little or no public discussion of trade custom or traditions, though court arguments often pivoted on defining custom in such issues as the length of time for giving proper notice. This absence is possible for at least two reasons. First, during the period there is no public or collective conflict concerning the reorganization of the labor process. Second, the rapid expansion of the industry was relatively recent, largely after the introduction of labor-enhancing machinery. In addition, many in the workforce were comparatively recent entrants into the trade, and as such there were thus fewer workers who could make claims to trade custom or have family work histories anchored in it. However, such absence did not obviate issues of workplace conflict, and to enhance their labor control regimes a number of employers turned to the local court.

THE COURT AND ITS JUSTICE

As I noted at the outset the town of Redditch came into its own shortly before the period of study. In a number of respects the development of the town and the needle industry and the transformation of commercial agriculture conjoined in the early 1860s to lead local economic elites along a path to the local court in creating their problem-solving regime for labor control. Both the district and the needle industry had expanded rapidly in the previous decade, and the recent consolidation of the latter in the district altered the manufacturers' economic landscape. Up until this period they had the option of investing capital in other manufacturing districts, such as Long Credon in Buckinghamshire, the long-standing center of needle production. Several manufacturers maintained production in both places, having established firms in Long Credon before setting up facilities in Redditch (Shrimpton 1897). However, as needle production converged on Redditch during these years, manufacturers became dependent on local labor. During the same period local landowners and farmers were adapting to the increasing commercialization of their production and the declining of a traditional rural order in part because of these changes, which included challenges of controlling labor that were less tied to the farm and farmhouse. Finally, the rapid growth of the town itself not only produced a rising and socially cohesive group of manufacturers, but also growing merchant and professional classes. All of these classes shared concerns of governing both a town and a region in the process of substantial transformations.

From the start local governance through the new boards was exercised by a mix of merchants, professionals, and more prominent needle manufacturers. While there was an occasional grumble that the last group did not receive adequate representation on the town's improvement board, there seems to have been little political discord among the town's various economic interests.[40] All of the town's major classes coalesced around new institutions of governance both to assert political authority and to manage economic development.

As with all borough courts the establishment of Redditch's bench required an act of Parliament. Leading members of the town requested the establishment of petty sessions because of the necessity of traveling to Alcester, seven miles distant, and their growing need for summary justice given the town's growth. The "police reports" in the *Redditch Indicator* in the few years prior to the establishment of the borough court show that both farmers and needle manufacturers brought prosecutions at the Alcester sessions with some regularity, suggesting that some reliance on master and servant law had been established prior to the installation of the Redditch borough court. However, no records exist from this court, so it is impossible to know how reliant Redditch area employers were on such prosecutions prior to the establishment of the Redditch petty sessions.

Though Redditch's initial request for its own petty sessions was turned down, in part because of concern that the town could not muster a sufficient magistracy, from its inception a reliable group of justices took control of the bench.[41] The petty sessional division encompassed a number of satellite villages with both farming and manufacturing interests, including Beoley, Feckenham, Inkberrow, and Webheath. For most of the first four years of its existence the petty sessions were chaired by George R. Gray, the hard-nosed vicar of nearby Inkberrow.[42] The remainder of the magistrates was divided between the landed elite, needle manufacturers, and barristers. Among the most prominent members was William Tabberer, a county magistrate and owner of about 250 acres. He and John Brown, also a landowner who also had previous experience as a Warwickshire magistrate, represented the agriculture interests. In the second group were the needle magnate Henry Milward, the next largest manufacturer Robert Bartleet, and two other prominent members of the industry, Edmund Holyoake and James Smith. Among those rounding out the magistracy were the local barristers John Doherty and Edward Waldron Haywood.[43] Throughout most of the period Gray, Milward, Holyoake, Haywood, and Tabberer were among the most stalwart members. This group thus combined knowledge of both the law and the two most significant sectors of the regional economy. It thus mirrored many other borough courts of the era in being controlled by the town elites. However, in this case the prominent landowners and manufacturers sat side by side.

During its first years the court met bimonthly, but by the summer of 1865 petty sessions were held on every Friday (*Redditch Indicator*, July 29, 1865). In most years the court would deal with somewhere around 230–80 cases of summary jurisdiction. It is not clear that this number was particularly distinctive relative to its population, but what is apparent is that an unusually high percentage of master and servant cases were taken before the Redditch court for most years during the period, as shown in table 6.1. Recall that from the early 1860s until the reform of the law in 1875, master and servant prosecutions represented about 2 percent of all prosecutions for summary offenses in England. During this period, Redditch's northern industrial neighbor, Birmingham, roughly paralleled these figures with a little over 2 percent of all prosecutions falling under the category. Worcestershire exhibited a higher rate at about 4.7 percent.[44] However, on average about 5 percent of the summary cases brought before the Redditch petty sessions involved master and servant offenses.[45] Moreover, as table 6.2 shows for the years 1866 and 1872, in some years the percentages for master and servant prosecutions rose to half of those for all forms of assault and in the case of drunk and disorderly charges almost two-thirds. Its peaks roughly parallel those of Hanley although, as table 6.1 shows, it had larger yearly swings than either that town or Hull. Partly this can be subscribed to Redditch's much smaller size.

From 1862 to 1875 a little under 170 master and servant cases were brought to the Redditch petty sessions, of which almost 90 percent were prosecutions by employers. Table 6.3 shows the percentage of cases by identifiable industry as well as an industrial breakdown for employers' prosecutions more particularly. Not surprisingly, because their economic dominance, agriculture and the needle and fishhook industries figure most prominently, and their numbers were identical. The engineering and metal

TABLE 6.1. Master and servant cases as a percentage of all Redditch petty session cases, 1863–1875

Year	Percentage
1863	6.7
1864	4.6
1865	2.3
1866	6.3
1867	5.4
1868	3
1869	1.3
1870	4.5
1871	5.8
1872	10.1
1873	7.2
1874	3.6
1875[a]	5.6

[a] Through July 29.

Sources: Worcester County Record Office, Redditch Magistrates' Register of Cases between the 16th day of July 1862 and the 25th day of December 1865 (b260.105/ BA5796/I) and Petty Sessional Division of Redditch, Register of the Court of Petty Sessions, 1865–1875, (b260.105/ BA 5796/ (ii–iii); *Redditch Indicator*.

TABLE 6.2. Selected offenses as a percentage of all summary prosecutions in Redditch, 1866 and 1872

Offense	1866	1872
Assault (all forms)	14.6	19.4
Bastardy	2.9	. . .
Begging	2.9	. . .
Breaches of the peace	. . .	. . .
Drunk and disorderly (all forms)	10.8	19.8
Malicious injury	4.6	. . .
Master and servant	6.3	10.1
Peddler's act (hawking)	. . .	3.1
Stealing	1.6	. . .

Sources: WCRO, Redditch Magistrates' Registers of Cases (b260.105/ BA5796/ i–iii); *Redditch Indicator*.

TABLE 6.3. Master and servant cases and employers prosecutions by industry, Redditch, 1862–1875

Industry	All Master and Servant Cases	All Employer Prosecutions
Needle and fish hook	52 (31)	51 (34)
Farming	60 (36)	51 (34)
Engineering and metal	22 (13)	20 (13)
Other and unknown	34 (20)	28 (19)

Note: Numbers in parentheses are percentages.
Sources: WCRO, Redditch Magistrates' Registers of Cases (b260.105/BA5796/i–iii); *Redditch Indicator*.

trades, which supported both the needle and fishhook industries, are also clearly represented.

Table 6.4 shows the percentage of cases that were decided in favor of the employer. As with the previous case studies this calculation includes those cases in which employers not only sought punishment of workers, but also alternatively a warning from the bench to their obstreperous workers about acceptable behavior along with an order to return to work, or the dissolution of contracts that the employer considered untenable. It thus includes cases that were withdrawn or dismissed, but where there is clear evidence that in doing so the magistrates dictated to defendants that they must return to work and obey their employers, or that their employers were taking appropriate action in discharging them.[46] The table shows that employers in agriculture and the needle industry received favorable judgments in about two-thirds of their cases, while those in other trades were somewhat less successful.

Table 6.3 shows the judgments broken down by the percentage rendered in a number of principal categories of decision. As noted in chapter 2, magistrates (particularly after 1867) had a number of options at their disposal in rendering a decision against a worker, including fines, damages, prison, and the provision of a surety to insure that the worker would return to the job and meet employers' expectations.[47] In addition, in a number of cases employers asked for severance of the employment contract because they found the continued employment of a worker untenable. Farmers brought workers before the bench with regularity as public exercise to recuperate their authority. They argued explicitly that they did not wish to pursue a particular punishment, but in doing so sought to have their right of deference affirmed.

While table 6.3 needs to be analyzed with some caution, there seem to be some interpretations that can be made concerning similarities and differences between the ways in which the two dominant groups of cases, the needle and fish hook industry and agriculture, were adjudicated. First, similarly as to what we found in Hanley, relatively few workers were imprisoned for their offenses. Generally there was little advantage for either type of employer in locking up workers. In Redditch, sentences of imprisonment usually were meted out to workers with a history of multiple transgressions of the law or in those few cases where the employer determined he needed to make an example of the worker because of the magnitude of the offense. In farmers' and needle manufacturers' cases, magistrates sometimes rendered decisions that provided the worker return to the job without penal sanction, such as the withdraw, dismissal, or adjournment of the case with a warning to the prosecuted worker. These cases are captured in the "Other" category.

Perhaps more striking are the differences in forms of punishment meted out to workers in these two groups. As shown in table 6.5, the percentage of

TABLE 6.4. Employers' prosecutorial success rates by industry, Redditch, 1862–1875

Industry	Successful Prosecutions (%)
Needle and fish hook	68
Farming	68
Engineering and metal	60
Other and unknown	60

Sources: WCRO, Redditch Magistrates' Registers of Cases (b260.105/BA5796/i–iii); *Redditch Indicator*.

TABLE 6.5. Percentage of type of decision rendered in judgments for employers, Redditch, 1862–1875

Industry	Fines	Damages	Surety	Prison	Discharge	Other
Needle	11	31	26	3	9	20
Farming	16	9	11	9	31	24
Engineering and metal	0	42	8	8	42	0
Other and unknown	12	6	18	0	12	52
Total	11	19	17	5	22	26

Sources: WCRO, Redditch Magistrates' Registers of Cases (b260.105/ BA5796/i–iii); *Redditch Indicator*.

those who were ordered to pay damages or find sureties, or were discharged, differs in each case by more than a factor of 2. In the needle trades damages and sureties were much more usual and in agriculture the discharge of farm laborers was the most common action, far outstripping the percentage in the needle industry.

These tendencies reflect divergent understandings and expectations both on the part of the magistrates and the employers. The bench often found itself hearing rancorous disputes that were frequently as much matters of personal enmity as they were about the particulars of employment. And in playing out the drama of justice the magistrates also pointedly insisted on their position as impartial adjudicators, which we have seen in the previous case studies. The hegemonic discourse of the state is precisely an impartial one, and thus the justices explicitly drew upon "the law" in rendering their decisions. As a magistrate responded to a father's protestations in a case concerning an apprenticed needle-driller, "No matter what you think, the law settles it; we have no voice in the matter, we only administer the law as we find it" (*Redditch Indicator*, May 4, 1872). Of course, what the magistrates "found" depended on how and where they looked. As I argue below, the decisions rendered in the needle trades cases angled more toward questions of the control and output of production, while those in agriculture focused more on the integrity of a rural patriarchal order.

Several cases typify the assumptions drawn upon both by farmers and magistrates in prosecutions concerning farm servants. All were issues of disobedience that employers took as an affront to their general authority and that the court, from a slightly different vantage point, saw as the violation of a proper hierarchical order. In one of the early cases heard before the newly constituted petty sessions a farmer from nearby Beoley prosecuted one of his servants in husbandry for persistent intransigence in the face of his orders.

> Mr. Nicholas, farmer, of Beoley, charged Clements with refusing to perform the work set to him. Mr. Nicholas stated that he had, in the month of April, engaged the defendant to work at stated wages, viz. £7 10 0, for a half-year ending in October; that he first worked at levelling a bank, and during that time the plaintiff saw he was a hardy fellow, and knew well how to manage horses, and he engaged him to do that and other general work, that he had sent him out with a team several times, but found he could not depend on his being home in proper time (instancing once taking ten hours to go to Redditch and back for manure when five would have been ample time), that subsequently he set him other work, and he

refused to do it, had also absented himself one week from his services, and had boasted that he would not do anything *but* go with the team.

Defendant when called on to give his defence said he was hired to go with the team, that was his work.

Plaintiff re-examination on this point said he was hired to do any kind of work, should not give as high wages to a mere waggoner.

The magistrates were trying to ascertain if defendant would go back and behave better, when plaintiff begged them to settle the matter as they could not go on well together. So the bench ordered £1 to be deducted from his wages on consideration of his leaving plaintiff in harvest time, one week for absence, and the balance was paid, and the defendant liberated.[48]

In this case the farmer was willing to divorce himself of a servant during harvest time, when labor was at a premium, because of what he took as intractable intransigence.

These cases became part of the stock and trade of the bench. Six and a half years later before the petty sessions another agricultural laborer was prosecuted for both leave without authorization and damages. The relationship between master and servant was clearly toxic.

James Shepherd was charged by William Court, of Ham Green, with leaving his service without leave on the 21st, causing loss or damage to the amount of 1s. 6d.

Defendant pleaded not guilty.

Complainant sworn, deposed: I am a farmer, living in the parish of Feckenham; the defendant is my agricultural servant. I hired him on the 9th of November, until Michaelmas. (To Mr. Gray; He was an in-door servant). He left my service on the 21st of December, about 5 o'clock in the afternoon without my leave, and returned about half-past eight; he has left on several occasions; he did not ask permission to go. (To Mr. Gray); He was to feed the cattle, and prepare food for them, and another man had to do it. On the 22nd he refused to work at all; he was destroying my property; was giving poisonous matter to the horses, which are now under treatment; I saw him, also, throw a new rope over the hedge into the snow; I asked him why he did not do it up? (he ought to have put it into the cart hovel). He said he would be ——— if he would do any more work; if he did he would break everything that came in his way. He did no more work that day.

[In response] To [magistrate] Mr. Gray: I hired him at his own home.

> Mr. Gray asked what was the defendant's reason or excuse for refusing to work. Complainant gave a long and rather digressing explanation; and in answer to—
>
> The Clerk's questions [the complainant] answered 'I had previously told him he deserved a good horse-whipping;' and he said I could not do it. I struck at him but did not hit him.
>
> The Chairman remonstrated with complainant for attempting personal chastisement to his servants; it lowered a man in the esteem of the public, besides rendering a master amenable to the law. 'Two blacks do not make one white—you should get a character with your servants.
>
> Complainant cross-examined by defendant; Did I ever refuse to do my work before you struck me? Ans. No.
>
> Defendant then said—in defence—that his master had struck and kicked him, and only gave him three meals a day.
>
> Complainant, to questions, said: There is about 14s. or 15c. coming to him. I do not want him back again.
>
> Defendant was ordered to pay 1s. 6d. for compensation and 9s. costs, to be deducted from his wages; The contract to be annulled.[49]

As characterized many of the cases concerning agricultural laborers, the farmer was as much concerned with the rebellion against his authority as in the incompletion of work. In such cases farmers often expressed dismay over transgressions of hierarchy. The magistrates echoed these concerns, though this came through most clearly in their remonstrance to farmer, not the defendant, when they admonished him to pay more attention to his esteem before the public. He was not upholding the station of the master as quoted earlier in the *Farmer's Magazine.* Here, arguably, there was a subtext of how a patriarchal rural order should function.

A final example resonates with the first two, illustrating that the target of the prosecution as insolence. In this case the immediate superior to a wagoner, the farm bailiff, seeks the assistance of the farm owner to reestablish order.

> William Simmons sworn. I am a farm bailiff in the service of the Hadens of Wallhouse farm parish of Feckensham and Hanbury. The defendant Wilks is also employed by him as wagoneer [*sic*]. On the 27th July last defendant went to Redditch with a steam Engine and four horses. He also took a boy with him. He returned about 2 o'clock without the boy. The horses returned by themselves. Defendant was 100 yards behind them. Defendant was drunk. He tumbled backwards into the chaff whole [*sic*]

> and was on his head or back with his feet outside. This was in the parish of Feckenham. I told him what to do and he used very bad language and took 2 kicks at me. He threatened me several times. He followed me into the house using bad language all the time. I was obliged to go over to my master at the Woodrow farm and tell him of defendant's conduct. When I came home Deft was covered up in straw in the stable. This was about 10 o'clock.
>
> Fined 2/6. Costs 18/ and in default of payment 14 days imprisonment.[50]

In this trial the brunt of the prosecution concerned the servant's surly intoxication.[51] The farm bailiff argued for neither lost work nor damages. Rather, it was the insolence of the servant that created a chain reaction of the bailiff appealing to the farmer and the tiff proceeding to court. All of the above cases seem to illustrate a particular masculine rebelliousness that disrupted the farmers' standards of patriarchal order and discipline. Most were also prosecutions of laborers who were or wished to be seen as having higher status than general servants in husbandry. As will be discussed further below, the gendered foundations of this order are also demonstrated in the handling of female servants.

Turning to the prosecutions brought by needle manufacturers, as summarized in table 6.5, we note a different trend. In these cases, which often contained personal conflicts and claims of defiance, the emphases are on securing damages or insuring that workers return to fulfill their contracts. Much as with the potteries cases in Hanley, employers emphasized the need for labor power or compensation for its loss. The magistrates' decisions resonated with their concerns in the ways in which they formulated rulings in terms of trade customs.

One such case emphasizing trade custom involved an adolescent girl in the employ of needlemaker John Emms. As noted above, manufacturers employed many children and adolescents in stamping and drilling processes. Though it is not clear what tasks the girl had from this account, it is likely that she engaged in one of these tasks.

> Emma Braithwaithe, a girl 13 years of age, was charged by J. Emms as above.
>
> Complainant said the girl had worked about two half-days, Friday and Saturday in the Whitsun-week; he paid her 2s. 6d. on account on the Saturday night, and she did not come on the Monday, nor since then.
>
> This being a trade matter, Mr. Holyoake and Mr. Smith [both needle manufacturers] referred it to Mr. Tabberer, who, pointing out to the

> complainant the serious effect on a young girl of a charge like this pressed to conviction, asked him if he wished so to press it, or would he be willing to take the girl again into work. Then Mr. Tabberer explained to the girl that she must know, or her friends must know, that the custom of all manufactories (and other such work), required at least a week's notice before leaving. That it is quite necessary to support this custom; and, if complainant had pressed his case, they, the Magistrates, *must* send her to prison.
>
> The mother of the girl then came forward and begged the Bench to hear some explanations; which she proceeded to give. She declared that complainant, not only neglected to pay the children the full wages due, but also shamefully ill-used a sister of the defendant's, and used very bad language to her, until it was quite impossible to allow the children to stay with him; she also—and the defendant—averred that complainant had distinctly told the girl that she *need not* give notice to *him*, or to the shop where she worked previously; she said, too, that if the children went back to work complainant would be hard on them.
>
> George Court, a person who had employed defendant since, came forward to corroborate their evidence.
>
> The Bench pointed out to the mother that her defence had not removed the necessity of upholding the rule between master and workman—a week's notice on *either* side—and, that if her children were not paid, or not treated properly, she had her remedy by applying to the Magistrates. Eventually, the charge was withdrawn, defendant paying expenses, and, the children to return to work (emphases in original).[52]

This prosecution is emblematic of the court's workings with regard to needle cases, and also demonstrates the particular legal formality that the magistrates exercised with respect to their positions and their hegemonic legal "neutrality." As unbiased state adjudicators, magistrates were not supposed to hear cases in their own industries, to protect against favoritism. In this instance, the matter was left to Tabberer, the landowner, to hear, though it is likely that his fellow magistrates remained throughout the proceedings. In so doing the court was able to enact a theatre of impartiality.

Tabberer, as the disinterested referee, emphasized the customary rules of the trade and the necessity of sending the girl to prison if she had violated them. And he pointedly noted that the protestations of the girl's mother only could be addressed through a separate civil suit before the bench. Here the magistrate found the law clearly aligning with trade custom, and there was to be no equivocation or allowance for the conduct of the employer or the gender and age of the worker.

In the next case (in which the magistrates Holyoake and Milward did not recuse themselves, even though it was a trade matter) a small sail needle maker, Benjamin Briscoe, prosecuted George Yates for not fulfilling a yearly commitment. As in many trades, skilled workers often tried to maximize their earnings by offering their services to rival employers at higher wages, and then abandoning their current position. Under the law, both the worker and the new employer were subject to prosecution for violating an existing contract, though the latter might argue ignorance. In this case, only the worker, George Yates, appears to have been pursued.

> Benjamin Briscoe: About 4 times before the 15th June defendant asked me to employ him and on that day I engaged defendant for 12 months to help a man named Bonall square big sail needles. On the 25th June between 11 and 12 defendant came. Sat to the block and began [?] the needles. I said I was sorry he didn't come on the Monday. He had said he had been to Bromsgrove fair. He worked till 29th July and then left and never came again. He drew 3/9 and left the work undone. I am sure I engaged defendant for 12 months. I want him to fulfill his contract. When I engaged defendant I gave him 5/ earnest money. This he offered me again to release him but I refused.
>
> John Bonall: The defendant worked with me at complainant's shop from Tuesday till Saturday. He said he was coming to work for Briscoe but did not say for how long. On the following Monday defendant did not come but left work undone. I saw complainant give defendant 5/ which was earnest money. Defendant offered it to him again since his former master had offered him more money to go back. Complainant declined the 5/.
>
> Alice Briscoe: Defendant came 4 times to my husband and asked him for work. He said he could get more money under my husband than his master.
>
> George Yates (Defendant): I took 5/ from complainant to go to work for him and enable him to get an order off. It was in June. I went for a few days. There was no agreement for any particular time. I offered him the 5/s because I thought him a poor man.
>
> Ordered to fulfill contract in a [?] and find one surety £10. Costs.[53]

For Briscoe the nub of his grievance clearly was the need for labor. The magistrates could have suggested to Yates that he return to work to give a proper notice (and return part of all of the earnest money), which we saw above was a week according to trade custom and which they did in several other cases.[54] Instead, the court seems to have readily accepted the parol evidence and mandated that Yates return to finish out his year under bond. In so doing it also affirmed the ways in which contracts of service limited freedom in the labor market and provided the employer significant authority and leverage in the workplace.

In the next example, a prominent manufacturer in the fishing tackle and hook trade, Samuel Allcock, sought damages from a worker, Saul Yardley, who had been absent without authorization for the better part of two weeks. The presiding magistrates were Milward and Holyoake, who again did not see reason to recuse themselves. The worker acknowledged his absence, but claimed that it had not hampered the shop's production.

> Defendant admits absence without leave but denies damages.
>
> Samuel Allcock: I estimate the damage done to me by defendant's absenting himself from my service since the 2nd instant at £5. Defendant left on the Thursday and I could not supply his place until the following Tuesday. The place of the man who then supplied him could not be filled up for 3 days afterwards. There were about 15 or 20 men depending on defendant for work and all lost time by defendant's absence. I positively swear I have sustained a loss of £5 thro' defendant's absence without leave.
>
> Damages £5. Costs 13/4 and in default 6 weeks imprisonment.[55]

From Allcock's perspective, of course, the disruption of production and the lost work that it entailed was an egregious offense. The magistrates were satisfied with his assertion concerning his idled workers, and they appear not to have requested testimony from other members of his shop to corroborate his story. The damages awarded were a heavy penalty—amounting probably to at least a month's wages—and suggested that they too viewed Yardley's absence as a major transgression.

These cases reflect the tendencies represented in table 6.5. Needle manufacturers faced obstinacy and irregularity in the workplace, but their stated efforts in court were less concerned with repairing their authority and more concentrated on the bottom line. They were most focused on the payoff from labor, whether it was of an adolescent girl or a skilled adult male. The magistrates' understandings of these disputes, anchored in the local knowledge provided by needle manufacturers such as Milward, Bartleet, Holyoake, and Smith, synchronized with the stories told by prosecutors. The petty sessions were not blunt instruments of industrial discipline. Needle manufacturers experienced adverse outcomes in about a third of the cases they prosecuted. Yet, as we have seen in the other case studies, what in local courts was considered criminal often depended less on the written law than on the standards of right and wrong constructed by the powerful within communities. Within small towns such as Redditch, where popular politics or organized labor offered little counterweight to elite control, the politics of production and its representation in custom was determined by those who controlled the levers of justice.

It is worth noting that, unlike the Hanley case, major manufacturers were not the most frequent prosecutors. Rather, medium and small producers, those who likely had a more difficult time recruiting and maintaining a workforce, brought the bulk of the cases. Several employers who prosecuted more than one case were also out-processors, especially stampers, whose lifeblood was the timely turnaround of orders from larger manufacturers. This pattern also possibly reflects a modicum of successful paternalism among the largest manufacturers such as Milward and Bartleet, though it could also indicate that they saw less need to prosecute because of the size of their workforces.

Another means of exploring the divergent conceptions of authority and motives for prosecution is to examine the master and servant cases involving female workers in both agriculture and the needle trade. As we saw in chapter 2, the annual parliamentary statistics on criminal prosecutions for the mid-Victorian period show that the percentage of females prosecuted generally ranged between 5 and 10 percent of the total.[56] For the years under examination the percentage of women in all Redditch master and servant cases was close to 11 percent, and 10 percent for cases specifically involving the criminal prosecutions of workers by employers. There are thus relatively few cases by which to scrutinize the treatment of females by the bench, but these prosecutions tentatively suggest differences in the disposition of their cases by economic sector. Among those cases involving agriculture, half of the six prosecutions of female workers were successful, and all of the three females who prosecuted farmers for ill treatment were victorious. To be sure, in the latter cases physical abuse or insufficient board were clearly proved. However, in the few criminal prosecutions of female servants the magistrates showed a different disposition than they tended to exercise in the needle industry cases. In the prosecution of Mary Clarke by farmer Thomas Fortman, the chairman opened the proceedings by noting that Clarke has applied for a warrant against Fortman for violent language, which he did not grant, but observed "it still made it somewhat like a counter charge".[57] Fortman admitted to "cussing" at Clarke and that the two had discussed, but could not agree on, the partial payment of her wages to sever her contract. Moreover, Clarke does not seem to have contested that she overslept in the morning and failed to make breakfast for the laborers. The magistrates dismissed the case, and then suggested to Clarke that she could take out a summons against Fortman for wages due.

In the prosecution of Jane Ireland by Thomas Baker, a farmer from Beoley, the former explained that when she arrived at the house from Tewksbury she saw another servant and decided that she was unwanted and left. She also said that Mrs. Baker had told her that the other girl had been hired because she preferred to have girls that were not so far from their homes, and Ireland even claimed that an anonymous messenger had met her at the train station on her arrival, informed her that the Bakers had hired another girl, and offered her half a crown to leave. Despite Ireland admitting that Mrs. Baker had never actually dismissed her, and having no verification of her story concerning the messenger (which was labeled as hearsay), the court dismissed the case and stated to Ireland that "They were sorry she should have come so far on a fruitless errand."[58]

In contrast, of the eight cases of prosecutions in the needle trade all but one were settled in favor of the employers, and the exception affirms the dominant pattern. These prosecutions were often of adolescent girls, such as the case of Emma Braithwaithe discussed above, who were often employed as stampers and drillers. As with Braithwaite, less consideration was given to them for their age, gender, or the conditions under which they worked compared to their rural counterparts. In early 1872, for example, Ann Druett was summoned by needle stamper Charles Craddock for twice leaving work without providing a week's notice. The bench made it clear to Druett that she must observe the custom of the trade and could do so as soon as she returned to work. To insure this they ordered her to find a £5 surety and pay court costs of 12s. The prosecutor offered to front these costs and to work out their repayment with Druett who, making only 5–6s per week, probably had her employment with Craddock extended by several weeks to meet the expenses.[59]

A couple of months later the court dealt with the prosecution of needle driller Elizabeth Vincent, who was apprenticed to Richard Lewis. Lewis was deposed by the magistrates' clerk, produced the apprenticeship papers that showed that her term did not expire until the following year, and described how Vincent's father and stepmother frequently kept the girl from fulfilling her stated hours. The *Indicator* describes a raucous proceeding in which young Vincent was frequently speechless and in tears, while her father was bellicose and defiant, claiming that his daughter was underpaid, overworked, and that Lewis was frequently "tipsy" and no longer had a wife to supervise the girls as had been the case when Vincent was originally bound. None of this moved the court, which found his interjections intemperate, and repeatedly explained to the father that he could avail himself of the law if he wished to pursue his complaints, but that he did not control his daughter: "You cannot take your daughter away until next July twelvemonth; and, if you do not intend to ruin your daughter you will obey the law, else *she* will go to jail" (May 4, 1872). The father stormed out of the court, at which point the stepmother interceded adding her own complaints, but eventually agreed to an adjournment of the case to find sureties for the completion of the apprenticeship.[60]

The final example is the prosecution of Cara Ann Harrison, a needle stamper in the employ of John Emms. He charged the defendant with leaving work without notice and never returning. Her solicitor (from Bromsgrove) attempted to make a complicated argument that she was a casual worker supplied by her father who also worked at the shop, but the bench gave no credence to the argument. Nonetheless, they dismissed the case because Harrison was married, and did not have her husband's formal consent to the contract. In addressing Emms when rendering the decision a magistrate remarked, "*When you* employ married women in the future take care to make their husbands parties to the contract."[61] In this instance the employer's control was in general affirmed, but only superseded by the patriarchal control of the husband.

Finally, the court records and newspaper accounts suggest that, as we saw in Hull, some employers turned to the court to discipline adolescent males apprenticed by poor law unions. Almost all of the cases in the engineering and metal trades were brought by two employers, Affifi Lely, an engineer and machinist and foundry owner, and Edward Dobson Monks, a file manufacturer who had works in Birmingham and Sheffield as well. The majority of the latter's prosecutions involved apprentices. In 1867 and 1868 Monks prosecuted three apprentices, one on several occasions, all from the Huntington Poor Law Union (in Hereford, the county to the west), and noted that he had also applied to the (nearby) Bromsgrove Poor Law Union for apprentices as well.[62] Monks' treatment of these apprentices became a matter of public debate when a letter writer using the pseudonym "Humanity" accused him of lying to the magistrates concerning the number of times he had prosecuted two of them and demanding too much labor from the boys.[63] Two fishhook manufacturers at various points prosecuted parish apprentices from Bromsgrove for refusal to work.[64] There are several other cases of apprentice prosecutions, but it is not clear that they were indentured by parishes.

Commercial farmers and needle manufacturers faced similar issues of labor recruitment though quite different problems of labor discipline in production. Both relied on relatively local markets to satisfy their labor needs. In commercial agriculture this involved some continued reliance on traditional statute or annual hiring fairs for servants in husbandry, though there was an ongoing shift to more seasonal laborers. In the needle industry manufacturers hired locally out of necessity: their national trade dominance paradoxically left them dependent on a circumscribed district workforce. However, the use of labor was markedly divergent. Commercial farmers, while hiring servants for some expertise, for instance in the keeping of animals, needed flexibility in their labor to meet the changing daily and seasonal challenges of farm production. The rhythms of farm labor varied; though farms were of moderate size, servants could work out of sight of their employers, and farmers depended on their servants to exercise diligence and competence in these varied circumstances. The labor control regime was predicated in a waning rural hierarchy, in which the patriarchal control of the farmer was reflected in a larger rural order in which deference from servants in husbandry was expected. Fewer servants were indoor (housed with the farm family) and there was more circulation of labor between farms. The increasing outward proletarianization of servants in husbandry, coupled with growing social divisions between farmers and servants, put strains on the traditional patriarchal authority that was at the heart of the labor control regime. To shore up their authority a number farmers in this corner of Eastern Worcestershire turned to the courts.

Needle manufacturers organized production with a very refined division of labor, one in which the labor process had long been broken down into many discrete parts. This elaborate division depended on a mix of skilled and unskilled labor, and an accompanying gender and age stratification to fill the requisite positions. Each task in the production chain involved prodigious output, and many involved extended periods of continuous concentration and repetitive movements. Larger manufacturers organized this production chain within their factories, while smaller firms relied on some workshops for a particular step in the production process. In the former, supervision was conducted by factory managers, while in the latter the workshop owner (or an adult family member) exercised direct control. While the breakdown of the labor process was extensive, it was in many ways still a handicraft system of production and depended on formal subordination. There were some technological advances that boosted production at particular stages, but the pace of production and quality of output still most immediately relied on the industriousness of the workers.

It appears that larger manufacturers in the needle district tried to practice paternalistic despotism. Throughout the period, and indeed for most of the nineteenth century, the district experienced relatively little collective organization among needle workers, even skilled males, and manufacturers had overcome the few attempts at resisting the introduction of new machinery in the 1830s and 1840s with few protracted battles. This might well signal the relative success of these efforts among the kingpins of the trade, though the bases of this labor quiescence are not entirely clear. As was the case in the Potteries, Redditch manufacturers based their binding of labor through a contract of service in which they could claim customary rights and authority. With so much of the total capital in production sunk into labor, all manufacturers needed to insure the output of their workforces. The data suggest that medium and small producers required recourse to the courts to bolster their labor control regime.

Thus both commercial farmers and needle (and fishhook) manufacturers turned to the local bench. At the same time a number of factors conjoined to lead these groups along with growing merchant and professional classes to create an infrastructure of local governance to address new town and district needs. Both the local boards governing the town's and district's infrastructure and the court were composed of a commodious cross-class alliance, a political construction that represented the interests of these economic sectors. There was little political factionalization and substantial agreement concerning issues of governance. Magistrates were elite landholders and the largest needle manufacturers. Assisted by barristers, they "found" the law based in their own experiential knowledge as landowners and employers, which not surprisingly generally synchronized with the employers who brought prosecutions before the bench. As with the previous case studies, these magistrates insisted on their impartiality. They generally did not recuse themselves in cases concerning their own industries, and their interpretation of custom and service accorded closely with most employers. Yet their decisions do not seem to have publicly renounced by workers, as in Hanley. In "finding" the law the Redditch magistrates were at once preservationists and prescribers, exercising a hegemony possible in small-town justice. In this hybrid agricultural-manufacturing district—with a system of stratification based on a melding of traditional rural hierarchy and industrial class divisions—the legal system successfully integrated authority in the workplace and the community into a broader stable order.

The result was two divergent patterns in the rendering of master and servant decisions. In the prosecutions of agricultural laborers the magistrates arguably offered a venue to affirm farmers' beliefs in patriarchal control and deference that historians have noted were increasingly threadbare. The theater of these cases provided both the landed magistrates and farmers (and in a few cases servants as well) with the opportunity to recuperate, albeit temporarily, a conception of rural hierarchy and order that was neither particularly achievable nor tenable in quotidian realities of agriculture. For farmers, particularly by the early 1870s as they faced the restive mobilizations of agricultural unionism not far from their region, this had an immediate significance. For the landowners who were at greater remove from this upheaval, these cases nonetheless were an affirmation of their status and their claims to their positions in rural life and on the bench. The theater was not only utilitarian but also confirmed a stratified world that placed them in positions of authority in a "natural" order.[65]

Alternatively employers in the needle trades established a "custom" that placed a premium on labor extraction. With some of the processes of production still found in workshops as well as factory departments, and the stations in the factory not regimented by real subordination, they sought out the law as a means of enforcing productivity. Master and servant prosecutions were more a disciplinary tool. The wedding of trade custom and legality provided a hospitable means of affirming their authority to regularity of work, pace, and performance standards for all genders and ages. Turning to the courts, mostly medium and small manufacturers were able to enforce a workplace discipline that was not embedded in the labor process itself. Given that the preponderant proportion of capital invested in labor, manufacturers had to insure that they were receiving their optimal return from labor in a production process that was based on high volume and intense and continuous work. With the district's largest manufacturers often sitting in judgment, the court was a largely reliable institution to affirm their authority and the subordination of labor.

As with the prior two case studies we thus find labor control regimes at least partly embedded in local legal institutions. In this case the concept of embeddedness must be used with caution. The court, as we saw, was a recent creation, and it is not clear how frequently employers had recourse to the petty sessions prior to its establishment. Reports in the *Redditch Indicator* for the two years prior to advent of the Redditch court suggest that both farmers and needle manufacturers brought cases to the petty sessions in Alcester, although Redditch elites complained of this as a hardship. It is thus difficult to know whether prosecutions had long-standing as a "problem-solving regime." Moreover, we have less information on the history of labor control after the period, so it is more difficult to make a case for clear path dependence.

We can make a plausible albeit cautious argument that the labor control regime in needle manufacture dampened enthusiasm for technological and organizational innovation. In a study of its relative, the pin industry, H. I. Dutton and S. R. H. Jones (also a historian of the needle trade; 1983) argue that among the factors that slowed automation in the first half of the century were a pliant and inexpensive workforce and wariness of inventors' claims. They note that their US counterparts forged ahead where the English lagged. Similarly, we have seen that there was little innovation in the needle trade during these decades, and none past the mid-1840s. Though dependent on a localized labor supply, needle manufacturers were able to maintain relative passivity and high productivity while largely dictating piece rates. They did this in part through a gendered division of labor, but by the 1860s the use of master and servant law in their labor control regime surely played a part as well. Manufacturers seem to have remained wedded to their production process in succeeding decades. An economic history of the district indicates that the number of workers in the industry actually declined in the 1880s and then remained constant for two decades, while there was probably a modest expansion in production. Work was increasingly consolidated within factories in Redditch proper, though there is no indication of a substantial transformation of the labor process or the broader politics of production. A US consular report from the early part of the twentieth century reported that production involved the "necessary dexterity" of the workers and that inexperienced labor would be incapable of the tasks, suggesting no further significant degradation of labor or real subordination (Allen 1929, 257–58, 326–37, 359; US Department of Commerce 1908, 86–87). This long arc of stability speaks to a steady path taken.

There are a few distinguishing features of this case compared with those of Hanley and Hull. First, the local elite had only recently established their petty sessions, and had actively pursued the establishment of a local court because of their perceived need for a more available system of summary justice. Whether considerations regarding the efficient prosecution of master and servant cases were part of their concern is unknown, but given the rapid expansion of the needle industry and the erosion of the rural order underpinning commercial agriculture it might well have been one consideration.

Certainly the local court was rapidly incorporated into the problem-solving regimes of the district's two major economic sectors. Second, and following, the court's handling of both shows the flexibility with which legal institutions could respond to diverse issues of labor control. The Redditch local court crafted decisions that were responsive to both rural and industrial orders, suggesting how this institutional mechanism provided solutions for a wide array of labor control regimes. We will consider this topic further in the conclusion. Before doing so, however, we go from bottom-up analyses to top-down, and turn to a rereading of one of the most famous institutional narratives of England's economic development, Karl Polanyi's *The Great Transformation*.

PART III

CHAPTER SEVEN

Retelling *The Great Transformation*

In the previous three chapters we have taken a bottom-up look at how labor control regimes were partly organized and pursued through master and servant law and the local courts. Employers faced control issues both in local labor markets and the production process and workplace. Their industries were not at the technological apex of production, much of their resources were sunk in variable capital, and their capacity to insure productivity and thus profit depended on the authority that they could wield in the service relationship. Oriented by the proposition discussed in chapter 2 that the embeddedness of such regimes is rooted in local configurations of institutional power, we examined how in Hanley, Hull and Redditch employers found in the local court a reliable aid to exercise discipline over their workers both in the labor market and in the workplace. In each case we charted specific historical trajectories of how political and economic factors conjoined during this period (and in some instances prior to it) down a path in which the politics of production was embedded partly in this local legal institution. These are only three cases, but as we saw in chapter 2 master and servant and other law and the contract of service were foundation stones for labor control regimes and struggles in other industries and regions around England.

Given political and economic transformations that occurred in the 1860s and 1870s, these local contests roiled upwards, and they became generalized in working-class efforts to fundamentally change existing labor law. These efforts crystallized into a national contest, involving the nascent Trade Union Congress, national federations of employers, the major political parties, and parliamentary politics. In dialectic fashion, what had been generalized by the consolidation of master and servant law in the 1820s and high court decisions in the succeeding decades, and made concrete practice in specific locales, returned as a national conflict.

In this sense our final look at labor law and control involves a top-down analysis, examining the ways in which embeddedness at the national level became the stage for significant transformation. As noted in chapter 2 one of the signal works that raised the question of how economic activity is embedded in societal institutions and has been the touchstone of many subsequent debates is Karl Polanyi's *The Great Transformation: The Political and Economic Origins of Our Time* (hereafter *GT*). Social scientists of disparate intellectual persuasions credit *GT* and Polanyi's subsequent work with spurring the examination of the economy as an "instituted" process. Proffering a vision contrary to neoclassical economics, his corpus provides theoretical and methodological bases for analyzing capitalist development and its market economy contoured, channeled, and at times abetted by a broad range of social and political institutions.[1] As important, the elaborations and debates on Polanyi's work are matters of historical analysis and serve as a touchstone for understanding contemporary global capitalism and the social and political movements fomented in reaction against its expansive reach.[2] Our reconsideration of Polanyi's narrative in *GT* thus has both contemporary and historical import.[3]

The ambiguities in Polanyi's writings have spawned a series of debates over the intellectual lineage of his vision and its affinities with other macro perspectives on capitalist development, as well as over core concepts such as embeddedness.[4] My aim in this chapter is to engage these issues in so far as they facilitate a rethinking of the narrative of the English Industrial Revolution and its consequences depicted in *GT*. My hope is that this retelling of the story will reflect on and add to these dialogues.

Confronting the great depredations of economic collapse, the rise of fascist states, and the carnage of war, Polanyi sought to find the institutional roots of the capitalist system that had led to this wreckage. His starting point was in nineteenth-century England, and his account of these transformations hinges on what is now termed the "double movement," that is, the rapid ascendancy of a market society in the mid-1830s and the societal countermovement in response to protect itself from the damages of a market-driven social order. In this chapter I return to this part of the narrative to provide a revised account of role of class dynamics in the transformation of market, economy, and society. Where in the case studies I have attempted to demonstrate that historical materialism requires a fuller institutional analysis to explain labor control, in this chapter I argue that understanding the institutional dynamics of this great transformation requires class analysis.

Polanyi's intellectual heritage from its Viennese roots onward was rich and complex, and scholars point to the integument of arguments in his work that suggest an indebtedness to his encounters with Marxist theory and politics. Despite these filiations, it is clear that Polanyi consciously rejected what he saw as a reductionist determinism in historical materialism, and with it a class analysis.[5] My aim is to preserve Polanyi's cogent concern with the role of institutions in capitalist development, but to do so with renewed attention to the ways in which class dynamics were central to the construction of what he termed "market society." I offer a retelling of the great transformation that is in some respects the converse of Polanyi's narrative that involves revisiting the ground covered by Polanyi and charting territory he neglected. My focus reprises the theme of this book, that is, class power and legal institutions. In this partial alternative account of the great transformation I turn to how capitalists at the national level embedded the relations in and of production in particular legal institutions in the early part of the Industrial Revolution as a problem-solving regime for labor control, and defended this institutional arrangement against a working-class movement for freedom from these legal bindings. This working-class movement, led by trade unionists, was ultimately successful in surmounting these legal fetters through union organization and their increased political power due to the expansion of suffrage. Paradoxically to Polanyi's narrative it is this successful fight for "free labor" that births its full commodification. Labor's triumph is accomplished by what Polanyi would see as a disembedding from state authority.

THE GREAT TRANSFORMATION, THE RISE OF THE MARKET SOCIETY, AND THE "DOUBLE MOVEMENT"

The Great Transformation, of course, is not solely about the rise of market society, but a more sweeping account of what Polanyi takes to be a set of unprecedented institutional changes that restructured the international system. In his long epochal sweep not only the rise of self-regulating market (abetted by the liberal state), but also the balance-of-power system among states creating the relative absence of international conflict and the gold standard anchoring international banking were critical mechanisms that kept European market society afloat, until its monumental crisis in the 1930s. Here, however, we concentrate on the first part of his narrative, the unique historical creation of a market society in England, for it is this part of the story that speaks directly to the questions raised in this volume.

As Margaret Somers and others have emphasized, Polanyi saw a key underlying impetus for the rise of a modern market economy in England not in the rise of modern capitalism, as for Marx, but in industrialization itself (1990, 156). More specifically, his obliquely stated causal analysis does not start with institutions, but with the rise of the factory system and how new technologies of production impelled institutional change (1947, 96–97; 1957a, 74–75). As he states in *GT*, "On the eve of the greatest industrial revolution in history, no signs and portents were forthcoming. Capitalism arrived unannounced. No one had forecast the development of a machine industry; it came as a complete surprise" (1957a, 89).

Industrial production transformed the functioning of the economy, installing commerce as the servant of industry where the relationship historically had been the reverse. To meet the demands of this new master,

> The extension of the market mechanism to the elements of industry—land, labor, and money—was the inevitable consequence of the introduction of the factory system in a commercial society. The elements of industry had to be for sale.
>
> This was synonymous with the demand for a market system. . . . As the development of the factory system had been organized as part of a process of buying and selling, therefore land, labor and money had to be transformed into commodities, as actually they were not produced for sale on the market. (1957a, 75)

A key part of Polanyi's telling of this first part of the tale of the "double movement" was that land, labor, and money fundamentally could not be transformed into commodities since they were not products of human industry; rather they became, in his terms, "fictitious commodities" (1957a, 72; 1971b, 148).[6] Nonetheless, starting in the late eighteenth century efforts began to subsume all three into the market economy. This prolonged process was part of a greater transformation by which social relations themselves became embedded in the market system. Whereas in the past economic activity had been ordered to maintain social relations, society was for the first time in history the handmaiden in the service of the economy. In Polanyi's narrative the rise of political economy, particularly the dominance of its ideas as expressed through Malthus and Ricardo, played an essential role in these developments (1957a, 75, 122–27; 1971a, 65).[7]

By Polanyi's account the most difficult part of this transformation was the commodification of labor, a protracted and sometimes tempestuous process that put the state and political action at the center of the birthing of a "market society." Initially society reacted against the creation of a free labor market with the construction of a system of poor relief that became known as the Speenhamland system, run through the local governments or civil parishes. This followed traditional forms of parish relief under the poor laws that had been part of an institutionalized order for hundreds of years to insure subsistence for the many workers displaced, dispossessed, and unemployed. Parishes adopting the plan also subsidized the wages of (largely agricultural) workers, who were remunerated below a subsistence wage for their households. These wage subsidies spread to many counties throughout the country.

As Polanyi himself tersely notes, however, "In the long run the result was ghastly," only furthering pauperism (1957a, 80).[8] The state, accepting what political economists regarded as the brute facts of nature, instituted sweeping changes in the social welfare system with the New Poor Law in 1834, abolishing such subsidies, and imposing stringent and punitive standards for assistance in dreaded workhouses. With subsistence no longer guaranteed through parish relief, the New Poor Law gave workers the stark choice of workhouse or factory discipline. "It is no exaggeration to say," Polanyi observed, "that the social history of the nineteenth century was determined by the market system proper after it was released by the Poor Law Reform Act of 1834" (83). Critically, this involved the application of free market principles to labor with the state receding from the employment relationship. "To separate labor from other activities of life and to subject it to the laws of the market was to annihilate all organic forms of existence and to replace them by a different type of organization, an atomistic and individualistic one. . . . Such a scheme of destruction was best served by the application of the principle of *freedom of contract*" (emphasis added; 163).[9] Labor was now fully commodified with the first half of the "double movement."

Polanyi argues that the working class was not sufficiently organized to protect itself from the deleterious effects of the labor market until the maturation of unions beginning in the 1870s (1957a, 82, 166). However, what the state had taken away the state could return, and so began the societal reaction to the laissez-faire system in the second part of the "double movement." A full-fledged market society, a world run on the singular principle of laissez-faire economics, was a dystopian project that would have led to economic, social, and cultural devastation. Recognizing this possibility, a variety of collective interests—including leading politicians, members of the landed elite, working-class leaders, and public intellectuals—spontaneously forced state action to re-embed the market. Factory legislation, public health provisions, education reform, and a host of other enactments that brought the state back in were part of a great collectivist countermovement to protect society as a whole from the chaos and destruction of unrestrained market capitalism.

In Polanyi's story, class interests themselves were too narrow an impetus for the explanation of such long-term macrosocial changes. He wrote, "Class interests offer a limited explanation of long-run movements in society. The fate of classes is much more often determined by the needs of society than the fate of society is determined by the needs of classes" (1957a, 152). The class interests of both workers and landowners are part of Polanyi's story of change, but he conceptualized them largely as reflexive, nonideological, and pragmatic responses to the disruptions by the market system, and argued that by themselves they were insufficient to be primary explanatory factors of the countermovement. Moreover, such interests, in the end, were not so material as they were moral and cultural, and concerned with integrity and standing in society. As he summarized the rise of a "collectivist" reaction to laissez-faire liberalism,

> The countermove against economic liberalism and laissez-faire possessed all the unmistakable characteristics of a spontaneous reaction. At innumerable points it set in without any traceable links between the interests deeply affected or any ideological conformity between them. Even in the settlement of one and the same problem as in the case of workmen's compensation, solutions switched over from individualistic to "collectivistic," from liberal to anti-liberal, from "laissez-faire" to interventionist forms without any change in the economic interest the ideological influences or political forces in play, merely as a result of increasing realization of the nature of the problem in question. (1957a, 149)[10]

And in reviewing his thesis on the rise of antiliberal interventionism he contended: "Briefly, not single groups or classes were the source of the so-called collectivist movement, though the outcome was decisively influenced by the character of class interests involved. Ultimately, what made things happen were the interests of society as a whole, though their defense fell primarily to one section of the population in preference of another. It appears reasonable to group our account of the protective movement not around class interests but around the social substances imperiled by the market" (1957a, 162–63).

Thus a response required a societal rather than a sectional countermovement.[11] The market economy was re-embedded through successive state actions into societal structures, and antiliberal collectivism gained traction against the destructive tendencies of laissez-faire economics and the market society it had advocated. In the second half of the "double movement" English society, at the precipice, caught a glimpse of the free market abyss and built institutional walls to protect itself from the plunge.

PROBLEMS IN THE NARRATIVE

One of the difficulties in understanding Polanyi's narrative of this great transformation is that it precedes his explicit and elaborated theory of institutional embeddedness by over a decade (Dale 2010; Gemici 2008; Randles 2003). Regardless of whether Polanyi offered more than one conception of embeddedness, how infrequently the term appeared in *GT*, or if his theory of instituted economies changed over time, *GT*'s narrative motor animating the story of the rise and taming of market society relies on some version of these core ideas.[12] In *GT* these theoretical insights are largely woven into the tapestry of his expansive analytic narrative of the demise of mercantilism and the abrupt turn to laissez-faire.[13] Unraveling the threads of this complex weave provides not only a chance to revisit particular pieces of the story, but to think about how the cloth itself was fashioned. This is particularly the case in terms of the place of legal institutions and class power and conflict in the contrapuntal movements of embedding and disembedding. Retelling the story of the great transformation involves threading power into the narrative of institutional change and, as I will argue below, this at times leads us to reweave the design of the tapestry.

Problems of institutional change arise at both ends of the narrative of the double movement. Both critics and sympathizers alike have noted that the initial impetus for disembedding the economy is an ad hoc explanation partly leaning on technological determinism. For all his attention to the institutional organization of economy and society, Polanyi provided no explanation for why contemporary institutions failed to resolve the dilemmas created by the demands of an increasingly technologically complex industrialism.[14] Rather, the narrative ambiguously suggests an inevitability of this transformation and focuses on the failed resolution to the problems of commodifying labor with the Speenhamland system.

Relatedly, the centrality of a spontaneous "societal" reaction to the rise of the market economy frequently hypostatizes society and the state at the expense of concrete analyses of institutional conflict and change.[15] Polanyi's narrative of organic societal response, however, provided no specific accounts of why and how these reflexive reactions against the perils of market forces were channeled into coherent actions for institutional change, or how the countermovement resulted in particular constellations of embeddedness.[16] As Gareth Dale argues, it pivoted between a voluntarism in explaining the rise of market society and functionalism in charting the countermovement response, and in the end offers no unified causal analysis (2010, 79). *The Great Transformation* suffers from this and the other dilemmas we have reviewed because it lacks an underlying theory of power generally and an analysis of institutional power more particularly.[17] As a result Polanyi was unable to pursue how the contradictions, tensions, and power dynamics within these institutions shaped the course of the double movement Concurring with Chris Howell that all industrial relations institutions are "congealed form(s) of class power" I offer a partial retelling of the double movement that emphasizes the class struggles within these institutions and their result in a new institutional path for capital and labor (2005, 23).

CLASS STRUGGLE AND THE EMANCIPATION OF COLLECTIVE LAISSEZ-FAIRE: A RETELLING

My retelling of Polanyi's story remains predicated on his insights on the embeddedness of the economy. Indeed, in response to some of his sympathetic critics who, as I have noted, observe that Polanyi did not fully realize the promise of this stricture in *GT*, this narrative focuses squarely on the ways in which economic relations were defined and mediated by the legal system. In a reversal from Polanyi, however, I argue that it was not until the last quarter of the nineteenth century, well beyond the heyday of laissez-faire liberalism and well into his claimed societal reaction of the double movement, that labor becomes "commodified" in his own terms. Additionally, I assert that this inversion of Polanyi's narrative is critical in understanding not just the labor market, but also the institutional embeddedness of the social relations in production. Whereas Polanyi rejects a focus on the production process when he eschews Marxist theory, the full importance and impact of institutional embeddedness can only be appreciated by a focus on *both* exchange and production relations. Unionists fought not only for a transformation of the labor market, but also change in how the law governed power in the workplace.[18] Finally, while Polanyi's story of reaction centers on a spontaneous societal response in the double movement, my narrative more directly focuses on a class struggle that was critical in refashioning the legal institutions that defined the employment relationship. This is not to say that other classes or groups were inconsequential; labor had influential reformist allies and friends of convenience in its struggles. And certainly structures of gender and race were integral in the construction of this new capitalist order. However, the transformation of labor's legal status was (Anglo-Scot male) union inspired and largely led, and both capitalist federations and labor unions were explicit that they were the principal actors in this political conflict. Just as important, the response of male-controlled working-class organizations was to *distance* themselves as much as possible from the protective reaches of the state once they had established the minimum conditions for their legal integrity. Contrary to Polanyi's story of the double movement, unions largely sought refuge *from* rather than *in* state institutions, opting for what has become known as "collective laissez-faire." For working-class leaders there were quite sound experiential reasons for this path in addition to a lineage in radical political ideology that affirmed it.

A BRIEF RETURN TO PRELIMINARIES

In chapter 2 we examined key aspects of nineteenth-century English labor and legal history that are the foundations of this retelling. To briefly review, England's legal system was thickly planted with statute and common law that governed the employment relationship. Born of increasing frustrations by capitalists in particular trades, new statute law started to accumulate in the mid-eighteenth century and ultimately was consolidated under the Master and Servant Act of 1823. As we saw, using novel language that surpassed centuries' old law on employment, these master and servant acts gave employers new powers and created what the legal historian Robert Steinfeld has termed a relation of "coerced contractual employment." While Polanyi asserted that labor was becoming a "fictitious commodity" within a market society, master and servant law complicates his account. Workers were bound to their employers under a standing order for service. In effect the free will of liberalism and the hierarchy of patriarchy were wedded together: (adult male) workers were deemed to be free agents to choose employment, but in making this commitment they bound themselves to the will of their employer. The law cast most enduring or exclusive employment relations as one of a hierarchical status arrangement of continual service. The intersection of master and servant law and the New Poor Law confounds Polanyi's analysis of the disembedding of labor in a market society. For, as we noted in chapter 2, under the New Poor Law workers were no longer able to request relief from the parish in which they currently worked. With the abolition of this right of settlement by hiring, the New

Poor Law reinforced the legal duty of service to the employer. Rather than increasingly labor mobility in a free market, the New Poor Law had the effect among some groups of workers of binding them more firmly to their employers.

As the century progressed, capitalists in particular industries and regions, such as Hanley, Hull, and Redditch, increasingly relied on the law as a punitive tool to maintain control of the workplace and, at times, redefine workers' tasks in the production process. Over the same period local legal institutions developed that made recourse to the law easier and, given the class composition of many urban benches, a more reliable venue for employers constructing labor control regimes. By the late 1850s, when national data became available, the use of master and servant law was entrenched in a number of areas and industries. In some of those industries in which it was sparingly used, it nonetheless hung as a shadow over the workplace. Master and servant law was also effective in putting a rapid end to spontaneous labor stoppages and in making strikes themselves more difficult. Workers had recourse through civil action against capitalists for ill treatment and nonpayment of wages, but evidence suggests that in practice, as in the title of the act, masters came first.

On a collective level workers found themselves in a legal netherworld with regard to their capacity to organize. The repeal of the Combinations Acts at the end of the first quarter of the nineteenth century removed statutory barriers criminalizing association, but workers could still be prosecuted under common law for conspiracy. This, too, was a relatively recent construction, and much as master and servant law, criminal prosecutions for conspiracy against workers groups were products of the industrial revolution (Orth 1991, 38; Wright 1887, 43). Its common law basis was solidified by superior courts from the 1840s onward, and along with newly enacted legislation against interference with other workers, and the lack of a legal status for unions themselves, these laws insured that organized labor lacked unambiguous state sanctification.

Employers also increasingly used the non-labor-related law and the courts to change the contours of custom. As the nineteenth century advanced, a wide array of capitalists in both mining and fabrication industries used criminal prosecution for larceny to eviscerate customary rights claimed by workers to the gleaning of waste or the taking of a set amount of inferior product for household use (Philips 1977; Woods 1979). In some instances, as in the woolen industries of Yorkshire, manufacturers created private police forces to eradicate what they redefined as theft (Godfrey 1999a, 1999b). In this case the law was used to emphasize the cash nexus of the employment relationship and reinforce capitalist conceptions of property rights.

From the start of the industrial revolution onward the employment relationship was legally entangled in ways antithetical to Polanyi's narrative of the double movement. Master and servant law ensured that labor never became institutionally unmoored, and capitalists in a number of industries increasingly turned to it as a form of labor control during the decades that for Polanyi mark the rise of the market society. During the repeal contests of the early 1870s the attorney general himself, drawing on Henry Maine's famous dichotomy, noted, "The truth is our law regarded labor as a matter of status, not of contract, and regulated wages and employments" (Curthoys 2004, 196).[19] In this sense, even with the passage of the New Poor Law, labor never became the disembedded "fictitious commodity" so central to *GT*'s narrative. Instead, in a number of areas around the country, labor became more institutionally entwined as employers in these areas embedded their labor control regimes in the threat and practice of the law.

As noted in chapter 2, despite the passage of the Combination Acts which putatively legalized unions, they remained in a legal netherworld. The 1825 act had legalized collective organization concerning wages and hours, but no other issues, and while collective agreements were no longer illegal, they had no binding standing in law. Workers had pressed for repeal of the old Combination Laws so they could be free from prosecution for common law criminal conspiracy, but the new act limited this exemption to these two issues. The law contained vague language concerning "molesting or . . . obstructing" and "threats and intimidation" that left strike activity at risk to legal sanctions, especially when workers engaged in picketing. And language concerning "endeavouring to force or prevent" made approaching and attempting to persuade fellow workers about a union position during a contract of service a possible criminal offense. More generally, while the 1825 act permitted union activity concerning wages and hours, it did not legally recognize unions themselves. This statutory law remained essentially in place for the next half century (Orth 1991, 86–92). Employers generally preferred the easier master and servant law as a means of labor control and as a means to combat strikes. However, by the 1860s unions were very aware that their efforts to exert collective control over the labor process and the workplace had no legitimation in law and were open to criminal prosecution.[20]

The 1825 act did not negate problems posed by the common law of conspiracy as unionists had hoped, and its ambiguous language invited court activism in similar ways as had the definition of service reviewed in chapter 2. During the course of the nineteenth century many superior court judges issued rulings based in a "dogmatic individualism" in exercising a "*quasi*-legislative role" (Curthoys 2004, 7). These rulings bolstered the application of conspiracy doctrine to strikes, since in a number of cases they found that attempts to dissuade workers to enter a struck workplace interfered with their right to make their own bargains and obstructed the employer's capacity to use his capital as he pleased.[21] Indictments for conspiracy were infrequent, but when they occurred in the 1850s and 1860s unions realized acutely that struggle against employers remained on legally tenuous grounds.[22] The implications for unions were foreboding.

From Polanyi's perspective it is reasonable to argue that the superior court rulings on strikes were part of the disembedding of economy from society in the first half of the double movement: superior courts sought to impose a strict laissez-faire doctrine on the employment relationship. Yet during the same period these courts also reinforced the subservience of labor under contracts of service. Moreover, master and servant law was consolidated during the rise of market society, and its use by capitalists in many industries to subordinate labor intensified during the period of the societal countermovement. Throughout these decades employment was legally embedded, but it was institutionally anchored by neither a state-imposed free contractual market relationship nor a societally imposed protective order. This is a part of a story of great institutional transformation, but it is one that belies the contrapuntal rhythms of *GT*'s double movement. The course of labor law confounds Polanyi's underlying its logic of embeddedness. It is a story of class struggle within institutions, one that takes a turn toward a new order of collective laissez-faire, driven by a working-class effort toward freedom from the status of servitude, in its own protective efforts to gain security within a market society.

While Polanyi's narrative of the countermovement emphasized increased state intervention and a societal reaction against the market liberalism, the struggle over labor laws offers an inverse picture. The efforts to change labor's legal status were dominated by trade unionists, though they had important assistance from Positivist intellectuals, several radical lawyers, and a few parliamentary allies. Their victory was achieved to a large degree because of increased working-class political power with the Second Reform Act of 1867, which significantly expanded the number of adult male workers on the voting rolls. Finally, while these reformers turned to the state for relief, their object was largely to secure legislation that would *insulate* them from oversight from the central government and the courts. What unions most desired, and what they partially achieved, was to be legitimated and then left alone to their own devices, what Kahn-Freund termed "collective laissez-faire."[23]

In the spring and summer of 1863 the Council of the United Trades of Glasgow met to discuss their grievances with master and servant and law. In an ensuing communication to other councils to take action for reform they asserted, "Here then, we have a law made by employers, made for employers, and by employers administered. Was ever anything so grossly unfair?"[24] The Glasgow meeting led to a call to action and a numerously attended conference the following spring in London, the first salvo in a twelve-year campaign that culminated in the reform of these laws and the passage of legislation securing the legal status of unions (Howell 1905, 1:151).

Most contemporaries and historians characterize these decades as ones of growing conciliation and reformism in which working-class and union leaders put behind the radicalism of Chartism to achieve gains within the existing system.[25] Nonetheless, both capital and labor explicitly recognized the struggle over labor law as one of class conflict, and their solutions were irreparably divergent. The substantive goal of the unions was for their legal security and the decriminalization of their relations with capital. "We ask for no privileges—no exemptions," argued labor leader George Howell. "Give us the protection of law, and make us amenable to law, as citizens of a free State; we ask for nothing more, and shall be content with nothing less" (*Bee-Hive*, Feb. 25, 1871). In a sense labor argued for negative liberty rather than positive state intervention, and this was predicated in a three-pronged rationale.

First, as a practical matter, the experience of the past half century had led working people to distrust the courts at all levels.[26] To the unions, "Involvement with the law meant, for them, as for the individual worker, exposure to a hostile environment, where the stakes were very high and where the dice were loaded."[27] Making employment a purely civil and private matter and insuring the legality of unions and their actions left workers free to confront employers on their own terms. This was a turn to liberalism, but for unions it represented a rebalancing of the employment relationship for collective or individual bargaining.

Second, as E. P. Thompson detailed decades ago in *The Making of the English Working Class*, working-class radical politics was based in a deep-seated suspicion of the state. From the planting of the roots of the Liberty Tree with Paineite politics in the 1780s onward through the Chartist movement that preceded the period of this study, many working-class radicals had advocated for a minimalist state. Within this radical tradition the state represented elite corruption and an impediment to freedom, and these ideas still held significant currency in contemporary working-class popular politics.[28] For union activists struggling to secure their collective freedoms this was a comfortable and cogent politics based also on decades of experience, and they likewise adopted a parallel posture of insuring against state intrusiveness.

Third, and relatedly, the campaign for universal male household suffrage leading to the extension of male suffrage in the Second Reform Act of 1867 reaffirmed an older artisanal theme of popular politics that focused on the property of labor as the basis of adult male freedom and citizenship.

> Counterpoised to slavery was freedom to sell his labour power in conditions of equity and justice: that a man should be able to maintain himself without recourse to charity or the state Poor Law; that he would have a degree of freedom in the regulation of his trade or job; and that collective organisation of the trade, informal unions or otherwise, was desirable, if not always possible. . . . The basis of a popular claim for universal manhood suffrage became the notion that the property which working men possessed was the property in their labour. . . . To be in possession of this property was to be free, to have possession of one's self and to have the potential to shape and dispose of one's labour and person. (McClelland 2000, 99, 101)

This conception of freedom was no simple valorization of individualism, since understandings of reciprocity and collective ownership of a trade were deeply embedded within this tradition. Nonetheless, for "working men" of the British "nation," state intervention was tainted with the mark of dependency.

Finally, working-class leaders and sympathizers frequently drew on popular political economy to construct their case for their class interests. In *GT*'s political economy, championed by Ricardo and Malthus, is an ideological juggernaut that displaced all competing ideas of economy and society in its wake. Polanyi recognizes the work of Robert Owen as providing an alternative to this ascendant discourse in the nineteenth century, but the rise of an oppositional discourse was more complex. From the early decades of the century working-class leaders and organic intellectuals had been appropriating facets of classical economics to create a popular political economy.[29] This discourse was used as a foil against the hegemonic claims of laissez-faire economists and politicians in a variety of economic and political struggles. Exemplary of such moves were the claims for working peoples' control over their own "property" their labor, and unionists frequently had recourse to this argument in their campaign of the 1860s and 1870s. In advocating for the legal freedom of trade unions, the secretary of the Amalgamated Society of Engineers, William Allan, responded to a series of questions before the Royal Commission on trade unions with precisely such an argument:

> [1774] What do you mean by "protection of trade"?—The protection of trade I can only understand as being similar to protecting my property, that is to say, to make the best of it I can by using all legal means. . . .
>
> [1778] I object to the illustration; I want to know the fact; what do you mean by "encroachments on the trade"? Do not give me any illustration, but tell me the fact?—I will explain it this way; I learned a trade, I served my time to a trade, that trade is my capital, and I consider that I have a right to protect it. . . .
>
> [1783] But there is no capital in labour?—Is not there? It is my capital.[30]

Popular political economy proved effective in legitimating working-class positions and refuting laissez-faire hardliners in advancing an alternative understanding of liberal freedom. However, it did so by conceding the centrality of markets in organizing the economy, and to this extent recognizing labor as a commodity.[31] Contrary to Polanyi's narrative, many union activists accepted the market principle, and they did so because in part because through their popular political economy that could make claims for institutional freedom for the control of their labor.

The push for transformation of labor law was spearheaded by a relatively small group of activists. From the inception of the Conference of Amalgamated Trades from 1867–71 and the Trades Union Congress (TUC) from 1868 (and more particularly its Parliamentary Committee established a bit later), much of the lobbying for reform centered around these organizations. Other craft and trade unions, local trades associations (such as the London Trades Council and the Sheffield Association of Organized Trades), and short-lived confederations also advocated for change throughout the period. Union activists obtained critical support from a small circle of sympathetic MPs and civil servants in the Home Office, and coteries of Christian Socialists and Positivists who, as public intellectuals, expended considerable energy championing the reform cause.[32] This was not a spontaneous societal reaction against market society.

A Royal Commission on trades unions in 1867–69 and a Royal Commission on labor laws in 1874 were partly the result of the concerted politicking of the unions and their associates, and the unions secured important allied support in the first commission through which their quest for reform was articulated in a minority report.[33] However resolution of their concerns over master and servant and conspiracy law remained slow. The former was partially reformed with an act in 1867 that mandated imprisonment only for "aggravated offences." These were not defined, though, leaving the issue in the hands of distrusted magistrates, and the offense itself remained criminal. One commentator in the workers' *Bee-Hive* noted in the renewed campaign for repeal that the law remained one of the "disgraceful relics of industrial barbarism" and flatly stated that "whilst such a state of the law exists, working men cannot fairly regard themselves otherwise than as a degraded class" (June 27, 1874). The legal integrity of trade unions was finally established with the Trade Union Act of 1871, but unions were sorely disappointed when the Liberal government also shepherded to passage the Criminal Law Amendment Act at the same time. The CLAA was the Liberal's simultaneous attempt to clear unions of restraint of trade charges and address the fears of capital, and it contained revised language on "threats" and "molestation" that left the door open for further prosecution of peaceful picketers (Curthoys 2004, 153–65). As one union tract declared with contempt, "If making the working-classes the victims of special criminal legislation, intended to hamper them in their efforts to improve their condition, is not class legislation, and with a vengeance, let the representatives in Parliament answer!" (Hunter 1873, 4).

With two high-profile cases in 1872 and 1873 that, from the unionists' perspective, saw strikers imprisoned with impunity, the campaign intensified and received more favorable press.[34] Moreover, as Curthoys notes, "During the early 1870s, when unionists believed that iniquitous laws were being perpetuated by the political influence of capital, their language assumed a very markedly "class" tone, and was viewed by some politicians with especial alarm" (2004, 4). Equally alarmed, if not more so, were employers who had been far more sluggish in organizing for their interests.

Employers' federations had an uneven history for several reasons, not the least of which was the pressure of competition. In part, some larger capitalists also saw accommodation to union organization as a way of insuring stability and eliminating smaller competitors. Throughout the mid-Victorian period local employers federations constructed for purposes of arbitration or conciliation boards had uneven and often inauspicious histories (Allen 1964; Fraser 1974, 106–17). The activism of trade unions for legal reform served as a more potent impetus for capitalist organization.

Several employers groups both regionally and nationally, were already active and vociferously anti-union by the early 1870s. As Arthur McIvor notes, "Frequently, employers formed and joined organisations when they perceived their ability to dominate the labour contract being undermined by the introduction of trade unionism in their workplace, or, alternatively, where the labour contract was deemed to require negotiation. . . . Through organisation, individual employers gained access to associations' sophisticated strikebreaking and victimisation machinery that could be exploited to undermine militancy during tight labour markets, restrict labour mobility and keep activists from the shop floor" (1998, 16–17). From the mid-1860s through the early 1870s a robust economy provided many such challenges. The industries involved included some of the largest and most heavily capitalized, including shipbuilding, engineering, coal mining, earthenware, and the iron trades.[35] In 1873, after several years of watching first the CAT and then the TUC Parliamentary Committee make headway in their public campaign to repeal laws, major associations of employers came together to found the National Federation of Associated Employers of Labour (NFAEL). Their purpose was "fundamentally an ideological attack on the TUC's programme" (Curthoys 2004, 186). They soon established their own periodical, *Capital and Labour*, whose masthead motto declared their agenda: "The Freedom of Labour—The Sanctity of Contract and of Law," and in its introduction stated that "Capital and Labour asks for nothing but justice, and desires to set labour wholly free" (Feb. 25, 1874, 1).

From 1867 with the first parliamentary committee, through the final transformation of the law in 1875, most employers' association representatives and the NFAEL maintained several fundamental principles. First, they insisted that a summary process and criminal penalties for violation of contract must be maintained in order that employers could maintain authority in the workplace: "It is only by a summary process and severe penalties that any real protection can be given to employers against the caprice or willfulness of workmen. . . . It furnishes to employers the only security for the due performance of work contracted to be done. If it were repealed, they would be absolutely at the mercy of the workmen."[36] Many employers and associations were convinced that without coercive power workers would simply walk away from fines, "the more irresponsible class of servants or workmen, and particularly workmen who have a Union at their back encouraging breaches of contract, not only in single file but en masse, will snap their fingers at decrees of damage, and carefully avoid all suretyship for performance" (*Capital and Labour*, July 21, 1875, 380). They argued that employers were dependable targets of civil suits and judgments because they had sunk capital in and responsibilities to their businesses.

Workers, however, were often footloose and did not have to be so responsible. Employers emphasized that the absence of a few workers could stop an entire production facility and perhaps even be the cause of substantial damage to equipment while putting many others out of work. Therefore the penalties that they sought to have maintained readily fit such "crimes," and their damage was an offense against the larger community.[37]

Second, in the battle over the CLAA, most employers' associations involved in the campaign fought stalwartly to retain some legal curbs on picketing. As a cotton manufacturer who was part of a NFAEL delegation to lobby the Home Secretary fretted, "I cannot see why they [the unions] want to get rid of this Act, unless they desire to be perfectly free to carry out their own avowed design of establishing an imperial government for the *working man*, which shall have the control of capital and labour" (NFAEL 1874, 22).[38] The Liverpool Master Builders' Association argued for a complete ban on picketing and proclaimed that "the liberty of all classes engaged in trade would be absolutely sacrificed to the intolerable tyranny of the trades unions" if any legislation short of this was passed.[39] Throughout this political struggle these capitalists and their sympathizers in Parliament and the press proffered a vision of the labor contract based on a strict laissez-faire individualism.

Not all employers and association representatives who participated in the debates were so openly hostile to either the unions or changes in the law. Some, following the lead of the parliamentarian A. J. Mundella and Rupert Kettle, a county judge, sought accommodation through formal boards of arbitration or conciliation, and several important union leaders concurred with the idea. Such boards had checkered records of both endurance and success, which varied greatly by region and industry. Two acts championed by sympathetic MPs and in consultation with several union leaders were passed during this period to facilitate such boards, but they were not used significantly.[40]

Ultimately a conjuncture of circumstances helped shift the tide in favor of the unions. A turning point in the push for reform came with the passage of the Second Reform Bill in 1867 that enfranchised well over 1,000,000 urban male householders and thus many workingmen. While the large majority of working-class males remained disenfranchised, this bolstering of numbers and the addition of urban seats through the reform made the skilled male worker, one who was more likely to be in an organized trade, a recognizable force. Second, government leaders, members of both parties and civil servants recognized by the 1870s that organized labor was an irremovable fixture of the British economy. Abstract principles gave way to concrete pragmatism, leading to a legal solution finally pursued by a Conservative government in 1875.[41] In these battles the unions proved to be the more organized and effective lobbyists than their capitalist counterparts.[42] Third, doctrinal nostrums of freedom advocated in laissez-faire economics, read partly through popular political economy and reformist liberalism, proved compatible with labor and union law reform. In the end, a majority in Parliament came to see that "the role of the legislature was to secure equal treatment under the law; but ultimately: 'the solution to these problems could be found only in absolute freedom . . . freedom between master and men'" (Spain 1991, 120).

The Employers and Workmen Act and the Conspiracy and Protection of Property Acts achieved many of the hard-fought goals of labor leaders and their allies. The former abolished all penal provisions in the old master and servant acts. Breaches of contract were treated as purely civil matters among equals and the law set out a series of damage penalties for infractions. With the latter Parliament sought to finally banish the issue of conspiracy from union collective action. Language regarding "molestation and destruction" disappeared and collective actions could only be construed as conspiracies when the action would be indictable as a crime if committed by a single person (Curthoys 2004, 224–33). The victors and even most disgruntled employers saw this as marking a new and final equilibrium in employment relations in which collective laissez-faire would become dominant. The state distanced itself from industrial relations as it discarded a system of law that had governed it for the better part of a century. Most all of the participants in this protracted struggle assumed that a mature market in labor was finally at hand.

Superior court judges, however, were not part of this settlement, and their insularity from other political institutions allowed them to continue to call into question the legality of unions. "The judges sought to curb union power either out of a conscious design to protect the existing economic and political order, which unions were perceived to threaten, or owing to a more subtle class bias that rendered judges simply incapable of impartially adjudicating trade union matters" (Klarman 1989, 1559). From the last part of the nineteenth century into the first decades of the twentieth century, judges remained committed to a strict theory of individual contracts of employment and they also exposed the unions again to conspiracy charges through tort law. A series of rulings, capped by the now-famous Taff Vale decision of 1906, forced Parliament to return to what they had assumed was settled law, to pass further legislation fully protecting unions from such continued judicial jeopardy, finally institutionalizing the system that became known as collective laissez-faire.

In the mid-1860s a small group of local union leaders shifted their horizons and began to question the fundamental inequity of the law in a more coordinated fashion. They realized that a top-down solution was necessary to redress their grievances. Joining forces with the nascent TUC and its Parliamentary Committee, which turned its sights to breaking the legal manacles on the labor movement, these working-class leaders forged a successive series of direct challenges to the legal status quo. Though crucially aided at key points by sympathetic intellectuals and select MPs, the campaign to repeal master and servant law and other legislation was nonetheless decidedly a working-class agitation. Employers had no illusions otherwise, and they rallied through several organizations in the latter part of the decade to stymie labor's efforts.

This transformation reprises our discussion of the role that critical junctures play according to historical institutionalists in chapter 2. The rise of the TUC, coupled with the passage of the Second Reform Bill in 1867, shifted the balance of class relations on the national political landscape in a relatively brief time frame. Liberals and Conservatives faced a new electoral landscape, and in the pull and tug of the early 1870s in which great champions of their parties—Gladstone and Disraeli—vied for power, it was the latter who ultimately delivered reform in 1875. On the surface this appears paradoxical: in this moment of opportunity in national political space, unions chose not increased national state intervention on their behalf, but the modified market solution of collective laissez-faire. Yet from the unions' perspective this made strategic sense. To achieve collective power over their labor required that they sever themselves from laws that had been used to enforce their subordination and advantage capitalists.

The result, though tenuous, was a new institutional path sought by trade union leaders, which insulated labor relations and, more particularly, the labor contract from capitalist power wielded through the law. Given the independence of judges in the high court system, and their overall enmity to collective action on the part of workers, it would take another thirty years to completely solidify this victory. Yet the victory of 1875 established a new course of labor relations in England that was to endure for many decades.[43] Important for my argument, and paradoxical to Polanyi's thesis, this new path established labor more completely as a commodity in the market.

In many respects the story above is a mirror image of the one told by Polanyi. In *GT* he argues that the English state disengaged from labor relations in the mid-1830s, whereas I focus on the growing legal infrastructure of the local state over the same period that could be used for such purposes. Polanyi's concept of a double movement is predicated on a "spontaneous" reaction to the process of fictitious commodification by diverse groups and forces. Alternatively, I emphasize a concerted and strategic class struggle as the dynamo of change. And while Polanyi characterizes the resolution of the double movement as a process of re-embedding, I argue that unions acted to buffer themselves from state power and sought haven in their preferred version of market relations. In the terms of *GT*, this was a relative disembedding.

This alternative narrative shares aspects of emplotment with stories told by a number of other social scientists and historians of nineteenth-century British and American labor. Though the specifics of their stories diverge significantly at points (both from my own account and one another's), a number of historians and social scientists make claims that American labor unions' continuing battles with and defeats by the courts and inability to insure gains through representative institutions led to the development of "business unionism."[44] Other analysts argue such strategies in the face of juridical obstruction are characteristic of Anglo-American union struggles as opposed to Continental labor histories (Steinmetz 2000a).

Yet while these analyses are in some respects inversions of Polanyi's, all nonetheless affirm the most fundamental claim of *GT* and Polanyi's larger corpus, that is, capitalist labor relations are necessarily institutionally embedded. The revised narrative offered above describes how capitalists in a number of important sectors of British industry relied on legal institutions to subordinate labor, enforce discipline in the workplace, and constrain labor markets, particularly during the rise of "market society." Ultimately unionists forced a transformation of these institutions in a pragmatic response to a structurally constrained field of action. This analysis confirms what Polanyi's sympathetic critics argue: that we need to attend to the political struggles that fashion these institutions and analyze how legal processes fashioned in these struggles are endogenous to capitalist organization of labor. Such struggles were (and are) never determined by market forces: the subjugation and commodification of labor are always dependent on complex processes of embeddedness. To fully understand these processes, however, requires us to navigate into the interior of institutional power, to understand the structural cleavages that animate it, and to see both recursive processes that reproduce it and contradictions that create the ruptures for change. In so doing we reveal the structured institutional matrices through which people acted and power worked.

CHAPTER EIGHT

Conclusion

We have pursued a detailed series of investigations of law, labor, and England's great transformation from both top-down and bottom-up perspectives. Most broadly, these analyses are motivated by the big question posed by Tilly on how we can increase our understanding of how large-scale structures and processes transformed both nineteenth-century societies and those of our own times. In *Durable Inequality* Tilly (1998) noted that one of the fundamental mechanisms through which such transformations occur is exploitation. In *The Remaking of the British Working Class 1840–1940* Savage and Miles argue that "for purposes of class analysis, focus should be directed to those exploitative social structures which define the antagonistic relations lying at the heart of the conflict" (1994, 18). True enough, but that small phrase "exploitative social structures" is heavy gravity produced by a complex of forces.

Through the studies in previous chapters I have made an argument for combining historical materialism and historical institutionalism to work through the many lattices of these durable exploitative social structures. In the three case studies we saw how an institutional analysis of these structures illuminated conjunctures of the labor market, the labor process, local politics and law, and the national statutory and common law combining into durable paths for exploitation. In the last chapter we also investigated how working-class mobilization against these institutions transformed some of the legal bindings of exploitation. My purpose in all of the analyses has been to consider how interweaving these perspectives provides us with new understandings of exploitation in the local mid-Victorian world of work and legal order. Let's not create another too-much-thumbed manual, but a study that offers some revised ways of thinking about large-scale structures and processes, and more particularly mechanisms of exploitation. I hope that none of my suggestions will be taken as formulaic. What I have intended to offer is *not* a scheme in which the social relations in and of production + legal institutions + gender structures + class politics = durable structures of exploitation. My purpose has been much more modest and limited.

To conclude this extended analysis I return first to the specific questions that motivated this study. Then I briefly address the question of class formation that was not the object of this work. Finally, I turn to some of larger theoretical issues that we have addressed on law, class and institutional analysis.

In what ways did the specifics of the production processes in their industries set the conditions by which the law became a strategy of choice? In each of the industries we have examined, the social relations in and of production posed both challenges and limitations for workplace organization and control. Both pottery and needle manufacturing had been organized through very refined divisions of labor, which in many respects gave the manufacturer greater control over the production process as a whole. Yet this division of labor, as Marx argued, did not readily lead to specific dominion in the workplace. Manufacturers lacked the capacity to inject further discipline into the labor process. The spatial organization of production (even within the factory), the accretion of labor processes into which production had been divided, the retention of what in shorthand terms was claimed as skill (by adult male workers), and the technical limitations of tethering production to powered task masters were all impediments to exerting more control. Pottery throwers and needle pointers maintained some leverage at the frontiers of control. Moreover, to the extent that adult male workers required subordinates to assist them, these manufacturers ceded their patriarchal authority in the workplace as a price of production.

The small producers in farming and fish trawling faced a different set of challenges. Their control was more immediate and personal, but they needed to exert it over labor that was not so neatly parsed. They required farm servants to drive animal teams and mend hedge rows, fourth and fifth hands to do varied tasks on deck. Both lacked the capacity to divide the production process beyond rudimentary lines. Farmers and fishing trawlers needed a means of both directing labor to specific tasks and insuring their effective completion. In Marx's terms all of the employers we have studied faced problems of formal subordination. However, this categorization is an incomplete explanation for why all turned to the law because, as we noted, capitalists responded to these concerns through an array of strategies in labor control regimes. Pursuing this question requires that we go beyond the labor process and even beyond the politics of production as addressed by Burawoy.

Going beyond means in part adding location. Space and place contoured the labor control regimes we have analyzed. Region mattered for the industries we have examined in a few respects. Skill and knowledge requirements tied pottery and needle manufacturers to local labor markets, and labor recruitment and reproduction through patriarchal household and kin networks fortified this dependence. Redditch-area farmers also drew from a circumscribed market, hiring from what may well have been a shrinking regional labor pool. Hull trawler owners increasingly confronted an inverse dilemma. Because local labor markets proved inadequate they became more reliant on poor law union apprentices from more distant places. In all cases the geography of the labor supply imposed constraints on employers both in terms of hiring and workplace control.

Place mattered as well in terms of political and legal power. For the sphere of production and the lives of working people state power resided most directly in the institutions of local governance. In the towns we have studied, blocs of capitalists, merchants, and professionals (and, in the case of Redditch, landowners as well) controlled borough politics and through it the inferior courts. Borough and/or stipendiary magistrates provided both large and small employers with a ready and dependable institution to exert and affirm workplace authority. Solidification and expansion of the administrative capacities and authority of the "police courts" over successive decades added surety and ease to prosecution. Workers still found a measure of justice in their civil claims, but the balance of court actions tipped decidedly toward their criminal prosecution. Local courts were a redoubtable presence for working people, whether they were of long standing as in Hanley and Hull, or recent creation as in Redditch.

The dilemmas of the production process mattered, and place too, but of course these factors were tied to one another through the law. By the mid-Victorian era the accumulation of statutory and case law on master and servant clearly defined a hierarchical relation of continual service. The labor contract connected the labor market and the workplace and tied worker to employer in a number of asymmetric relations. The contract of exclusive service in each of our cases was realized through specific control strategies. Most fundamentally the law expected practices of obligation, and defined potential penal consequences for their transgression. At times obligation was impressed, as Price contends, by controlling custom. In quite different ways pottery manufacturers and farmers metered the intensity and variability of work through their claims of long-standing expectations. Trawler owners defined what was expected of "good lads" in their service. Hull magistrates sometimes reproached them for the severity by which they imposed these standards, and occasionally fined them for their brutal discipline. But as hundreds of apprentices learned, employers' expectations of obligations were generally currency in court.

For a number of workers in these industries workplace resistance was often played out in the shadow of the law. On the individual level, disputes over responsibilities, productivity, pay, and other issues could turn into criminal disobedience. On the collective level, work stoppages and strikes could be pursued without the potential for prosecution only in narrow legal corridors given obligations defined in a contract of service. Employers in all of these industries found in longer-term (often yearly) agreements of exclusive service the opportunity to exercise authority in the workplace when their options were otherwise limited. Forms of annual bonding, for example, in pottery and farming advantaged employers not only in the labor market but also the workplace. Apprenticeships allowed trawler owners to dominate fisherlads. In each case the bundle of practices locally institutionalized as master and servant law significantly shaped the labor process and the politics of production.

Why did pottery manufacturers, fishing trawler owners and other employers discussed adopt strategies of labor control that significantly depended on the law? We already have stated some answers above, but another piece of the explanation concerns timing: why depended partially on when. In each of our cases employers faced problems of labor control and the confluence of circumstances led to a legal turn. In Hanley in the later 1830s pottery manufacturers sought a way of securing their victory over defeated unionists, and found a beneficial course in the appointment of the stipendiary magistrate. Redditch-area needle manufacturers during a period of significant expansion and landowners facing tighter labor markets likewise pressed for and then drew on the local bench in the early 1860s. During a robust expansion of their trade Hull trawler owners solved a chronic labor shortage with cheap and available apprentice labor and a sympathetic magistracy to discipline it. The legal turn in all of these cases was a pragmatic response, an exercise in Haydu's terms of creating problem-solving regimes. When employers confronted their problems, the path to a solution through the law was more apparent and possible than alternatives. Our answer relies on a soft version of path dependency. We cannot show specific critical event conjunctures in a delimited causal ordering. But in each case we demonstrated how a confluence of circumstances led employers to incorporate master and servant prosecutions into their labor control regimes.

How did recourse to the law for workplace control become embedded in the routine governance and organization of the production process?

Here our answer involves following the paths, some of which were admittedly longer and more amply documented than others. What we can say is that in all cases employers found responsive local legal institutions (in two cases partly of their own creation). Rates of successful prosecution were high, and expense (in terms of both time and money) modest. But the legal turn involved more than calculations of assured economic return: it also reinforced class orders in the politics of production and beyond. Successful prosecutions affirmed employers' standing as *masters* in larger systems of patriarchal or paternalistic despotism. Many fine legal strokes confirming authority and hierarchy combined over time into a composition reproducing class relations.

To what extent did these capitalists' reliance on the law affect the ways in which they considered alternatives to the organization of the production and ultimately changes in the law itself? And to what degree and in what ways did these legal strategies of labor control affect the trajectory of these enterprises within their industries? Our answers to these questions are necessarily more cautious and circumscribed, since responding to them edges us into the territory of counterfactuals. As we noted at the outset, social scientists and historians maintain that the course of technological innovation in a number of industries was shaped (and compared to other countries dampened) by the labor supply, systems of craft control, patriarchal subcontracting, and gendered divisions of labor. We can make plausible arguments that in several of these industries the legal turn was part of a buffer to technological and organizational innovation. The case is firmest for the pottery industry, which was ensconced in a labor control regime involving master and servant law from at least the later 1830s. Four and five decades on, Potteries district manufacturers were adding steam-powered machinery that had been introduced early in other smaller areas of production in England and in Scotland. They slowly adapted the production process within the well-worn path of their labor control regime as their once-vaunted supremacy in Britain and Europe waned. We can make a similar though less confident case for the Redditch needle industry in comparison to its US counterpart. In the trawling industry we witnessed a different course, one in which a well-trodden path between the ship and the bench was abandoned. With the rewriting of master and servant and merchant shipping laws Hull trawler owners relinquished their reliance on apprentice labor, no longer having the capacity to coerce fisherlads to remain in their service or set out to sea.

In answering the above questions through the case studies we highlighted the importance of the labor contract in labor control regimes. From the bottom up we examined how these contracts bridged labor markets and workplaces. Through them capitalists combined and institutionalized asymmetries of power that gave them leverage over their labor forces. The law became part of a bundle of established practices in the routine class and gender micropolitics of production. It also was often salient in waging of contests of subjugation and autonomy at what Price terms the "frontiers of control." The particular construction of the labor contract under master and servant law made claims to authority portable: what employers could not effect at the point of production they could insist upon in court. Capital and labor were keenly aware of these institutionalized advantages when on the national level they squared off in a protracted struggle beginning in the mid-1860s over the legal structure of employment.

Through both bottom-up and top-down analyses we demonstrated that Burawoy's political apparatuses of production encompass larger institutional orders than he theorizes. In our case studies production and state politics were always entwined in a circuit of control that passed back and forth, through factory and workshop gates, from workplace to court bench. Through our analyses we have provided more systematic mappings of how the law was implicated in the "chains of connection" that Price maintains configured the systems of authority at the heart of nineteenth-century labor control. We have extended his perspective on the frontiers of control by demonstrating how institutionalized recourse to the law, given specific configurations of constraints and opportunities capitalists faced, contoured the boundaries of these frontiers. Employers pursued legal action to define "custom" and the structure of autonomy and obligation in the workplace, and these became central features of their labor control regimes.

These labor control regimes were predicated on varied forms of patriarchal authority in the workplace, some of which were also tied to a broader paternalistic despotism exercised by manufacturers. In different ways in pottery and needle manufacture and trawling, adult males, either as workers or supervisors, exercised authority over women and children, many of whom were legally precluded from exercising independent judgment. Both the case studies and the reconsideration of Polanyi's narrative reveal that at issue in many contests of authority were claims of adult male workers' masculine independence. In the national struggle for labor law reform this involved a complex gender politics. Adult male workers, either recently enfranchised or still seeking full inclusion in the polity, risked compromising their claims of civic independence by pursuing state protection. In both the state and production politics of the time masculine independence dovetailed in the unions' campaign to curb the power of the courts in relations between capital and labor. Combined with a popular political economy through which male workers claimed rights over their "property," collective assertions for masculine autonomy led union activists to a new liberal legal order keeping the courts (and the state more generally) at greater distance in their relations with capital.

Gender may have been at work as well in the court, but as noted the data pose problems for making such a case. As we saw, over 90 percent of all prosecutions involved males. Arguably, governing understandings of gender difference mattered most in determining what behaviors were recognized or engaged in as transgressions and who was prosecuted for them. Adult male workers might well have been more defiant in the face of authority and their employers could also have interpreted their actions as troublesome assertions of masculine independence. However, once before the bench the charges against workers and the resulting sentencing rarely were cast in specifically gendered terms. The reasons for this absence are unclear. Hegemonic gender expectations might have been so implicit that all parties did not raise them. In the prosecution of the potter George Tittensor for his absence and drunkenness, conceivably no one needed to acknowledge that he had fallen short of a workingman's respectability. It is also possible, though, that within the specific context of the court and the law the gendered dimensions of the employers' claims and workers' defenses could be subsumed through the particular discourse of the law. As we heard from the magistrates in the case studies they determined the "facts" and "followed the law." Hull magistrates were not unsympathetic to Charles Taylor's claims so that he could be a good husband and father; but even as they deemed his sentiments worthy they found that they had no bearing on the issue at hand. Finally, it is also plausible that what was paramount for some employers was restoring authority and securing reliable labor. Needle manufacturers did not distinguish between male and female stampers whom they saw as failing in their obligations. What motivated their prosecutions was deficient productivity.

Beyond these particular questions larger concerns have motivated this study. One was to better understand law's materiality in productive relations. Several decades ago E. P. Thompson reflected that "'law' was deeply imbricated within the very basis of productive relations, which would have been inoperable without this law." The law, he concluded, was a terrain of struggle over "actual practice" (1975, 261). Our study affirms his insight. Workers and employers certainly engaged in ideological struggle through the law, as we witnessed in the fierce campaign for legal reform. The law provided a basic conceptual map of labor relations. But the law was also always "functions in the world," as Duncan Kennedy (1985, 998) maintains, as well as hanging above it in the realm of ideology. Labor process theory does not lead us to envision capitalists leading with the law as the tip of the spear in struggles in and about work. Yet the case studies demonstrate that law was in some situations a weapon of choice. It was, however, not generally a blunt instrument of coercion, though at times it was used as such when applied to the fisherlads. Law was the transfer of control over labor as "property" and the class and gender practices of domination and consent involved in these relations. It involved the ordering of the workplace and the measuring and enforcement of productivity. Law was part and parcel of the hierarchical structuring of authority and deference, and was the means by which the latter was enforced when not readily given. It is also important to remember that while the number of workers' civil claims (usually concerning wages) was generally much smaller than that of criminal prosecutions, they did win about two-thirds of their suits. And when adult male workers won reforms in 1875 they substantively changed realities in the spheres of exchange and production. They affirmed claims of "independence," but they also restructured the social relations through which they pursued it. In all of these ways law was a piece of a "regulated set of social forms of life" through which capitalist relations of production unfolded. It was also "a continuously contested terrain of relational power," even if on the whole one side often held clear advantages (McCann 1994, 283).

A second broad concern was to pursue a working alliance between historical institutionalism and historical materialism through their perspectives on durable asymmetric systems of power. Both our analyses of the national development and transformation of the law and its use in the micropolitics of production demonstrate how the former offers key conceptual tools for the latter. We have explored how capitalists and workers made pragmatic choices within institutional constraints, the ways in which these decisions were shaped by when they were taken, and the enduring results embedded in institutional repertoires. The conceptual tools of historical conjunctures, path development, and embeddedness enhance class analysis, sharpening our ability to pursue the dynamics of subjugation, resistance, and accommodation in the workplace. Focusing on institutional dynamics also furthers intersectional analyses of structural inequalities. In our bottom-up and top-down investigations we illuminated how structures of class and gender combined in the development, use, and transformation of master and servant law. Gendered practices and expectations of in/dependence intertwined with the balance of class authority in the workplace and enacted through the law.[1]

The benefits are mutual. In our examinations of the development and transformation of master and servant law, particularly in the revision of Polanyi's narrative, class analysis offered critical insights. Underscoring how legal institutions were crucibles of class power, cleavage, and conflict deepened our analyses of path development and rupture. From master and servant law's origins as a solution to specific trade strife in the eighteenth century, capitalists in an expanding array of industries turned to Parliament for assistance with their labor problems. Capitalist interests cut an increasingly deep and broad trough through which master and servant law was generalized. Class politics, writ large on the national stage of Westminster and small in borough politics, were central in producing the institutional structures through which master and servant law became a durable and reliable practice in labor control regimes. And after at least a half century of this institutional order class politics produced its undoing. Our top-down and bottom-up analyses affirm that to understand the creation and transformation of durable structures of inequality requires the insights of both perspectives.

In the introduction to this study I struck a theme by inviting readers to go beyond with me. Through a complex investigation we have traveled a considerable distance, but in these closing pages let us go a bit further. Charles Tilly frequently argued that we have only the past as a guide to interrogate the present. The questions we have pursued concerning law, labor, and capitalist transformation are being played out in sites today around the globe, albeit in quite different contexts from Victorian England.

Ching Kwan Lee opens her insightful examination of labor protests in contemporary China with what she terms "haunting parallels" between Engel's depiction of the Manchester mills and a Chinese migrant worker's account of the grueling realities of a Shenzen factory. She finds "a uniquely Chinese path of contentious politics that pivots on a politics of the law" in analyzing the transformation of class and citizenship formation, the state restructuring of the economy and contradictions in these processes that animate labor unrest. Over the past two decades the central state's increasing efforts to "rule by law" has made the law "a viable terrain of struggle" even with its lopsided asymmetries of power (2007, 237, 238).

Lee and many other scholars and activists have dissected how an authoritarian state has attempted to engineer capitalist development by transforming production based in a collective social contract to a "market-oriented, voluntaristic and individualistic 'labour contract'" (Friedman and Lee 2010, 509). This process of labor commodification through law (which both Marx and Polanyi would recognize) has been protracted, contested, and replete with institutional contradictions. As the state both dismantled the "iron rice bowl" of state-owned enterprises (SOEs) and opened the doors to foreign capital from the late 1970s onward, it gradually promulgated policies that encouraged the new relationship of the labor contract. A key turn was made in the mid-1980s when regulations on new employment in SOEs introduced labor contracts (Lee 2007, 41; Ngok 2008, 47). The state's decisive step was in 1994 with the passage of the Labor Law, which "codified the use of the labor contract system to manage the labor relationship" (Gallagher and Dong 2011, 40). Encompassing both SOEs and private enterprises, it was the first legal system to establish a unified labor regime. The 1994 law mandated labor contracts and social insurance, set standards for fixed and open-term contracts, created mechanisms for dispute resolution, established the principle of a minimum wage, defined a formal work week, and set limits on overtime. The Labor Law was part of a larger state objective to construct "rule by law" both reconstructing its legitimacy as a protector of the people and creating institutional mechanisms to channel and manage discontent.

Over the next decade institutionalization of the state's project proved uneven and contradictory for many reasons. Lacking significant punishments for noncompliance, many firms simply ignored the law, with the compliance rate among non-SOEs being estimated in 2007 at only 20 percent. Firms opted for short-term fixed contracts to avoid long-term legal entanglements and many increasingly turned to "dispatch" services, subcontracting labor from employment agencies so that they could bypass legal responsibility. Monitoring systems were weak and labor arbitration committees and courts were incapable of handling the surge of claims made by workers. Workers found the dispute resolution process itself frustratingly slow and expensive.

Critically, from the perspective of this study, implementation of the law depended on an institutional system of what Lee terms "decentralized legal authoritarianism" (2007, 7). While the central state pursued legitimacy and stability through "rule by law," it left implementation to local governments, creating contradictory forces. Faced with greater fiscal responsibilities, pressures to achieve economic expansion, and increasingly intense regional competition to attract investment, many local governments saw implementation of the law as an impediment to their economic and political security. Arbitrators were officials from the Labor Bureau, and thus subject to administrative pressures from the Communist Party and the local government. The All Chinese Federation of Trade Unions, the sole official collective agent for workers, also faced contradictory pressures to represent workers interests but also as an arm of the Party to maintain social stability. Compliance and enforcement evolved as an uneven patchwork both between SOEs and private enterprises and across different locales. Many workers who engaged in the dramatic increase in the filing of complaints in the dispute resolution system developed what Mary Gallagher (2006) terms a legal consciousness of "informed disenchantment." As Lee (2007) demonstrates, the promise of empowerment coupled with the realities of execution led in different ways to heightened labor protest.[2]

The central state responded by instituting further rules in the Labor Contract Law that took effect in 2008. The process of consultation leading up to its passage was highly contentious. Lan and Pickles comment that "it was arguably the most politically debated law in the history of the Peoples Republic of China" and the number of public comments on the draft law substantially outstripped those on other high-profile legislation (2011, 3). Representatives of capital, particularly foreign capital such as the American Chamber of Commerce in Shanghai, engaged in robust lobbying to weaken some of the draft law's provisions regarding employment security.[3] Intense politicking by different factions within the state and divisions on the draft law between northern and southern interests also determined the law's final content.

Despite the concessions incorporated during the drafting period, the Labor Contract Law contains provisions to enhance employment security and workers' rights, especially for migrants who lead a precarious existence within the industrial order. Written contracts are required within a month of employment, and penalties are increased for violation. Probationary periods are delineated given the length of contract. There are greater restrictions on fixed-term contracts accompanied with a mandate for open-ended contracts after two fixed-term agreements. The law includes more restraints on labor subcontracting. Changes in work rules require employee consultation (though veto power by trade unions was removed after heavy objection from capital). The law also makes mass layoffs more difficult and enhances claims for severance pay.[4]

During the first year under the new law the number of recorded disputes doubled nationally and in some economic development zones increased by 300 percent. Chinese courts faced a surge of labor cases, which also almost doubled nationally the same year and saw even more dramatic increases in some export zones. To Gallagher and Dong, "the wave of filings initiated by workers against their employers can be seen as a type of bottom-up enforcement of the new law in direct response to the lackluster official measures to implement and enforce" the law (2011, 59).

Predictably, the Labor Contract Law has yielded mixed results. While limited data suggest that some workers were emboldened to pursue their rights, enforcement remains problematic because of the continuing problems posed by decentralization. Administrative units and lower courts are still subject to the pressure of local governments focused on growth and the legal process is too costly for many workers. There are indications that while the percentage of workers with written contracts has increased, it remains far short of general, especially for migrants. Many firms, more often private enterprises, insist that workers sign blank, covered, or English-language contracts subverting the intent of the law. There has been increased flight by foreign capital to such countries as Vietnam, where formal regulations are less onerous. Perhaps most germane to the issues of this study, "there is little reason to believe that the new law will adequately address the deep power asymmetry at the point of production."[5]

Given that Lee sees parallels between nineteenth-century Manchester and twenty-first-century Shenzen, it is worth considering whether some of the questions that motivated this study provide insights for a very different time and place. Scholars and activists are now posing questions of how the institutionalization of labor relations through the labor contract shapes asymmetries of class power, involves both national and local state institutions in the contouring of workplace relations and constrains, and channels and stimulates class conflicts through contradictory dynamics. They are probing variations in the embeddedness of the law according to enterprise types, labor forces and markets, regions, and industries and the frictions between the micro- and macro-politics of institutionalization.

One prominent example is Steven C. McKay's *Satanic Mills or Silicon Islands?* In a systematic comparative analysis of export zones McKay teases out how combinations of national and local regulatory regimes, the gendered division of the labor force, and transnational capital conjoin to produce the "political apparatuses of flexible production" (2006). He analyses how neoliberal policies produced more devolved regimes through localization of state capacities. McKay finds despotic, panoptic, peripheral human relations and collectively bargained regimes, and maps out their institutional configurations. Transnational employers use local regulatory institutions as part of their scheme to create social structures of exploitation. These vary from the privatized police forces in despotic regimes, to labor management councils, to zones laws that disperse workers' housing, all laden with distinctive institutional configures to control labor markets and the labor process. And he reminds his readers at the end that "the national state is also complicit in its strategic *non*enforcement of constitutional laws that explicitly promote full employment, equal opportunity, security of tenure, human workers conditions, and even a living wage" (2006, 218–19).

McKay urges us to reject the vision of the frictionless flow of global capital subordinating the mass of global workers in its wake. Instead, he illuminates for us a fractured landscape of labor control regimes forged in the changes needs of capital and the varying local capacities of advantage, hued by national neoliberal regulations. His is a complex picture, and a heuristic exercise for us now is to further consider the complexities we've unearthed in this study. Let's not try to find doppelgangers of Hanley, Hull, and Redditch in twenty-first-century China or the Philippines. However, as with Lee's reflections on Manchester, I ask readers to consider how they provide a basis to reflect on their possible comparisons with the contemporary world.

There is one more reason to consider the larger implications of our study, and it returns us to nineteenth-century England. The British empire imposed many exports on its subjugated populations, and one was its legal system. Through colonial legislation, versions of master and servant law were spread throughout the empire. As a relatively simple means of regulating labor markets and enforcing work performance it "was immensely adaptable, and much adapted" (Hay and Craven 2004, 56). Particularly after abolition, master and servant law became a key means not only of extracting labor power, but also of doing so by reinforcing distinctions of race, gender, and age. Hay and Carven argue that as "low law" it was insulated from disputes over other aspects of criminal law that were fodder for later high court scrutiny and popular democratic transformation. In investigating the contemporary great transformation of globalization we do well to keep sight of the imperial legacies of master and servant law.

While my previous work partly focused on historical processes of class formation, that question has not been my concern in this study. However, I think it is possible that the fusion of historical materialism and historical institutionalism offers a new angle for understanding the institutional dynamics of "class making." In his reflections on the comparative-historical analysis of class formation Aristide Zolberg (1986) notes that that there is a recursive relationship between political organization and economic structures, but that it is difficult to disentangle state versus regime effects. In the analysis of the juridical in labor control regimes I have demonstrated how legal institutions shaped the course of exploitation in different industries and labor-control regimes. In a sense this was part of the larger process of the making of the English working class. Others might see further possibilities from these case studies for fuller comparative analyses.

Reflecting on the greater purposes of social sciences Charles Tilly addressed how analysis and ethics are intertwined: "Social science complements moral philosophy by ordering comparison of what actually exists with what could be and by asking which moral principles could be realized, and how, in the sort of world we know. Whether or not the aspiration to grand design drives them, social scientists who reliably identify past or present social life inevitably form propositions, however suppressed, about what could happen, about what can be, about what might happen next" (1997, 19).

In this study I trust I have reliably identified some relations between law, labor, and England's great transformation. My analysis has not been motivated by a grand design. If I have partly succeeded in my more modest aims, I hope I provide others with propositions they can use to understand what could happen in other times and places, particularly with regard to exploitation. As important, I hope I have provided some conceptual tools that help others to understand how to confront asymmetries' power and ask what it would mean to go beyond them.

NOTES

CHAPTER ONE

1. *Hull and Eastern Counties Herald*, May 17, 1866. This sentence represented the magistrate's leniency, for until he heard of Taylor's noble act of marriage, he had been prepared to send the apprentice to prison for ten weeks.

2. *Staffordshire Advertiser*, June 2, 1866.

CHAPTER TWO

1. Marx characterizes the capitalist's mandate here as follows:

> It is here that the supervisory responsibility of the capitalist enters. . . . He must also see to it that the work is performed in an orderly and methodical fashion and that the use-value he has in mind actually emerges successfully at the end of the process. At this point too the capitalist's ability to supervise and enforce discipline is vital. Lastly, he must make sure that the process of production is not interrupted or disturbed and that it really does proceed to the creation of the product within the time allowed for the particular labour process and its objective requirements. This depends partly on the continuity of work which is introduced by capitalist production, partly however on controllable external factors. . . . The capitalist forces the worker where possible to exceed the normal rate of intensity, and he forces him as best he can to extend the process of labour beyond the time necessary to replace the amount laid out in wages. (1976, 986–87)

2. "The work may become more intensive, its duration may be extended, it may become more continuous or orderly under the eyes of the interested capitalist, but in themselves these changes do not affect the character of the actual labour process, the actual mode of working" (Marx 1976, 1021).

3. For useful summaries see Cain and Hunt 1979, 62–101, and Phillips 1980, 168–87.

4. Marx does note at an earlier point in *Capital* of "the pretensions of capital in its embryonic state, when it cannot yet use the sheer force of economic relations to secure its

right to absorb a sufficient quantity of surplus labour, but must be aided by the power of the state" (1976, 382).

5. And in the *Critique of Political Economy* he states, "The first exchange between labour and capital is a *formal process*, in which capital figures as *money* and labour capacity figures as *commodity*. The sale of labour capacity takes place notionally or legally in this first process, although labour is *paid for* only after it has been done, at the end of the day, of the week, etc." (1994, 132; emphases in original).

6. As he notes in *Wages, Price and Profit*,

> As to the *limitation of the working day* in England, as in all other countries, it has never been settled except by *legislative interference*. Without the working men's continuous pressure from without, that interference would never have taken place. But at all events, the result was not to be attained by private settlement between the working men and the capitalists. This very necessity of *general political action* affords proof that in its merely economic action capital is the stronger side. (1965, 74; emphases in original)

See also his retrospective comments in his inaugural address to the International (1975, 10–11).

7. See, e.g., Cangiani 2011 and Dugger and Sherman 2002.

8. For a similar argument, though one that ultimately argues for a different direction than this study, see Hodgson 2001.

9. Geoffrey Hodgson observes that "for Marx, the surface juridical phenomena were closely related to the underlying reality. Accordingly, legal formalities are not mere surface phenomena that can be ignored, but critical expressions of an underlying socio-economic reality" (ibid., 288). However, he never explains how legal and economic form and substantive affect one another.

10. In elaborating and amending Marx's perspective, LPT analysts from the 1970s forward have focused on the dynamics and transformation of the social and technical relations in the labor process. Building on Marx's legacy contemporary LPT theorists continue to focus on (a) the exploitation of labor by capital, (b) the capitalist logic of accumulation that has determinant effects on these relations, both in terms of how they are constrained and how they are transformed, (c) the exercise of specific managerial strategies by capital to realize exploitation, and (d) the ways in which the fundamental conflict produced in exploitation creates specific configurations of control and struggle, resistance and consent within specific workplace regimes (Thompson and Vincent 2010, 48). However, while LPT has a lineage in Marx's materialism and class struggle, its proponents do not always accept that conflict in the workplace is tied to broader social and political conflict and societal transformation (Edwards 1986; Thompson and Smith 2010).

11. Analysts of the English case have argued that both the timing and completeness of this transformation were different and varied significantly by industry. See, e.g., Knox 1986; Lazonick 1979, 1981; Littler 1990; More 1980; and Price 1982, 1984a, 1984b, 1986.

12. Burawoy 1979; Edwards 1986; Haydu 1988, 2001; Hyman 1987; Knights and Willmott 1989; Littler 1990; Meiksins 1994; Smith 1994; Spencer 2000.

13. In a retrospective discussion of the trajectory of his studies Michael Burawoy acknowledges that Braverman's work was a basis for framing two big questions that he has

pursued: (a) "how do managers elicit the cooperation of workers in the production of surplus value" and (b) "what is the role of production on working-class formation?" (2001, 21–22).

14. Burawoy 1985, 29; 1984, 250–52; 2001, 41; Burawoy and Krotov 1992, 18.

15. "Production politics are struggles shaped within the arena of production over relations in and of production and regulated by production apparatuses. State politics, on the other hand, are distinctive in that they cannot be characterized over any particular set of relations. . . . What is distinctive about the state is its global character, its function as a factor of cohesion for the entire social formation. . . . State politics include as their core the politics of politics" (Burawoy 1985, 254).

16. He does, however, concur with Marx that there was considerable degradation of work in the nineteenth century. "It does not require a great deal of historical knowledge to appreciate the extreme forms of deskilling prevalent during the early years of capitalism. A cursory glance through Engel's survey of various branches of industry in the first half of nineteenth-century Britain makes it clear that few workers had much control over the labour process" (ibid., 49).

17. "In reality, there is a high degree of inter-penetration of control strategies from one productive stage to another and it is highly problematic that an historical typology may be developed on the basis of a linear movement from one kind of market to another" (Price 1984b, 98).

18. Price 1982, 198; 1984a, 223–24; 1984b, 119; 1984c, 107; 1986, 95. As he observes, "The labour process under capitalism can only be understood as a struggle for authority and control; the technical and material elements in the labour process, important though they are in closing off or opening up the potential for resistance, are in the final analysis subsidiary to the imperatives of authority. . . . More than in any other previous economic and social formation, industrial capitalism depends on authority over the labour process: without industrial discipline the very foundations of capitalism are threatened" (1982, 197).

19. Price 1980, 79; 1982, 199; 1983, 61–62, 68; 1984a, 222; 1984b, 121–22, 128; 1986, 72. "Autonomous regulation was the main feature of work-place relations and although the extent to which it could be exercised varied widely over time and place its practice was the major legacy of the period to labour organisation and relations. Across those large sectors of industry where the labour process remained unchanged there was no fundamental challenge to the practice of work control" (1986, 77).

20. Price 1984a, 217; 1984b, 124–25; 1984c, 97; 1986, 35, 39, 64, 82.

21. "For the first three-quarters of the nineteenth century, the nature of labour law expressed the central continuities of social relations throughout the period of industrialisation" (Price 1986, 39).

22. Price 1983, 70; 1984b, 124–25; 1986, 39, 42. Elsewhere he urges that law be seen across its social and economic as well as its intellectual dimensions, maintaining the we need to see the law "not simply as a restraining agent, nor as something that was just received, but also as a site where labour met and negotiated with state and society. This is true not only at the level of legislation and statutes, but at the more important level where common law was actually determined through contests that emerged from the fabric of social relations" (Price 1991, 259).

23. Busfield 1988; Cowman and Jackson 2005; Freifeld 1986; Morgan 2001; Schwarzkopf 2004; Valenze 1995.

24. As Sonya Rose (1991) observes, conceptions of masculinity were also raised in debates on the various factory acts. Critics questioned why men would allow their wives and daughters to enter the factory and whether they were hiding behind petticoats to advance their own interests concerning work regulations.

25. Rose also observes that machinery itself was gendered, as devices often were constructed with their presumed typical (male or female) workers in mind (1992, 29–30).

CHAPTER THREE

1. Forms of "structural" Marxism widely drawn on in the 1970s and 1980s emphasized the "relative autonomy" of politics and the law, within a base/superstructure model. As Barry Hindess argues, in both the dominant model and the structuralist variant "Marxist political analysis characteristically operates in two different registers, with little connection between them: there is the analysis of the ultimate determinants, and there is the analysis that gives other elements their due" (1987, 95).

2. And she elaborates further on,

> There are, then, at least two senses in which the juridical-political "sphere" is implicated in the productive "base." First, a system of production always exists in the shape of specific social determinations, the particular modes of organization and domination and the forms of property in which relations of production are embodied—what might be called the "basic" as distinct from the "superstructural" juridical-political attributes of the productive system. Second, from a *historical* point of view even political institutions like village and state enter directly into the constitution of production relations and are in a sense prior to them (even where these institutions are not the direct instruments of surplus appropriation), because relations of production are historically constituted by the configuration of power that determines the outcome of class conflict. (Wood 1995, 28)

See also Taiwo 1996, 55; Sayer 1987, 77.

3. Jessop and Sum 2006, 249; Sayer 1987, 25–27; Wood 1995, 49–75. As Duncan Kennedy notes, Marx's "whole definition of commodity production is in terms of and therefore presupposes the legal concepts of private property and contract. The legal concepts are built into the definition of the 'social formation' or 'mode of production'" (1985, 978).

4. Bidet 2007; Fine 1984; Marsden 1999; Taiwo 1996.

5. As Richard Kinsey observes, "The juridical relation is thus an abstract but determinate theoretical construct appropriate to the analysis of the capitalist mode of production, whilst the law is one historically specific mode of expression of that relation. The mediation and realisation of the juridical relation as law occurs in the material practices of its administration—primarily through the courts, . . . but also in customary and conventional and private legal systems" (1978, 214).

6. Taiwo on this point quotes Marx, who observed that "the various stages of development in the division of labour are just so many different forms of property" (1996, 61).

7. Jacques Bidet makes the case that the struggle over surplus value extraction emerges from the contradictions inherent in the dialectic unity of the economic and the juridic (or what he also terms the "political") forms of capitalist labor relations. He argues that the division of property over labor power is never wholly settled through the labor contract; for while the worker sells it to the capitalist he never renounces his ultimate rights of ownership to it. For Bidet the capitalist must have some recourse to political domination in the labor process to maximize his proprietary control over labor power: economic compulsion in and of itself cannot maximize surplus value extraction (2007, 48–51, 70–72; see also Kinsey 1978, 222).

8. Christopher Tomlins likewise notes in a discussion of authority and subordination through labor law that "to investigate the legal history is to investigate the nature of law's participation in the basic routines by which different kinds of ascendancy obtain recognition in daily social life, and in turn the extent to which law is determined in detail by the course of those social practices and ideologies" (1995b, 66; see also 1993, 29–32, and 1995a).

9. In his study of legal mobilization for pay equity Michael W. McCann makes a parallel argument: "Just as legal consciousness develops through experience in material life, so do legal discourses *become material* in the very process of action within different social spaces and institutional sites" (1994, 283).

10. Other social scientists are promoting forms of dialogue between Marxism and institutionalisms that are distinct from what I offer here. They are based in theoretical perspectives such as "postmodern" Marxism (Garnett 1999), and "overdetermination" (Cullenberg 1999), or societal evolution (Dugger and Sherman 2002). In different ways they lean toward systems-centered approaches that I believe have less purchase for understanding the temporalities of developmental paths and their transformations and historical variation. The effort here is also distinctive from perspectives in institutional economics, such as the work of Douglass North (1990) in which formal state institutions are seen as levers of economic change in guaranteeing property rights and facilitating market transactions, or the perspective of Joel Mokyr (2008) who focuses more on informal institutions that created normative expectations for "gentlemanly" exchange.

11. Haydu 1988, 1998, 2002, 2008, 2010; Lyddon 1994; Pontusson 1995, 2005; see also Peck and Theodore 2007.

12. Campbell 2004; Clemens 2005; Coates 2005; Hall and Thelen 2009; Immergut 1998; Mahoney 2000, 2003; Sayer 1987; Wood 1995. In a series of important and fine-grained historical studies Jonathan Zeitlin and his colleagues offer a "neo-institutional framework" for the analysis of workplace control to counter Marxist approaches. He argues that they all contain an errant evolutionary determinism in which an inner logic of capitalist development predetermines capitalists' and workers' interests and compels managers to adapt specific control regimes. Alternatively he maintains that analyses must start at the firm level, investigating how historically specific constellations of enterprise and workplace organization, autonomous interests of state actors pursued through formal institutions, and union and employer relations contingently produce specific regimes of shop floor management. From this perspective "interests emerge from an interaction between social actors' prior interpretative framework and the specific situation in which they find themselves, in a context which includes the discourses and practices of institutions"

(1991, 22). Zeitlin offers an important admonition to foreground historical context, but his studies do not lead to a broader perspective on institutional bases of labor control and conflict. Cast in detailed accounts of employer-worker friction and accommodation, it is unclear why these narratives are presented in class terms, since Zeitlin posits that interests are fundamentally institutionally, contextually, and contingently determined. Finally, it is questionable whether these studies, anchored in the late nineteenth- and early twentieth-century skilled metal and engineering trades, are adequate bases for generalizing about labor relations in most other English industries, especially for the bulk of the nineteenth century (Sabel and Zeitlin 1985, 1997; Tolliday and Zeitlin 1991a, 1991b; Zeitlin 1985, 1987, 1989).

13. These arguments have some parallels with Charles Tilly's perspective on exploitation (1998; Tilly and Tilly 1998). He also emphasizes how well-established historical contexts set the conditions for the organization of and struggles over control in the workplace. Tilly argues that this creates an embeddedness that influences employers' decisions on control strategies and that there is an element of path dependence in this process. My argument also resonates with Tilly's more general proposition that structural and institutional perspectives must be combined to understand the relational dynamics of durable inequality.

14. Robin Stryker makes a more general theoretical argument that law and economy exist in a mutually endogenous relationship (2003; Edelman and Stryker 2005). Legal constructs and practices are incorporated into economic fields and organizations, while legal systems assimilate the economic interests and logics of the conflicts they routinely adjudicate. Stryker makes the case for a form of top-down and bottom-up analysis I pursue in this study by insisting that analysis must examine the interplay between everyday practices and formal legal institutions: "Because law exists in a broader social context, its social embeddedness affects both how formal law is constructed, mobilized, implemented and enacted in everyday economic life, and whether and how these everyday constructions from 'above' and 'below,' by capitalists, managers and professionals, workers and unions, and diverse race, ethnic, gender and religious movements, feed back into formal law and the state" (2003, 347).

15. Hattam 1993; Hepple 2000; Marks 1989; Orren 1991; van der Linden and Price 2000. In broad terms this parallels the arguments offered by Zeitlin, but most of these analyses stop short of his social constructionist claims that interests should be understood as developed within specific institutional contexts without recourse to more generally perspectives on structured class or other hierarchical antagonisms. Scholars analyzing union development in the British and American cases have noted how both statutory and common law and judicial governance significantly influenced the rise of "collective laissez-faire" and "business unionism" respectively in these countries (Curthoys 2004; Fisk 1994; Forbath 1991; Fox 1985; Hattam 1993; Orth 1991; Rubin 2000; Voss 1993).

16. "For most of the nineteenth century, work relations in industrializing countries were described by a multiplicity of legal forms, some referring to specific work categories within or beyond the category of wage labour, and in which elements of status and contract were intermingled. Different elements of these legal types coalesced to form what became the 'contract of employment,' but they did so in ways which reflected distinct legal traditions and different conditions across national systems" (Deakin 2009, 470).

17. Clemens 2005, 503; Hay and Wincott 1998, 954–56; Immergut 1998, 18–20; Martin 2003, 48–49; Orren and Skowronek 1996, 139; Streek and Thelen 2005, 27.

18. See also Mahoney 2000, 2003; Thelen 1999, 2003, 2004.

19. Thelen, for example, discusses processes of layering and conversion as part of ongoing adaptation of institutions to meet new exigencies (2003, 225–27; 2004, 35–37; see also Pierson 2004, 137–38). John Campbell portrays change as a process of bricolage through which existing elements are recombined in novel forms and translation and in which innovation is pursued by integrating new externally produced practices (2003, 68–71, 80–87)

20. Deeg and Jackson 2007; Hall and Thelen 2009; Haydu 2010; Immergut 1998; Orren and Skowronek 1996; Pierson 2004; Schneiberg 2007; Schneiberg and Clemens 2006; Streek and Thelen 2005. Orren and Skowronek (1996) term this development of contradictions as "intercurrence." In some explanations of contradictory forces there are hints of parallels with Marx's dialectical analysis. Streek and Thelen, for example, observe, "As argued most famously by Marx, social arrangements may set in motion dynamics that sow the seeds of their own destruction" (2005, 29). Schneiberg and Clemens also reference this dialectic logic, noting that some "studies argue that an institution (to echo Marx) 'produces . . . its own grave-diggers' or, less dramatically, its own patterns of challenge and contention" (2006, 218).

21. Ron Martin makes the general case for locality: "It is at the regional and local levels that the effects of institutional path dependence are particularly significant. Institutions are important 'carriers' of *local* economic histories. Different specific institutional regimes develop in different places, and these then interact with local economic activity in a mutually reinforcing way. If institutional path dependence matters, it matters in different ways in different places: institutional-economic path dependence is itself place-dependent" (2003, 80). For the case of English industrialization see Stobart 2001. Rosemary Hopcroft (2001) presents a more general critique that neo-institutional theory has failed to acknowledge regional differences in the effects of state governance.

22. Burawoy, as I noted in the last chapter, makes a similar argument.

23. Herod 2001; Rainnie, McGrath-Champ, and Herod 2007; Massey 1984; Peck 1996, 2005. Jamie Peck suggests specifically in the case of Burawoy that he "demonstrates how political apparatuses are shaped by and subsequently shaped by the labor process under different historical and geographic conditions, but stops short of considering the theoretical implications of spatially uneven development in the politics of production" (1996, 137). Susan Hanson and Geraldine Pratt (1995) offer parallel arguments for the gendering of work.

24. Behagg 1990; Berg 1994; Bythell 1978; Hudson 1992; Joyce 1990; Pollard 1992; Rule 1988; Sabel and Zeitlin 1985; Samuel 1977. Though as Lazonick (1981, 1990) has shown even in this case Marx presented an idealized account of a system that involved male worker discretion and paternalistic control.

25. Deakin and Wilkinson 2005; Hay 1998, 2000, 2004; Jaffe 2000, 2003; Klarman 1989; Orth 1991; Rubin 2000; Steinfeld 2001, 2000b.

26. The feudal vestige argument has been made by Karen Orren (1991).

27. Robert Steinfeld likewise observes, "In the absence of effective strategies for supervision in these industries, many employers may well have chosen to use penal sanctions to make shirking more costly to workers to elicit higher levels of effort as an alternative to paying higher wages" (2001, 72). Christopher Tomlins make a similar argument for the development of master and servant law in the American case (1993, 2010).

28. As Deakin and Wilkinson emphasize,

> at every point in the development of the employment relationship in British labour law, contract and status have been intertwined. It has never been possible to give an exhaustive account of the employment relationship using the logic of contract alone. Thus there was no general movement from status to contract at the time of industrialization, nor does the welfare state mark a reversion to pre-modern forms. In the period of industrialization, contract was complemented by the disciplinary code of master and servant regime and poor law conceptions of the legal duty to work. (2005, 37)

29. Likewise David Galenson maintains that "the status of free labor . . . did not exist for most workers in England prior to 1875" (1994, 130).

30. Craven and Hay 2004; Deakin and Wilkinson 2005; Frank 2010; Hay 2000, 2004; Napier 1975; Steinfeld 2001.

31. A number of these statutes concerned theft and embezzlement, which masters in outwork trades especially highlighted as a chronic problem.

32. When discharged, servants lost all claims on wages that had not been paid. Gravenor Henson, an activist framework knitter, and George White, a clerk committees in the House of Commons, saw 6 Geo. III, c. 25 especially oppressive in both validating masters' imperiousness and providing magistrates with judicial fiat on what was deemed a transgression. "As to misbehavior, one justice is to be the judge of what may be so called; a few angry words, singing, appearing dirty, smoking tobacco, workman not finishing his work to please his master, or not doing enough,—in short everything that the master chuses to style as misbehavior, has been construed into an offence before one justice, who send the unfortunate man to the gaol, or house of correction, without an appeal" (Henson and White 1823, 91). Henson and White also argued that masters deceptively had servants sign contracts that they did not understand, which were later used for prosecuting misconduct (91–93). They unsuccessfully urged for reform in terms of injecting greater reciprocity into the acts, though as Steinfeld observes they did not question "the traditional obligation to perform but enforcement of the reciprocal obligations of employers," and at no point objected to the penal provisions (2001, 99–100).

33. The acts provided appeal of the warrant and wage abatement to the regular county court sessions (quarter sessions), but not commitment to prison. This would change with later legislation and higher court rulings in the nineteenth century, making it virtually impossible to appeal any conviction. Hay notes that the country elites who controlled Parliament in the eighteenth century sought some balance between the interests of capital and labor since their goal was to maintain political and social stability. However, the balance shifted toward capital as sentencing in successive acts became increasingly punitive (Hay 2005, 83). Exactly who was covered under the acts was at issue for many decades, and a periodic subject of high court adjudication, which I examine below. 20 Geo. II, c. 56 covered servants in husbandry as well as "artificers, handicraftsmen, miners, colliers, keelmen, pitmen, glassmen, potters and other labourers" and 6 Geo. III, c. 25 added calico printers (Hertslet 1850, 28).

34. Hay 2004, 66; Hertslet 1850, 28–30, 51–54, 63; MacDonald 1868, 66–72; Napier 1975, 103–4; Simon 1954, 166. 17 Geo. III, c. 36 might have been used less frequently to

prosecute neglect in part because, unlike its predecessors, it required the presence of at least two magistrates (Hertslet 1850, 56).

35. *Justice of the Peace*, May 19, 1866, 311. Since magistrates' court minute books often do not indicate the specific act under which a defendant was prosecuted it is difficult to know how often employers chose to prosecute under the earlier legislation. Hay suggests that into the nineteenth century the earlier statutes were cited as the bases for conviction by courts (2004, 86).

36. Frank 2010, 55; Hay 2004, 86; Hertslet 1850, 90–101; MacDonald 1868, 72–74; Napier 1975, 103–4. This statute was extended still further in 1830 by 10 Geo. IV, c. 52, which specifically mentions the cotton, flax, fur, fustian, hemp, iron, leather, linen, mohair, silk, and woolen trades (Davis 1868, 37–38; Napier 1975, 103 n. 6). Under 6 & 7 Vict., c. 40, passed in 1843, piece workers in the cloth trades who neglected to fulfill a contract, were absent from work for seven days, or damaged work could be fined up to £2 or be imprisoned for up to two months at hard labor by two or more justices. This act encompassed all outworkers in these trades, not just those under exclusive service (Davis 1868, 39–40; Hertslet 1850, 103–4; Simon 1954, 166). Miners were similarly covered for breach of contract by 39 & 40 Geo. III, c. 77 (Davis 1868, 33; Edgar 1860, 689).

37. Legislation was proposed in 1844, but it was successfully beaten back by activist workers and their allies (see Frank 2010, chaps. 1–2).

38. I discuss the reform campaigns in chapter 7 when I amend Polanyi's narrative of the double movement.

39. All previous acts had allowed only the testimony of the master in prosecutions of servants, though both servant and master could testify in civil claims pursued by servants against masters. As a matter of practice it is not clear, though, that magistrates pursued the letter of the law in this regard. In a number of the cases I examined for the analyses of the case studies below it is clear that magistrates called on workers to give their defense prior to the 1867 act.

40. Given reforms of local courts under the Jervis Act of 1848, which I discuss below, it is not clear how often magistrates issued warrants by the 1860s. The difference under previous legislation nonetheless was a source of serious grievance of inequity among workers. Under warrants, as opposed to summonses, they could be arrested and held in prison awaiting their trials, while under their civil actions against employers no such possibility existed (MacDonald 1868, 238–39; BPP 1866 XIII [449], 3–4, 34). Imprisonment had been a punishment for some masters under previous statutes, but the grounds were narrower than for servants (Hay 2004, 67 n. 29). As Steinmetz observes, the law provided a formal measure of parity between workers and employers since both were now subject to fines of up to £20 and up to three months in prison for "aggravated offences." However, he notes that between 1868 and 1872 only six employers were sent to prison for seven days a piece (2000b, 277).

41. From 1868 onward the annual number of workers imprisoned under the act dropped by two-thirds (Steinfeld 2001, 203).

42. Steinmetz 2000b, 277; see also Davis 1868; MacDonald 1868, 192–98; Simon 1954, 185–86; Steinfeld 2001, 203–4.

43. Another issue that had significant consequences for the balance of power between capitalists and workers was the legality of trade unions, which we will examine in chapter 7.

44. Parliament responded to these rulings by passing 6 & 7 Vict., c. 40 in 1843, but it specifically only mentioned seven trades and thus was read narrowly by the courts. An attempt to shepherd a bill to cover all piece-rate workers through Parliament the following year was met with a concerted response by working-class activists and their allies a year later and failed (Frank 2010, chap. 2; Steinfeld 2001, 135–41).

45. Frank 2010, 29–31; MacDonald 1868, 75–82; Napier 1975, 106–20; Steinfeld 2001, 125–35, 143–53. An important exception, as I discuss below, were domestic servants, who in most interpretations of the law were outside its boundaries (Frank 2010, 35–36; Hay 2004, 65–66).

46. MacDonald 1868, 76, 78, 83; Napier 1975, 122; Simon 1954, 165–66; Steinfeld 2001, 59–60, 105–24; *Justice of the Peace* 30 (May 16, 1866): 310–12; *Law Times* 41, no. 1223 (Sept. 6, 1866): 768.

47. As Corrigan and Sayer remark more generally of the nineteenth-century English state, "Magistrates continue to be, in large measure, 'the State' until the later nineteenth century" (1985, 157).

48. Barry Godfrey notes that in the heavily industrialized counties of Lancashire and the West Riding of Yorkshire the percentage of industrialists on the county bench were only 5 percent and 12.5 percent respectively in 1840–80 (1999b, 62). However, in his study of the industrialized area of Worcestershire and Staffordshire known as the Black Country, D. C. Woods shows that close to half of all county magistrates in this region were coal and iron masters by midcentury (1979, 97).

49. Hay 2004, 105; BPP 1866 XIII [449] 1, 91.

50. And Wood continues, "They not only administered the law, but helped to make it as well. In this sense the manufacturers, iron and coal masters, merchants and factors, complemented their formidable economic power with control over local administration and justice" (1979, 102). The approval by the Lord Chancellor of the appointments was essentially pro forma. For additional discussion of this control see Godfrey 1999a, 1999b; Philips 1977; and Trainor 1993.

51. BPP 1866 XIII [449], 1. In testimony delivered a bit later the Sheffield unionist William Dronfield maintained, "we know from the surroundings in which they are connected, their feeling generally is in favor of the employing classes, as they themselves are, to a large extent, employers of labour" (36).

52. Christopher Tomlins (2010) offers a parallel argument for the American case, demonstrating the distinctive regional development of the law.

53. As Pat Hudson notes in the case of the role of government in the Industrial Revolution, "When one comes to analyse the role of the state directly and specifically in promoting British regional growth it is the role of *local* government at the county and sub-county level which requires attention" (1989, 30).

54. See, for example, the testimony of union representatives and activists given before the Select Committee on Master and Servant Law in 1866 (BPP 1866 XIII [449], 3, 9, 36–37, 87, 91).

55. French 1967a, 227–29; 1967b, 270; Manchester 1980, 77–78.

56. Frank 2010, chap. 7; Woods 1979, 101. The working-class paper *Bee-Hive* characterized stipendiaries in the following terms: "Their salaries, through a mistaken economy, are

fixed so low that no counsel of good practice would accept the office; their appointments are obtained through political influence, and have not infrequently been given as a consolation to some aspirant for parliamentary honours, or to a writer that has consistently supported the government with his pen. In fact it is from the class who have failed in their profession that these situations have too often been filled" (Sept. 17, 1870, 493).

57. As Hay suggests, some of this shift could have occurred with the advent of the county courts in the late 1840s in which civil claims of up to £20 could be summarily adjudicated. Workers claiming wages might have shifted their claims to these venues hoping for a more favorable outcome (2004, 105–6).

58. Woods 1979, 341–42; BPP 1866 XIII [449], 45, 103.

59. Data is collected from annual parliamentary reports: Judicial Statistics (England and Wales): Part I. Police. Criminal Proceedings. Prisons, BPP 1865 LII [445], 25: 1866 LXVIII [483], 25; 1867 LXVI [523], 25; 1867–68 LXVII [947], 25; 1868–69 LVIII [737], 25; 1870 LXIII [753], 25; 1871 LXIV [231], 25; 1872 LXV [235], 25; 1873 LXX [247], 25; 1874 LXXI [251], 25; 1875 LXXXI [259], 25.

60. Deakin and Wilkinson 2005, 70; Galenson 1994, 131; Simon 1954, 165; Steinfeld 2001, 66, 71; Woods 1979, 131.

61. BPP 1874 XXIV [391], 141; XXX [1157], 130

62. BPP 1874 XXX [1157], 155. The manager of an iron and coal works in Wales employing 11,000 observed, "I see that taking a man down to [the town of] Merthyr and fining him, and in default of his paying the fine sending him to prison, restrains scores and scores of men from committing the same act probably for a month or so" (147).

63. BPP 1866 XIII [449], 67, 110; BPP 1874 XXX [1157], 144–47, 154–55, 163.

64. Frank 2010, 44–47; Jaffe 1991, 101–4; Simon 1954, 172.

65. Dutton and King 1982, 66–67; see also Curthoys 2004, 356; Hay 2000, 251–52; Longe 1860, 24–26; Philips 1976, 180; Steinfeld 2001, 65–66; Woods 1979, 313, 321, 331. Metropolitan London did not distinguish itself as an area of high prosecution, reporting very roughly 400 some cases for most of the period in an area of over one million people.

66. In his study of the Black Country, Woods finds that women were treated fairly leniently by the courts, with most cases being settled by their promise of a return to work and the payment of court costs (1979, 337–39). One legal dimension sometimes raised in prosecutions was the inability of a married woman to bind herself through contract without her husband's consent. The issue seemed to trouble some magistrates and their clerks, as subscribers occasionally required clarification from the *Justice of the Peace* as to whether married women could be prosecuted under master and servant law. The question became even more vexatious with the passage of the Married Women's Property Act of 1870, which provided women with control over their wages or other earnings. However, the high court ruled in 1875 that a married woman could not enter into a contract of service without her husband's consent. It is not clear that married women used their status to subvert prosecution, or that many magistrates routinely considered the question, though we will see an instance in Redditch in chapter 6 (*Justice of the Peace*, Feb. 23, 1861, 124; Oct. 5, 1867, 639; Oct. 19, 1867, 670; May 7, 1870, 30; Aug. 28, 1875, 548–49; Sept. 18, 1875, 600–601; see also *County Courts Chronicle*, March 1, 1871, 341; *Capital and Labour*, June 23, 1875, 304, and Sept. 29, 1875, 583).

PART TWO

1. I spent many hours at a table in the Hull City Archives pouring through their exceptional collection of court records. For a number of days a doctoral researcher sat opposite me intently studying large stacks of considerably older documents. I finally asked him what he was studying: the use of Latin in medieval town documents he told me. And why Hull? Well, that answer was simple: because this archive has great records.

2. In the case of Hanley the archival records I use are for the borough magistrates and through the local paper I capture stipendiary court decisions.

3. For Hanley I also drew on a briefer run of the *Potteries Examiner* for 1871–75.

4. Burton 1999a; Clark 1995; McClelland 1991, 1996; Rose 1992, 1993; Tosh 1994, 2005.

5. Clark 1995, chap. 5; D'Cruze 1999; Emsley 2010, chap. 4; Wiener 2004.

6. The issue of youth raises another compounding factor. Apprenticed labor is policed in all three of these industries through master and servant law. It might have been the case that youth were not subjected to gender strictures in the same ways as adults.

CHAPTER FOUR

1. An earlier version of this chapter was published as "Capitalist Development, the Labor Process and the Law: The Case of the Victorian English Pottery Industry," *American Journal of Sociology* 109, no. 2 (2003): 445–95

2. *Penny Magazine* 12, no. 716 (1843): 201.

3. Dupree 1995, 52; Moyes 1979, 43, *Penny Magazine* 12, no. 716 (1843): 204.

4. Dupree 1995, 52; Moyes 1979, 42, 46; McCarthy 1885b, 301; McCarthy 1886a, 15; Whipp 1990, 22; BPP 1863 XVIII [3170] 1, p. 1; *Staffordshire Advertiser*, Nov. 11, 1871, 5.

5. Botham 1982, 302–3; Lamb 1977, 55; BPP 1863 XVIII [343], xl.

6. McKendrick 1961; Pollard 1965, 177–78, 184, 261; Wedgwood and Ormsbee 1947.

7. Supervision of female labor was quite different. As producers, women and girls were employed largely in the finishing portions of production. Many women were used in turning (a preparatory process of smoothing the rough ware prior to dipping and firing) and in the printing, painting, and burnishing departments as well as the warehouse. In printing women and girls were confined to transferring, while the painting department (a skilled occupation) was a female realm. Employers hired women finishers, paintresses, and warehouse workers directly. Paintresses were supervised by a senior female of the department and were in shops of between 10 and 30 workers (Dupree 1995, 149–50). Women were occasionally used in other departments, but faced fierce resistance among male potters who took their workshops as a masculine preserve (see, e.g., Staffordshire County Archives—SCA/PA/Hob/70/H.P.U.R.B, June 4, 1866).

8. Whipp 1990, 55; Dupree 1995, 149–50; McCarthy 1885b, 299; Moyes 1979, 45.

9. Dupree 1995, 149; Evans 1846, 26–30; Hall 1986, 14–16; McCarthy 1885a, 163–66; BPP 1863 XVIII [3710], 2–3, 14. Hall notes that about half of the women working in the pottery industry in 1871 were under twenty and that data from the turn of the century suggest that in many districts about one-third were married (1986, 22, 26).

10. Dupree 1995, 153, 157–59, 166; Whipp 1990, 73–75; BPP 1863 XVIII [3170], 20.

11. BPP 1865 XX [3473] 429, 10.

12. Celoria 1973, 15; Lamb 1977, 56; Moyes 1979, 48; Whipp 1987, 226; BPP 1863 XVIII [3170], 2.

13. Shaw 1977 [1903], 185; BPP 1865 XX [3473], 10.

14. BPP 1834 XX [450], 61, 71; BPP 1863 XVIII [3170], p. 4; see also Shaw 1970 [1903], 185–90; Warburton 1931, 40–41.

15. Botham 1982, 281–83, 290–95; Burchill and Ross 1977, 121; *Staffordshire Advertiser*, Dec. 16, 1871, Aug. 8 and 24, 1872; *Potteries Examiner*, Nov. 2 and 9, 1872.

16. Chamber of Commerce n.d., 12; Burchill and Ross 1977, 126; Warburton 1931, 143–44; Wedgwood and Ormsbee 1947, 93; BPP1856 XII [343], 206, 216; *Staffordshire Advertiser*, Jan. 1, Feb. 13, March 6, April 17, and July 10 and 24, 1869; July 13, Aug. 31, and Oct. 5 and 19, 1872; *Potteries Examiner*, Nov. 18, 1871; June 9, and Oct. 5, 19, and 26, 1872; Jan. 25 and March 1, 1873; Hollow-ware Pressers Union Record Book, Jan. 1, May 28, and July 16, 1866; Aug. 8 and 30, 1868; March 1, 1869, PA/Hob/70, Stoke-on-Trent City Archives.

17. Chamber of Commerce n.d., 8; Boyle 1838, 39–40; Warburton 1931, 56–60, 64–68, 82–84.

18. The Chamber claimed that the union asked for the insertion of a clause in the bond affirming that workers engaged in work "to the best of their ability," mandating the distribution of "good work" evenly among them regardless of skill and essentially usurping employers' control in the workplace (n.d., 14).

19. The Chamber also noted that any disputes over whether a worker was doing adequate ("a fair and reasonable quantity") work under the bond could be taken before the magistrates. According to Owen, "the workmen were not distinguished by their faith in the decisions of the magistracy in disputes between 'master and servant' . . . and pointed out, reasonably and truly enough, that the employers were maintaining a system which, even if it admitted the remedy suggested, 'would make an appeal to the law a daily necessity" (1970, 33).

20. *Potteries Examiner and Workman's Advocate* 1, no. 4 (Dec. 23, 1843): 29. It appears that Rose made such pronouncements to make working people fear the power of the law. In the small town of Lane End in his circuit it is claimed that he asserted that he would "make people so dread breaking the law that I shall be able to hang my watch in Market Square overnight and go the next morning to find it there" (Stuart 1985, 185).

21. *Potteries Examiner and Workman's Advocate* 1, no. 4 (Dec. 23, 1843): 29.

22. Owen 1970, 198; BPP 1863 XVIII [3170] 1, 14.

23. Hiring Books 1853–70, E46-29245/1-84, J. C. Wedgwood Papers, Special Collections and Archives, Keele University. The hiring books remaining from these years are few, so it is possible that printed agreements were used even earlier. The standard agreement for 1853–70 emphasizes that each worker is consenting separately to the contractual arrangement, possibly to negate any legal authority of union representation. It provides that workers can leave service for insufficient work if they have not been given at least sixteen hours/week for four successive weeks and at that time give a month's notice. It also mandates an arbitration process for disputes over piece rates or wages (though not for issues of workplace organization or control). Workers must give written notice within fourteen days of the dispute, and within seven days after the notice provide three representatives to a six-person board, who selects an umpire and a time and place for the hearing. If representatives

are not provided, the board is to proceed with its adjudications, and all decisions are final (ibid.) This was a system that the Chamber of Commerce decided would be part of all hiring agreements starting in 1852 (Warburton 1931, 145). There is a little evidence in the few agreement books that remain that specific verbal agreements were made concerning each worker's responsibilities. Agreement books for biscuit-oven men (the men who worked the large kilns in which pottery was fired) provide detailed counts for the firing of different types of ware, divide the men into sets, and establish the weekly schedule for firings and the responsibilities of each senior and junior member of the set (E-46–29222: Agreements, Biscuit Oven Men, Wedgwood Papers).

24. BPP 1866 XIII [449] 1, 60.

25. Botham 1982, 380; *Bee-Hive*, Oct. 8, 1864, 4; *Staffordshire Advertiser*, Nov. 11, 1866, 4–5; Nov. 14, 1868, 4.

26. BPP 1863 XVIII [3170] 1, 13–15, 322

27. Dupree 1995, 230; *Staffordshire Advertiser*, Nov. 16, 1867, 4; Nov. 20, 1869, 4; Nov. 18, 1871, 5; Nov. 15, 1873, 5; Nov. 19, 1875, 5.

28. *Staffordshire Advertiser*, March 5, 1864, 6; Feb. 22, 1865, 4; Oct. 12, 1865, 5; Jan. 11, 1868, 5; Feb. 1, 1868, 5; April 18, 1868, 5 ; Jan. 20, 1872; 5, May 18, 1872, 5.

29. It seems that not all of the branches in all of the towns relied equally on the law. A manufacturer in Longton noted that given his specialty and the local labor market, "we cannot enforce the law over them, for if we sent one to prison, we could not get another man who would take his place" (BPP 1863 XVIII [3170], 19).

30. The borough corporation was composed of twenty-three councilors, six alderman elected from that group, and a mayor selected from their ranks. Between 1860 and 1875 virtually all of the mayors were pottery factory owners (Crapper 1882, 33, 36; Greenslade 1963, 158). Separate boards of health, education, and highways were similarly populated (*Staffordshire Advertiser*, July 2, 1870, 4; Warrilow 1960, 401).

31. Halfpenny 1984, 190; Stuart 1985, 62; *Staffordshire Advertiser*, April 4, 1867; Jan. 29, 1870; and Aug. 26, 1871.

32. *Staffordshire Advertiser*, July 19, 1873, p. 6; Feb. 1, 1868, 5, Nov. 19, 1870, 6, July 19, 1873, 5; Stuart 1985, 53.

33. *Staffordshire Advertiser*, Jan. 2, 1869, 4; April 4, 1869, 4; April 23, 1870, 4; Dec. 3, 1870, 5–6; Jan. 1, 1872, 5; Sept. 28, 1872, 5; Burchill and Ross 1977, 118; Dupree 1995, 219, 223; Warburton 1931, 145; SCA/SA/CC/1, North Staffordshire Chamber of Commerce, Minute Book, April 1874–1897, April 20 and Oct. 20, 1874.

34. *Staffordshire Advertiser*, June 4, 1870, 4; Aug. 3, 1870, 7.

35. BPP 1866 XIII [449] 1, 130–31. Davis continued to advance this argument in a treatise that he wrote after the revision of the law in 1867 and even after its reform in 1875 under which breaches were made a civil offense (1868, 1875). He also maintained that some of what workers considered the most odious features of the acts be reformed, by allowing the worker to testify, allowing for the possibilities of sureties and fines besides imprisonment, and restricting petty sessions to the adjudication of written contracts, leaving parol agreements to the county courts as a civil matter (BPP 1866 XIII [449] 1, 131–32). As noted in a previous chapter, he also stated in a hearing that in his experience "the employers care little about the money, about getting actual compensation, and that they wanted labour" (BPP 1874 XXIV [391] 1, 139, 141).

36. Warrilow 1960, 401: *Staffordshire Advertiser*, March 16, 1867, 4; Oct. 28, 1871, 4; Oct. 12, 1872, 5.

37. *Staffordshire Advertiser*, July 27, Oct. 26, 1867; Feb. 5, 1870, 2; Feb. 4, 1871, 4; May 18, 1872, 5; *Potteries Examiner*, June 1, 1872, 5.

38. BPP 1866 XIII [449] 1, 60.

39. *Staffordshire Advertiser*, Jan. 2, 1875, 5. My thanks to Thalia Padia and Ron McDonald for this translation.

40. The aggregate annual data for Hanley in the parliamentary reports only started to appear in 1871. I do not know the reason why.

41. The minute books are not quite a continuous run for the period. They cover June 1864–March 1866 and May 1868–December 1875 (Court Registers, D26/1/1–8, Borough of Hanley, Staffordshire Record Office [hereafter SRO]).

42. Reporting only starts in 1871, though the borough maintained a magistrates' court for more than a decade before, as I noted.

43. The *Examiner* was published from 1864, but is only available at the British Library Newspaper Library from March 1871.

44. Only prosecutions for which some action is known are included in these counts.

45. Borough of Hanley, Draft Minute Book, D26/1/1, July 7, 1864, SRO; *Staffordshire Advertiser*, Sept. 16, 1871, 7; *Potteries Examiner*, Feb. 2, 1872, 5.

46. *Staffordshire Advertiser*, Nov. 17, 1866, 5; Nov. 16, 1872, 5; Nov. 15, 1873, 5.

47. While 88 percent of pottery workers had listed occupations, this was true for only 68 percent of all other trades.

48. One exception to this generalization is recorded in 1872, when an entire shop of decorators was prosecuted by the firm of Messrs. Davis and Son for a stoppage to demand higher piece rates. Also exceptionally, eleven of the twelve workers were female. The case was resolved when their solicitor persuaded them to return to work to avoid large damage payments and possibly worse (*Potteries Examiner*, Feb. 3, 1872, 5).

49. D/26/1/4, Nov. 9, 1872, SRO.

50. D/26/1/5, Oct. 21, 1873, SRO.

51. D/26/1/7, Sept. 6, 1975, SRO.

52. As noted above, workers could lodge claims for wages in amounts up to £10 in petty sessions, and suits of any size could be pursued before the separate county courts. A few county court cases are recorded by the newspapers, though none of them were successful. The stipendiary magistrate for the Worcester and South Staffordshire county court circuit, Isaac Spooner, was nicknamed "Cruel Isaac" by local workers, suggesting that his court would not have been the preferred venue for such cases (*Staffordshire Advertiser*, Nov. 13, 1869, 7; April 16, 1870, 7; March 4, 1871, 7; Oct. 26, 1872, 6; May 10, 1873, 5; Woods 1979, 101).

53. Hollow-ware Pressers Union Record Book, PA/Hob/70, Stoke-on-Trent City Archives.

54. Statistics on the number of prosecutions under the 1875 act were not published in 1876 and 1877. From thereon they were again published with the annual criminal reports though this was technically incorrect since they were civil prosecutions (Steinmetz 2000b, 283).

55. BPP 1893–94 XXXIX [7603-I], pt. 1, 7, 414; Whipp 1990, 135–38.

56. Burchill and Ross 1977, 154; Whipp 1990, 135–37, 140–42; BPP 1893–94 XXXIX [7603-I] pt. 1, 7, 398–99.

57. The secretary of the hollowware pressers' union, for example, testified in the early 1890s that in his first fourteen months in office he had personally been involved in 130 deputations regarding disputes (BPP 1893–94 XXXIX [7603-I], pt. 1, 7, 404).

58. Lamb notes, however, that the promise of such machinery in the production of ware was greater than its performance (1977, 57).

59. As assistant commissioner for the Children's Employment Commission, Francis Longe, noted in the early 1860s, "In some manufactories in Glasgow and Newcastle, steam power is used to a much greater extent than in any of the manufactories in Staffordshire." An important Hanley manufacturer reported to Longe that "the north competes successfully with us through the machinery they use" (BPP 1863 XVIII [3170], 8, 13; see also 31 and 33 for reports by Glasgow manufacturers).

60. Bremner 1869, 395–97; Burchill and Ross 1977, 154; Celoria 1973, 35–40, 45; Lamb 1977, 57, 60; BPP 1893–94 XXXIX [7063-I], pt. 1, 7, 401; BPP 1893–94, XXXVII [6984-XXIII], pt. 1, 545, 61.

CHAPTER FIVE

1. An earlier version of this chapter was published as "Unfree Labor, Apprenticeship and the Rise of the Victorian Hull Fishing Industry: An Example of the Importance of Law and the Local State in British Economic Change," *International Review of Social History* 51, no. 2 (2006): 243–76.

2. Bellamy 1971, 39–46; Brown and McLaren 1969, 227; Sheahan 1864, 284–85, 585–86; Starkey 1996, 74.

3. Gender differentiation by occupation was considerable. Half of all women concentrated in domestic service and another third involved in the textile or dress trades (Bellamy 1952, 39–40).

4. Ibid., 39; Bellamy 1971, 31–34; Brown 1972, 8–9; Sheahan 1864, 284, 582, 586, 589–91, 596; Starkey 1996, 73–75; *Trade and Commerce* (1878), 11, 17, 113–17; *Beehive*, March 9, 1872, 10–11.

5. Lorenz 1984; McClelland and Reid 1985; Pollard and Robertson 1979; Reid 2010.

6. *Hull and Easter Counties Herald*, Feb. 15, Dec. 13, 1866, Jan. 17, 1867. In the beginning of 1867 a Trades' Council was formed comprising seven unions and about 650 members and a month later boasted an additional ten unions as members. By this period many of the larger trade groups had formed unions, including the seed crushers, coopers, tailors, typographers, and various building trades. Brown suggests that the council was largely ineffectual until the 1880s (Brown 1972, 20; *Beehive*, Jan. 7 and 14, Sept. 16, and Oct. 7, 1865; March 30, 1872; *Hull and Easter Counties Herald*, Sept. 7, 1865; Dec. 13, 1866; Jan. 17 and Feb. 24, 1867).

7. Starkey 1996, 84; *Trade and Commerce* (1878), 126–30.

8. *Hull and Easter Counties Herald*, Feb. 2, 1866; Sept. 19, 1867; June 4, 1868.

9. Brown 1972, 20; *Hull and Easter Counties Herald*, May 7 and 14, and Aug. 20, 1874; *Beehive*, April 25, May 9, 16, and 23, June 13, July 18, and Aug. 22, 1874. In response to the joiners strike, Earle's appears to have outsourced some of the work.

10. In 1871 the major shipbuilding firm Humphry and Pearson used master and servant law to force a group of platers back to work on the claim of insufficient notice (*Hull and Easter Counties Herald*, Jan. 26 and Feb. 9, 1871). The following year the largest shipping firm, Messrs. Wilson and Sons, prosecuted several replacement dockers for pulling out of their agreements (April 4 and 25, 1872). The most active prosecutor during disputes appears to have been the major shipbuilders Messrs. Earle, which used a combination of prosecutions for nonperformance and intimidation in responding to several strikes during the period (May 5, 1864; Oct. 3, 1867; June 4 and 11, 1868; May 5, 1874).

11. Shipping magnates did run for and occupy parliamentary seats. In fact, a Tory populist and solicitor and steamship owner was instrumental in convincing the Conservative government in 1875 to pursue the final signal reforms of master and servant law in 1875 (Curthoys 2004, 222–23).

12. *Hull and Easter Counties Herald*, June 8, 1871, 6. Exactly who should be appointed as borough magistrates was a subject of periodic squabbling (July 7 and 26, 1866; June 8 and 22, 1871).

13. On several occasions over this period there were rancorous debates about increasing the salary of the stipendiary and his clerk that divided the borough council (*Hull and Easter Counties Herald*, March 9, 1865; July 26, 1866; June 5, 1873).

14. *Hull and Easter Counties Herald*, April 25, 1872. Travis was probably echoing the opinions of many of the town's capitalists, who in a variety of industries seem to have been hostile to unions and who often succeeded in defeating strikes. They were also antagonistic to state regulation of labor. C. N. Norwood was a Liberal M.P. for the borough and his family's firm was one of the major shipping lines. In responding to an article concerning the abuses to merchant seaman he remarked, "Over-legislation has done much to destroy the individuality and self-reliance of the sailor. He is now, Mr. Norwood remarked, coddled and fenced round with so-called safeguards and protection, as if he were a big baby, unable to comprehend or protect his own interests, the result being that he took no trouble to make needful inquiries" (Feb. 2, 1875).

15. Case data extracted from Kingston-upon-Hull City Archives, Magistrates' Court Minute Books, DPM/1/76–83, 85–91, 93–4 96–102, 1864–1875.

16. Katrina Honeyman (2007) demonstrates that for the early decades of the Industrial Revolution pauper apprenticeships were vital not only for textile factory labor, but also for smaller more established forms of manufacturing.

17. Dunlop 1912; Lane 1996; Hopkins 1994; Pinchbeck and Hewitt 1969; Rose 1989; Snell 1996; Tuttle 1989.

18. Public Record Office (PRO) MH/32/99, Baldwin Fleming, Correspondence and Papers Related to the North Midland District, "Treatment of Pauper Apprentices in the Grimsby Fishing Trade," June 19, 1873, fol. 45; Ansell 1883, 7; Boswell 1973, 15; Holdsworth 1874, 25, 69, 257; Robinson 1987, 47–48; Robinson 1996, 67; BPP 1866 XVIII [3596-I], 156, 163; *Hull and Easter Counties Herald*, Aug. 7 and Nov. 13, 1873.

19. The vast majority of these were before 1870 though (*Hull and Easter Counties Herald*, Jan. 1, March 24, April 7, May 26, and June 6, 1864; Feb. 22 and Oct. 18, 1865; April 18, June 27, Aug. 15, and Nov. 14 and 28, 1867; Jan. 1, Feb. 11, June 10, Oct. 12, and Nov. 11 and 15, 1869; May 5, 1874).

20. Data come from Kingston-upon-Hull City Archives, Registry of Ships DPC/1/15,

1858–1861, Port Number: 18/58 to 8/61; DPC/1/16, 1861–1864, Port Number: 9/61 to15–64; DPC/1/17, 1864–1867, Port Number: 16/64 to 15/67; DPC/1/18, 1867–1871, Port Number: 9/67 to 64/71; DPC/1/19. 1871–1873, Port No. 65/71 to 60/73; DPC/1/20, 1873–1876, Port No. 61/73 to 43/76.

21. Joyce Bellamy has noted that the industry was largely detached from the other commercial sectors in the town (1971, 56).

22. BPP 1866 XVIII [3596-I], 156, 160.

23. *Hull and Easter Counties Herald*, Nov. 11, 1869. To place this amount in perspective, the largest shipping firm, Thomas Wilson and Sons, had a capital of about £99,000 (Bellamy 1963, 30).

24. Markchow also observed that large capitalists did not invest in the trade, affirming its petty bourgeois foundations (BPP 1866 XVIII [3596-I], 160; BPP 1878–79 XVII [2449], 112; BPP 1882 XVII [3432], 60).

25. During fleet voyages, which could encompass as many as seventy boats and lasting perhaps eight weeks, smacks would regularly offload boxes of their iced catch to cutters that would speed the fish to a principal port for sale. Boxes were placed in small boats manned by a couple of hands who navigated them to the waiting cutters. Fisherman objected to the system, particularly during the winter, because of the precariousness of negotiating the sea (PRO MH/32/99, Fleming, fol. 8, 51; Ansell 1883, 19–20, 22; Boswell 1973, 10, 93, 96; Holdsworth 1874, 257–61; Horn 1996, 176; Levi 1883, 26; Robinson 1996, 71; Rule 1976, 384–87).

26. During the period under study the local paper reported a number of apprentice deaths, though probably not nearly all of them, *Hull and Easter Counties Herald*, April 20, 1870; April 20, 1871; Dec. 19, 1872; April 24, July 7, Sept. 11, and Dec. 25, 1873; May 7, Oct. 29, and Dec. 3, 1874.

27. While the system was started with the inception of the trade in the 1840s, it became common after it was used to break strikes of fishermen's unions in 1852 and 1856 (Robinson 1996, 75).

28. Rule 1976, 391, 405; Ansell 1883, 19; Holdsworth 1874, 258; *Trade and Commerce* (1878), 134; BPP 1882 XVII [3432], 28.

29. PRO MH/32/99, Fleming, fol. 10, 15–17, 20; Boswell 1973, 27; Chance 1985, 281; Rule 1976, 386.

30. PRO MH/32/99, Fleming, fol. 23; BPP 1882 XVII [3432], 2–4; Boswell 1973, 49–50, 58, 76; Robinson 1996, 55–56.

31. Horn 1996, 177–80; Robinson 1996, 58. This assumption of property in the apprentice was reflected in the questioning of Henry Toozes, mayor of Hull and a smack owner, before the 1882 parliamentary committee, when he was asked, "No man should *own* an apprentice who does not own a smack or part of one?" (emphasis added) (BPP 1882 XVII [3432], 86).

32. Likewise David Boswell, a historian of the trade for nearby Grimsby, has termed these apprenticeships "as much a peculiar institution . . . as was slavery in the United States" (1973, 5).

33. Boswell 1973, 67, 96, 104, 107, 117; Horn 1996, 184–86; Rule 1976, 395–97, 403. One major smack owner, Alfred Ansell, appearing before the magistrates during an absconding case, noted that many fisherlads preferred jail time particularly "in the winter,

when the weather is rough, rather than at sea" (*Hull and Easter Counties Herald*, Dec. 15, 1864).

34. PRO MH/32/99, Fleming, fol. 26–27; see also BPP. 1882 XIV [3432], 18.

35. In late 1864 and early 1865 the skipper and smack owner Thomas Hamlyn and his second hand, John Anderson, were brought before the bench on a charge for the death of an apprentice named Kisner. However, at the time the court deemed there was insufficient evidence. It is unlikely that Hamlyn was convicted of this charge, since court records show him as a prosecutor of fisherlads in 1866 and in intermittent years throughout the period (*Hull and Easter Counties Herald*, Dec. 22, 1864; Jan. 5 and 12, 1865).

36. Boswell 1973, 109; Rule 1976, 398; *Hull and Easter Counties Herald*, June 27 and Dec. 12, 1867; Jan. 30, 1868; Dec. 16, 1869; Sept. 8, 1872; Feb. 13, 1873; July 16 and Aug. 20, 1874; Feb. 25 and Nov. 11, 1875; Kingston-upon-Hull City Archives, Magistrates' Court Minute Books DPM/1/89, Feb. 16, 1871, DPM/1/93, Sept. 2, 1872.

37. BPP 1882 XVII [3432], 57.

38. *Hull and Easter Counties Herald*, Nov. 6, 1873. One, Henry Toozes, in partnership with Richard Vivian, had one of the largest smack fleets. He was a leading member of the South Myton Reform Association and one-time president, an officer of the Humber Masonic lodge, and would later become mayor. Alfred Ansell was one of the largest fleet owners, also a member of the Reform Association, and also a Worship Master of the Masonic lodge (*Trade and Commerce* [1878]; *Hull and Easter Counties Herald*, Feb. 2, 1869; Dec. 3, 1875).

39. *Trade and Commerce* (1878), 132. Despite their readiness to prosecute, smack owners were frustrated with the legal machinery to do so. As noted in chapter 2, under the Act of 1823 a warrant could be issued directly upon receiving a complaint from a master. However the 1867 act required that a summons had to be issued first for a servant believed to have left work without permission. If the summons could not be delivered, a warrant could then be obtained. Smack owners, through the Hull Guardian Society, a prominent commercial association, complained that they were required to take out summonses for absconding apprentices, knowing full well that they were fleeing and that the possibility of having a policemen arrest them in the process was diminished since they had to return to court for a warrant (*Hull and Easter Counties Herald*, Oct. 2 and Nov. 13, 1873).

40. In 1869 the borough opened a new jail with a capacity of holding 400 prisoners, which might have facilitated this strategy (Kelly 1872, 388).

41. *Hull and Easter Counties Herald*, March 3 and April 15, 1869; Feb. 3, 1870; April 13, 1871; April 18, 1872; April 24, 1873; April 9, 1874; and April 8, 1875.

42. Fleming claimed that "a considerable proportion of the fishing apprentices contract venereal disease and it was stated to me that lads purposely committed offenses when so diseased in order that they might receive medical attendance in Lincoln County Prison" (PRO MH/32/99, Fleming, fol. 42).

43. PRO MH/32/99, Fleming, "Treatment of Pauper Apprentices," fol. 40–1; see also Boswell 1973, 79–83; Horn 1996; Robinson 1987; BPP 1882 XVII [3432], 64. My thanks to Martin Wilcox for clarifying the legal bases of prosecution in Hull and Grimsby.

44. J. W. Beeton was a basketmaker who had repeated run-ins with several of his apprentices in the first half of the period.

45. PRO MH/32/99, Fleming, fol. 46.

46. Ansell 1883, 23; BPP 1882 XVII [3432], 41.

47. BPP 1882 XVII [3432], xii, 64.

48. An 1894 parliamentary report noted that one-third of all Grimsby apprentices absconded in the years 1881–93 (Chance 1985, 279).

49. For further details of the parliamentary investigation see BPP 1882 XVII [3432], "Report of a Committee . . . To inquire into . . . the relations between the Owners, Masters and Crews of Fishing Vessel." Horn notes that between 1880 and 1909, 5,176 boys signed indentures for Grimsby masters, about half of whom came from about 170 poor law unions, though the numbers were declining in the 1890s. As many as one-quarter of these fisherlads were imprisoned during this period and the 1883 revision of the Merchant Shipping Act actually provided greater powers for the local marine superintendent to issue warrants for absconding apprentices (1996, 177, 184, 187).

CHAPTER SIX

1. Gaut 1939, 310; Land 1986, 40, 73; Richardson 1986, 66, 78; Rollins 1984, 65, 70; *Redditch Indicator*, July 5, 1862.

2. Caunce 1997; Gritt 2002; Howkins and Verdon 2008; Moses 1999.

3. In his classic study of rural contention J. P. D. Dunbabin remarks that "in purely economic terms there may be some justification for describing the 'labourers in husbandry' as the only real Marxian proletariat England ever had. But in practice they often thought in terms of localities" (1974, 248).

4. Caunce 1997, 53; Howkins and Verdon 2008, 475, 481; Newby 1987, 120.

5. Caunce 1997, 50–52, 59; Dunbabin 1974, 235; Newby 1977, 45, 48; 1987, 81.

6. Gaut 1939, 318, 321; Snell 1985, 91–93; Stephenson 1861, 799; PP 1868–69 XIII [4202], App. Ai, p. 260; *Redditch Indicator*, Oct. 15, 1870, Sept. 5, 1874.

7. A reformer who sought to replace the statute fairs with hiring registries claimed that the fairs were only held in the county on Michaelmas (September 29), which had been traditional throughout the country, but local court records and newspaper accounts give a range of dates for fairs in the region (Stephenson 1861, 799). John Maynard claims that by the 1830s both customary rituals and pastimes and paternalism at the fairs were already waning (2005, 266).

8. *Farmers' Magazine*, n.s., 29 (1866): 517.

9. Armstrong 1988, 91; Caunce 1997, 52; Dunbabin 1974, 241; Miller 1992, 199; Newby 1977, 120.

10. Horn 1976, 63–65, 71–73; Howkins 1985, 19–20; 1990, 118; Kebbel 1893, 162–65; Miller 1992, 200; Snell 1985, 82.

11. See also Armstrong 1988, 91; Dunbabin 1974, 67; Horn 1984, 90.

12. Cadle 1867, 462; Dodd 1979, 18–19, 24; Gaut 1930, 336; Noake 1868, 27, 207; Walton 2000, 393, 396; Willis-Bund 1906, 310–11; Yelling 1973, 23, 31–32; BPP 1856 XXVIII [2088] 1, 64–65; BPP 1896 C [7400], 4:424. On a couple of occasions the *Indicator* made mention of the introduction of reaping machine and a steam-driven threshing machine on area farms, noting that they were not generally used (*Redditch Indicator*, Aug. 19, 1866, and March 21, 1868).

13. Cadle 1867, 462; Gaut 1930, 307, 311–13, 356; BPP 1896 C [7400], 4:424; BPP 1919 [Cmd. 25], 2:371; PRO Census 1871, England, RG 10/3075–6.

14. Cadle 1867, 463; *Farmer's Magazine* (1869), 317; Gaut 1930, 357; Purdy 1861, 335–36; BPP 1868–69 XIII [4202], App. 1, 57; App. Ai, 260–65; App. Di, 299–300.

15. Gaut 1930, 356; *Redditch Indicator*, March 9 and 16, and April 27, 1872.

16. In his study of the change and dislocation of agricultural labor in Worcestershire from 1790–1841, John Maynard notes that "there was a noticeable increase post-1830 in the number of cases of disobedient servants coming before the courts and labourers taking farmers to court for non-payment of wages" (2005, 245). Maynard makes this assertion based on readings of newspaper reports during this decade. It is not clear whether this marked a permanent and important shift in recourse to the courts. According to Maynard enclosure of farmland largely had been accomplished by the period and the advent of the New Poor Law sharply reduced relief in rural parishes, accelerating the debasement of farm labor.

17. *Penny Magazine*, suppl., 12 (1843): 33; Dickens 1852, 543.

18. Burritt 1868, 342; Jones 1980, 173; Land 1986, 35, 40; Morrall 1866, 18, 28–32, 36; *Redditch Indicator*, Aug. 26 and Sept. 23, 1865; Jan. 1, March 17, and Oct. 6, 1866; March 7, 1868; March 5, July 2, and Sept. 10, 1866; PRO Census 1871, England, RG 10/3075.

19. Burritt 1868, 342; Curzon 1883, 75; Noake 1868, 305. About 30 percent of the total (30 million per week) was shipped to the United States, while remaining exports found their way to France, Germany, Russia, Australia, and New Zealand. The sizable US market might explain why a relatively small town had a US consul office.

20. Noake 1868, 306; see also Land 1986, 41; Morrall 1866, 22; Richardson 1986, 66. A number of the larger manufacturers opened new factories during the period (*Redditch Indicator*, Nov. 10, 1866).

21. Curzon 1883, 74; Dickens 1852, 543; Morrall 1866, 34; *Penny Magazine*, suppl., 12 (1843): 35. Cutters processed about 100,000 pieces per day (Curzon 1883, 74).

22. The steel and grindstone dust created in the process, even with the advent of safeguards in the 1840s, produced lung disease, and many pointers were said to live no longer than about thirty-five (Morrall 1866, 26).

23. Morrall 1866, 16; *Penny Magazine*, suppl., 12 (1843): 36.

24. Curzon 1883, 74; Dickens 1852, 544; Morrall 1866, 35; *Penny Magazine*, suppl. 12 (1843): 37–38.

25. Morrall 1866, 25; *Penny Magazine*, suppl., 12 (1843): 39.

26. Dickens referred to a sett as a "disgusting black 'roly-poly' dumpling" (1852, 544).

27. Some of the larger factories used steam power to operate their scouring machines, but most operations relied on water power from the Arrow River (Morrall 1866, 19).

28. Curzon 1883, 75; Land 1986, 36; Rollins 1981, 19–20; *Penny Magazine*, suppl., 12 (1843): 39–40.

29. Bartleet and Woodward 1967 [1866], 199–200; Curzon 1883, 75; Morrall 1866, 20–21, 35; Rollins 1981, 19–20; *Penny Magazine*, suppl., 12 (1843): 40–41.

30. The pointers were out for almost a year resisting the extractor fans installed for their health and safety, believing that a reduction in danger would mean a diminution in their wages.

31. Personal communication with S. R. H. Jones, June 29, 2012.

32. The largest factory owner, Henry Milward, was a devote Anglican and stopped work at the factory each morning for compulsory prayers. Victor Milward observed, "We pride ourselves that our men get through as much work, and consequently, work more steadily than any other set in town; . . . We have not a 'Monday Man' on our premises; nay, more, there is not a man who does not come to work on Monday with as great regularity as any other day in the week" (*Redditch Indicator*, May 28, 1865, and May 18, 1872; Richardson 1986, 66).

33. Morrall 1866, 21–22; *Redditch Indicator*, May 6, 13, 20, and 27, 1865; Jan. 27 and May 14, 1866; May 5, 1872. With a few provisions, the large manufacturers supported the extension of the acts so long as they were applied to all establishments in the production process. They strategically requested that under the extension "every place shall be deemed a factory where any person or persons are employed in any process connected with the manufacturing or preparation for sale of needles, fish-hooks, fishing tackle, or pins" in order to prevent smaller workshops from gaining any advantage (*Redditch Indicator*, April 14, 1866). As with other industries subject to these acts, it is likely that the large manufacturers believed that because of their scale such regulations worked to their comparative advantage.

34. In a town with a housing shortage due to its rapid expansion, larger manufacturers built and leased housing for their skilled male workers in order to retain them (Jones 1980, 186). According to Jones the labor shortage became more problematic after the end of the American Civil War and continued up to the depression starting in 1875 (personal communication, June 29, 2012).

35. Personal communication with S. R. H. Jones, June 29, 2012.

36. In late November of 1870 the 800-square-yard Redditch Steam Needle Mills, including the building replete with machinery and surrounding land, sold for £1,250, suggesting that the fixed capital costs were far more modest than a textile factory (*Redditch Indicator*, Dec. 3, 1870).

37. Personal communication with S. R. H. Jones, June 29, 2012.

38. *Redditch Indicator*, March 16, April 20, May 18, and June 22, 1872.

39. Littlebury 1873, 578; Noake 1868, 306; Richardson 1986, 66; *Redditch Indicator*, June 6 and 17, Aug., 26, Sept. 23, and Oct. 7, 1865; Jan. 20, Feb. 24, March 17, Oct. 6 and 13, and Dec. 22, 1866; Jan. 4, March 7, July 25, and Oct, 10, 1868; Aug. 7, 1869; March 5, June 18, July 2 and 30, and Sept. 24, 1870; Jan. 27, and May 18 and 25, 1872; Aug. 1, 1874.

40. Littlebury 1873, 577–81; *Redditch Indicator*, June 6, July 8, and Nov. 11, 1865; Jan. 6, 1866, Feb. 8 and March 28, 1868.

41. Redditch was not to be made a local government district until a decade later (Rollins 1984, 71).

42. Gray was eventually forced out of the seat over public outrage of his insistence on a harsh sentence for a little girl who had stolen a penny (*Redditch Indicator*, March 24 and May 5, 1866).

43. PRO, England, Census, RG 9/2234, 2235, RG 10/3053, 3075, 3076, 3212. Haywood had experience as magistrate and deputy lieutenant, and Doherty was also a registrar.

44. Figures for Birmingham and the county are derived from annual parliamentary reports previously cited above.

45. Figures calculated from the Worcestershire County Record Office (hereafter WCRO), Class 260.105, BA 5796/ I (i) (for 1862–65) and BA 5796/1(ii–iii) (for 1865–75), Petty Sessional Division of Redditch, Register of the Court of Petty Sessions, with additional information from the *Redditch Indicator*.

46. Alternatively, cases were coded as not decided in favor of employers not only when the magistrates ruled in favor of the defendant, but also when they were dismissed or withdrawn with no accompanying evidence that the magistrates were reflecting employers' wishes.

47. The final category, "Other," contains a variety of outcomes including withdrawn and dismissed cases in which the worker is specifically told to return to work under his or her employer's conditions, outstanding warrants, and adjourned cases during which a worker is under a probationary caution from the magistrates. There were a few cases which fell under multiple categories, such as a damage payment and the need for a surety. In these cases I coded the outcome in terms of severity of cost to the worker. For example, a damage payment was a direct out-of-pocket expense for the worker as opposed to finding someone who could arrange for a surety, and thus the case was coded under "Damage."

48. *Redditch Indicator*, Aug, 30, 1862; WRCO, BA 5796/1(i), Aug. 27, 1862.

49. *Redditch Indicator*, Jan. 1, 1870; WRCO, BA 5796/1(ii–iii), Dec. 29, 1869.

50. WRCO, BA 5796/1 (ii–iii), Feb. 3, 1875.

51. Contemporary commentaries bemoaned that drunkenness was a common malady among agricultural servants, who were often partially compensated with cider or beer. An assistant commissioner on the employment of women and children in agriculture remarked to the Worcestershire Chamber of Agriculture that payment with cider was "a great piece of extravagance, and said that supposing a man in a higher class of life receiving £600 a-year spent £100 on drink for himself, it would be though the most unpardonable extravagance; but these labourers did it every day of their lives" (*Farmers' Magazine*, 3rd ser., 36 [1869]: 317). See also "The Midland Farmers' Club: The Labour Question," *Farmers' Magazine*, n.s., 41 (1872): 422, "The Cider Question," *Farmers' Magazine*, n.s., 41 (1872): 14–15.

52. *Redditch Indicator*, June 9, 1866; WRCO, BA 5796/1 (ii–iii), June 6, 1866.

53. WRCO, BA 5796/1 (ii–iii), July 24, 1872.

54. The magistrates articulated this customary understanding in other cases as well. In a dispute between a needle manufacturer and his worker concerning wages and discharge, a magistrate noted that "it is well understood in the trade; a week's notice ere leaving" and he suggested that any other arrangement should be written in a manufacturer's record books (*Redditch Indicator*, July 30, 1870).

55. WRCO, BA 5796/1 (ii–iii), Jan. 15, 1873.

56. They often, however, had roughly the same rates of conviction.

57. *Redditch Indicator*, April 2, 1864; WRCO, BA 5796/1 (ii–iii), March 30, 1864.

58. *Redditch Indicator*, Oct. 29, 1870; WRCO, BA 5796/1 (ii–iii), Oct. 26, 1870.

59. *Redditch Indicator*, Feb. 24, 1872; WRCO, BA 5796/1 (ii–iii), Feb. 21, 1872.

60. WRCO, BA 5796/1 (ii–iii), May 8, 1872.

61. *Redditch Indicator*, Feb. 6, 1864; WRCO, BA 5796/1 (ii–iii), Feb. 3, 1864.

62. WRCO, BA 5796/1 (ii–iii), Jan. 1, Dec. 23, 1867, Jan, 22, March 13, 1868.

63. *Redditch Indicator*, Jan. 4, 11, and 18, 1868. One apprentice, John Parker, was prosecuted several times in a period of a year and a quarter and eventually was sentenced to

one month in prison being unable to pay court costs, though in this last instance he was released from his indentures. If "Humanity" was correct in his charges Monks was an ornery master, since the former accuses him of prosecuting his two stepsons a total of six times.

64. WRCO, BA 5796/1 (ii–iii), June 1, 1870, and Sept. 16, 1874; *Redditch Indicator*, June 4, 1870, and Sept. 19, 1874.

65. Cases involving dismissal are also significant because, given legal precedent, farmers could release servants from service without recourse to the court. In a famous case in 1817, Spain v. Arnott, the high court reversed earlier common law understanding by ruling that a farmer could terminate a servant without payment of wages for insubordination without judicial intervention. It is unclear whether the Redditch magistrates misunderstood the law or simply enacted a version that suited the reinforcement of their conception of hierarchy. In at least one case in late 1863 they incorrectly told a farmer that he had improperly dismissed a servant without court approval, but the specifics of the case are not entirely clear (*Redditch Indicator*, Dec. 24, 1863).

CHAPTER SEVEN

1. Beckert 2009; Block and Somers 2014; Dale 2010; Krippner 2001; Krippner and Alvarez 2007; Mjøset 1985; Olofsson 1999; North 1977.

2. Many scholars and critics invoke Polanyi's work both to analyze and critique processes of global capital and to explain the rise of global justice movements. See for a sampling Birchfield 1999; Burawoy 2003; Hann and Hart 2009; Kirby 2002; Munck 2007; and Silver and Arrighi 2003.

3. See also Block and Somers 2014 for a different discussion of contemporary relevance.

4. Barber 1995; Beckert 2009; Block and Somers 2014; Dale 2010; Gemici 2008; Krippner 2001; Krippner et al. 2004; Krippner and Alvarez 2007; Lie 1991.

5. Birchfield 1999; Block and Somers 2014; Cangiani 2003; Dale 2010; Jessop 2001.

6. Several scholars have noted parallels between Polanyi's concepts and Marx of commodity fetishism and alienation. Block and Somers suggest that the concept of fictitious commodities deepens Marx's critique (2014, 79). However, for Polanyi alienation occurs in the sphere of exchange, whereas for Marx it is in productive relations.

7. See Block and Somers (ibid.) for a systematized perspective on what they term "ideational embeddedness" and the change to the market society.

8. Block and Somers (ibid.) have demonstrated that Polanyi overestimated the significance of the Speenhamland system.

9. And as he noted elsewhere,

> Justice and law, which were embodied in the institutional structure of earlier societies, had worn thin under the market organization of society. A man's property, his revenue and income, the price of his wares were now "just" only if they were now formed in the market and as to law, no law really mattered except that which referred to property and contract. The varied propertied institutions of the past and the substantive laws that made up the constitution of the ideal *polis* had now no substance to work upon. (Polanyi 1977, 16)

10. And at a slightly earlier point in the analysis he notes that "the change from liberal to 'collectivist' solutions happened sometimes over night and without consciousness on the part of those engaged in the process of legislative remuneration" (Polanyi 1957a, 146).

11. Polanyi describes this in general terms as a kind of existential crisis,

> A social calamity is primarily a cultural not an economic phenomenon that can be measured by income figures or population statistics. . . . Not economic exploitation, as often assumed, but the disintegration of the cultural environment of the victim is then the cause of degradation. The economic process may, naturally, supply the vehicle of destruction, and almost invariably economic inferiority will make the weaker yield, but the immediate cause of his undoing is not for that reason economic; it lies in the lethal injury to the institutions in which his social existence in embodied. The result is a loss of self-respect and standards, whether the unit is a people or a class, whether the process springs from so-called "culture" conflict or from a change in the position of a class within the confines of society. (1957a, 157)

12. As Krippner asserts, whether Polanyi deployed the concept of the disembedded economy as an ideal type or as an empirical description, "Polanyi left no room for doubt that nineteenth-century Britain exemplified the disembedded end of the spectrum" (2001, 193).

13. Gareth Dale suggests that a significant part of *GT*'s history reflects the historical writing of Henri Pirenne. He also notes that the Fabian socialist historians R. H. Tawney and G. D. H. Cole voiced objections to Polanyi's technological determinism and his analysis of Speenhamland among other aspects of the narrative (2010, 50, 81–85). Ellen Meiksins Wood similarly argues, "The main outlines of Polanyi's historical narrative, then, are in some respects not entirely different from the old commercialization model: the expansion of markets goes hand in hand with technological progress to produce modern industrial capitalism" (2002, 25).

14. As Mitchell Bernard comments, "Precisely because agency is ascribed to an autonomously evolving technology . . . change cannot be understood in terms of the social forces deploying technological innovation and the power relations, institutions and ideologies that shape the context in which they emerge" (1997, 81–82). See also Birchfield 1999, 38; Hechter 1981, 423; and Wood 2002, 23.

15. As Halperin observes, "Particularly problematic are his treatment of society as an organic and sociologically undifferentiated whole, and his conception of the state as a neutral mechanism for aggregating interests" (2004, 291). See also Dale 2010, 79; Hechter 1981, 420; and Krippner and Alvarez 2007, 232

16. As Randles summarizes the problem,

> *There does not appear to be, within* Polanyi's framework an explicit mechanism for institutional change, since competitive struggle and innovation do not (paradoxically given our interest both in Polanyi, and in the study of innovation and competition) feature in the Polanyian frame at all. What we might need to add, using Polanyi as an essential start point, is a mechanism for subsequent tensions and struggles which potentially or in actuality produce a *re-instituting* of whatever arena of substantive study we are interested in. Further, our *developed* analysis would need to explicitly

provide for this re-instituting to occur at a *range of temporal-spatial scales*, more than likely bringing groups of vested interest into competitive confrontation with each other (or alternatively mutual accommodation of each other. (2003, 423)

17. Birchfield echoes these same concerns when she concludes, "Though Polanyi laboured to reveal the deliberately political nature of economic organization, his main concern was to present the economy as a necessarily embedded social structure, not to articulate a political theory or fully specify the role of agency" (1999, 38). Likewise Dale suggests that Polanyi had a "tendency to leave power relations unspecified" (2010, 79) and Beverly Silver observes that "the concept of 'power' is largely missing from Polanyi" (Silver 2003, 18). See also Bernard 1997, 80, 82, and Halperin 2004, 264, 272.

18. Polanyi's neglect in this regard might stem from the theoretical foundations on which Polanyi drew in developing his concept of fictitious commodities. Dale suggests that this was predicated on Toënnies' perspective in which labor was treated as an empirical entity rather than as a social relationship in Marx. "By reducing commodities to things, Polanyi's concept contributes to the sort of reified understanding of social reality of which he is otherwise so critical" (2010, 77).

19. As Dale notes, in his essay "Aristotle Discovers the Economy," Polanyi recognizes the lineage of his concept of the disembedded economy in Maine's division, as well as in the work of Hegel, Marx, and Toënnies (2010, 93).

20. My analysis departs from Thelen's analytic narrative of the evolution of the apprenticeship system in the nineteenth century. "The legal framework in place in the nineteenth century discouraged the formation of unions among unskilled laborers while encouraging skilled workers to organize around the provision of friendly societies. Responding to this set of incentives and constraints, early trade unions organized strategies around the attempt to influence wages and employment by manipulating the supply of skilled labor" (2004, 92). In contrast I argue that union organization occurred despite labor law during these decades. As Curthoys maintains, "Governments kept unions outside the law by denying them the legal rights granted to friendly societies, the voluntary societies they most nearly resembled" (2004, 46). As I suggest below, increased union capacity to control labor was a result of their concerted efforts at institutional transformation in the latter part of the century.

21. Curthoys 2004, 30–37; Klarman 1989, 1491, 1562; Orth 1991, 93–98. Klarman notes the ironic nature of the judicial doctrine propagated in these decades: "The judges' position was, of course, internally inconsistent, for they delighted to require workers to abide by their employment contracts; it was only enforcement of agreements to withhold labor, or to work under prescribed conditions that violated the workers' free will" (1989, 1561).

22. In a significant case at midcentury, for example, members of the National Association of United Trades, who had organized a strike against a tin manufacturer who had introduced machinery to intensify production and lower piece rates, were sentenced to three months' imprisonment for obstruction and molestation. The message sent to the union by the presiding justice and the Queen's Bench in an appellate ruling was that "calling a strike was illegal under the statutes, and conspiring to call a strike was illegal under common law" (Orth 1991, 98).

23. As Kahn-Freund noted, the situation was quite unique: "The determination of the trade unions not to rely on sanctions of the law has given to the autonomous forces of

industry a position of strength in the British Constitution which is hardly paralleled elsewhere. What the State has not given, the State cannot take away" (1959, 244).

24. *Bee-Hive*, July 25, 1863. The committee also critiqued local courts where prosecution was pursued: "We object to the Justices of the Peace being judges in the cases, as they are with few exceptions employers, either as manufacturers or agriculturalists; hence it is but as appealing from Caesar to Caesar."

25. For reviews of the historiography on working-class reformism see Hall, McClelland and Rendall 2000; Kirk 1998, 21–37; Lawrence 1998, 11–69; and Savage and Miles 1994, 8–20.

26. As Paul Johnson observes, in the Victorian period "there was a deeply entrenched middle-class mid-Victorian prejudice against the character and behaviour of manual workers as a class, a prejudice which was embodied in the civil law and which exerted a powerful long-term influence on class relationships and self-perceptions. . . . Far from manual workers being seen as endowed with middle-class puritan virtues, they were repeatedly characterized in juridical discussion and in more general middle-class social discourse as morally different in a fundamentally inferior way" (1993, 147, 168).

27. Pelling 1968, 71; Field 1990, 459. John Orth comments that for organized labor "the lesson learned from its history was to see common law as inherently hostile to its organizational aspirations and to use parliamentary power to avoid as much as possible the law and the legal profession" (1991, 155).

28. Biagini 1992, 85, 139; Prothero 1997, 22–25; Spain 1991, 113; see also Epstein 1994; McCalman 1988.

29. Claeys 1987; McNally 1993; N. Thompson 1984; Steinberg 1999. Drawing on cultural institutionalism other sociologists have examined how the transposition of scripts between institutions was strategically important in economic and political change (Clemens 1997; Haydu 2008). My analysis here draws more on the dialogism that I have pursued earlier that emphasizes the continuing struggles over meaning within a discourse.

30. BPP 1867 XXXII [3873], 66–67. In arguing against anti-union commentators one unionist argued, "Those who live by labour are, by *right*, entitled to their revenue by the simple action of the principle of exchange equally with the other three great divisions of society, as opposed to the confused idea of wages being derived from the relation of master and servant, involving a sort of benevolent patronage on the one side, and obligation on the other. . . . It is only by trade combinations that the *free* exercise of this principle can be secured by working men" (Dunning 1860, 7).

31. Thus, for example, W. P. Roberts, the "miners' attorney general" and radical lawyer most famous for defending workers' and unions' rights during this period, specifically agreed with his interlocutor during the 1866 committee hearing on the reform of master and servant law that he "would treat labour as you would any other commodity, merely as an article to buy and sell" (BPP 1866 XIII [499], 103).

32. Curthoys 2004; Fraser 1974; Harrison 1965; Howell 1905; Kaufman 1974; McCready 1955, 1956; Spain 1991.

33. BPP 1868–69 XXXI [4123], xii–xxxiv. As Howell argues, state commissions can be crucial in the transformation of industrial relations institutions by offering a "class telling" of their workings, and this and subsequent commissions provided critical platforms for unionist politics (2005, 41).

34. In December 1872 five leaders of the London gas stokers strike were sentenced to a year in prison at hard labor for conspiracy to coerce, a sentence four times greater than that which could have been imposed under the molestation clauses of the CLAA. In May 1873 sixteen women, most of whom were wives of striking agricultural laborers, were sentenced to 7–10 days in prison at hard labor under the CLAA. Both cases drew widespread attention and condemnation and boosted the unions' efforts for reform (Curthoys 2004, 162–64, 174–81; Fraser 1974, 192, 195–96; Howell 1905, 1:237–53).

35. Fraser 1974, 105, 117; McIvor 1998, 44–46; Yarmie 1984, 153. Curthoys observes that the most vocal defenders of the Master and Servant Act of 1867 were some of the country's largest employers (2004, 186). Particularly active on both the local and national levels in the mid-1860s were the master builders who were battling craft unions over workplace control and wage policies. The General Builders Association, which played a prominent role in battling law reform, was founded in 1865 and two years later had eighty-four town branches (Price 1980, 105–28). The classic industry of the Industrial Revolution, cotton, had largely stabilized both piece-rate negotiations and workplace control issues by this period. On the whole, cotton manufacturers rarely resorted to master and servant law as a means of labor control and were less involved in politics over labor laws (McIvor 1998, 47–52).

36. *Capital and Labor*, March 4, 1874, 23. It also proclaimed that removing the possibility of criminal prosecution "would be a mockery of justice" (ibid.). John Robinson, chairman of the NFAEL, testified, "We want to have the means of enforcing contracts. We have felt the trades-unions have become so powerful, that is to say, since they have extended themselves so entirely through the trades, that it is exceedingly difficult to get men to carry out their contracts" (BPP 1874 XXIV [1094], 163).

37. BPP 1866 [499] XIII, 58, 67, 108, 118, 126; BPP 1874 XXIV [1094], 130, 135, 145, 154–55, *Capital and Labor*, Feb. 25, 1874, 5; March 4, 1874, 21. On the whole, the legal press argued that reform should make fines the initial punishment, but that the threat of imprisonment should be retained for workers' failure to pay so that the law could retain its bite (*County Courts Chronicle*, Feb. 1, 1867, 31; *Law Times*, Sept. 8, 1866, 768; Jan. 19, 1867, 221; *Solicitors' Journal and Reporter*, Feb. 9, 1867, 328).

38. *Capital and Labour* was equally blunt in its observations, noting that "no one possessed of common sense and candour will pretend to say that the stationing of pickets day after day is not a species of moral terrorism," and that the term *picketing* "is derived wholly from the practice and phraseology of war, and that in the hands of the Unionists it has only a meaning and application worthy of its origin" (May 12, 1875, 202; May 19, 1875, 219). For a variety of employers' and association representatives' statements concerning the importance of retaining the CLAA see BPP 1875 XXX [1175], 49–51, 59, 67, 77, 79, 84, 93.

39. BPP 1875 XXX [1175], 49; see also 50–51, 67, 79, 84.

40. BPP 1866 XIII [499], 88; BPP 1867 XXXII [3873], 11–12, 89; Curthoys 2004, 90–93, 139–40; Deakin and Wilkinson 2005, 223; Fraser 1974, 106–16.

41. Howell also suggests that in the end "the Press and the public had got a little tired of the question. Labour leaders had been much in evidence for ten or fifteen years. They could not be put down, but they could be quieted by legislative concessions, and for these the time had come" (1905, 2:370).

42. Curthoys 2004, 107, 243; Fraser 1974, 193–95; Kaufman 1974; Klarman 1989, 1496; Napier 1975, 127; Pelling 1963, 72; Spain 1991.

43. Chris Howell contends that the critical institutional transformation occurred in the 1890s with the advent of new forms of conciliation boards, and that previously the "state had played a minimal role in regulating industrial relations, and it had acted primarily to maintain order and safeguard property relations, rather than a conscious agent of economic intervention" (2005, 46). This argument makes sense if we focus only on new national administrative systems, but not, as I have maintained throughout, if we attend to statutory and common law concerning the labor contract. While diverging from my thesis, Howell's temporal parsing of industrial relations history also calls into question Polanyi's thesis of the countermovement.

44. Fisk 1994; Forbath 1991; Hattam 1993; Voss 1993; Tomlins 1985, 1995a, 1995b.

CHAPTER EIGHT

1. Given space limitations I have not pursued all of the intersections in this study. As both Rose (1992) and Bronstein (2008) note, the factory acts affirmed the status of adult female workers as "unfree agents" in the workplace, incapable of independent judgment. The lattice work of protective legislation, including the Mine, Workshop and Merchant Shipping acts were all institutional orders in which class and gender intersected.

2. Chan 2009; Gallagher and Dong 2011; Friedman and Lee 2010; Ngok 2008; Tsui 2009; Wang et al. 2009.

3. Gallagher and Dong 2011, 47–51; Lan and Pickles 2011, 4; Wang et al. 2009, 487, 497.

4. Gallagher and Dong 2011; Lan and Pickles 2001; Wang et al. 2009.

5. Friedman and Lee 2010, 525; Becker and Elfstrom 2010; Chang 2009; Gallagher and Dong 2011; Lan and Pickles 2011; Tsui 2009; Wang et al. 2009.

BIBLIOGRAPHY

ARCHIVAL SOURCES

British Public Record Office (Kew). MH/32/99, Baldwin Fleming. Correspondence and Papers Related to the North Midland District. "Treatment of Pauper Apprentices in the Grimsby Fishing Trade." June 19, 1873.

———. Census. 1861. RG/9/2234–2235

———. Census. 1871. RG/10/3075–3076, 3212

Keele University Library, Archival and Historical Collections. Wedgwood Manuscripts., E46–29245/1–85.

Kingston upon Hull City Archives, Magistrates' Court Minute Books, DPM/1/76–100, 1864–1875.

———. Registry of Ships DPC/1/15, 1858–1861, Port Number: 18/58 to 8/61, DPC/1/16, 1861–1864, Port Number: 9/61 to 15–64, DPC/1/17, 1864–1867, Port Number: 16/64 to 15/67, DPC/1/18, 1867–1871, Port Number: 9/67 to 64/71, DPC/1/19. 1871–1873, Port No. 65/71 to 60/73, DPC/1/20, 1873–1876, Port No. 61/73 to 43/76.

London School of Economics, British Library of Economic and Political Science, Sidney and Beatrice Webb, Collected Papers, Section A. Manuscript Sources, Trade Unions/A. XLIV. "Potters: Conciliation and Arbitration."

Staffordshire Record Office (Stafford), Borough of Hanley Court Registers, Draft Minute Books, D26/1–8.

Stoke on Trent Archives, Stephen Hobson Collection, Hollow-ware Pressers Union, Record book of the transactions of the Executive Committee for the Hollow Ware Pressers Union, Feb 16th 1864–Jan. 9, 1871, PA/Hob/70.

———. North Staffordshire Chamber of Commerce, Minute Book April 1874–1897, SA/CC/1.

Worcester County Public Record Office. Petty Sessional Division of Redditch, Register of the Court of Petty Sessions, July 1862–December 1865 BA 5796 (b260.105/ 5796/1 (i) Class 260.105.

———. Petty Sessional Division of Redditch, Register of the Court of Petty Sessions, 1865–1875, BA 5796/1(ii–iii) Class 260.105.

PARLIAMENTARY PAPERS

Reports from Commissioners: Factories Inquiry: Part II. BPP 1834 XX [450].

Report from the Select Committee on Masters and Operatives (Equitable Councils of Conciliation), BPP 1856 XIII [343].

Judicial Statistics (England and Wales): Part I. Police. Criminal proceedings. Prisons, BPP 1865 LII [445], 1866 LXVIII [483], 1867 LXVI [523], 1867–68 LXVII [947], 1868–69 LVIII [737], 1870 LXIII [753], 1871 LXIV [231], 1872 LXV [235]; 1873 LXX [247], 1874 LXXI [251], 1875 LXXXI [259].

First Report of the Commissioners on the Employment of Children in Trades and Manufactures. BPP 1863 XVIII [3170].

Third Report of the Commissioners on the Employment of Children in Trades and Manufactures. BPP 1864 XXII [3414-1].

Reports of the Inspectors of the Factories . . . for the Half Year ending 31st October 1864. BPP XX 1865 [3473].

Report from the Select Committee on Master and Servant, 1865. BPP 1866 XIII [449].

Report of the Commissioners on the Sea Fisheries of the United Kingdom. BPP 1866 XVIII [3596-1].

First Report of the Commissioners Appointed to Inquire Into the Organization and Rules of Trade Unions and Other Associations. BPP 1867 XXXII [3873].

Second Report of the Commissioners Appointed to Inquire Into the Organization and Rules of Trade Unions and Other Associations. BPP 1867 XXXII [3893].

Royal Commission: Eleventh and Final Report of the Royal Commissioners Appointed to Inquire into the Organization and Rules of Trades Unions and Other Associations. v. 1. BPP 1868–69 XXXI [4123].

Second Report of the Commission on the Employment of Children, Young Persons and Women in Agriculture—Reports from the Assistant Commissioners, Pt. 1, BPP 1868–1869 XIII [4202].

First Report of the Commissioners Appointed to Inquire into the Working of the Master and Servant Act, 1867, and The Criminal Law Amendment Act, 34 & 35 Vict. Cap. 32. BPP 1874 XXIV [1094].

Second and Final Report of the Commissioners Appointed to Enquire into the Working of the Master and Servant Act, 1867, the Criminal Law Amendment Act, 34 & 35 Vict. Cap. 32, and for Other Purposes. BPP 1875 XXX [1157].

Report of the Inspectors of Fisheries and Commissioners for Sea Fisheries. (Frank Buckland and Spencer Walpole). BPP 1878–79 XVII [2449].

Reports from the Royal Commission on Agriculture, v. 3, Pt. II, BPP 1881 XVII [3096]

Report of a Committee . . . To inquire into . . . the Relations between the Owners, Masters and Crews of Fishing Vessel. . . . BPP 1882 XVII [3432].

Royal Commission on Labour. v. III, Textile, Clothing, Chemical, Building and Miscellaneous Trades. Minutes of the Evidence, with Appendices Taken Before Group "C," P.P. 1893–94 XXXIX [7063-I], pt. 1, 7.

Royal Commission on Labour. Reports on the Employment of Women. Report of Miss Clara E. Collett on the Conditions of Work in Birmingham, Walsall, Dudley, and the Staffordshire Potteries. BPP 1893–94 XXXVII [6894-XXIII] pt. 1, 545.

HISTORICAL PERIODICALS

The Bee-Hive
Capital and Labour
County Courts Chronicle
The Farmer's Magazine
Hull and Eastern Counties Herald
The Justice of the Peace
Law Times
Penny Magazine
Potteries Examiner
Potteries Examiner and Workman's Advocate
Redditch Indicator
The Pottery and Glass Trades' Journal
The Solicitors' Journal and Reporter
Staffordshire Advertiser

SECONDARY WORKS

Allen, V. L. 1964. "Origins of Industrial Conciliation and Arbitration." *International Review of Social History* 9 (2): 237–54.

Ansell, Alfred W. 1883. *On Trawling*. London: William Clowes and Sons, International Fisheries Exhibition.

Armstrong, Alan. 1988. *Farmworkers in England and Wales: A Social and Economic History, 1770–1860*. Ames: Iowa State University Press.

Barber, Bernard. 1995. "All Economies Are 'Embedded': The Career of a Concept, and Beyond." *Social Research* 62 (2): 387–413.

Bartleet and Woodward. 1967. "On the Manufacture of Needles and Fish-Hooks." In *The Resources, Products and Industry of Birmingham and the Midland Hardware District*, edited by Samuel Timmins, 197–206. London: Frank Cass and Co. Originally published in 1866.

Becker, Jeffrey, and Manfred Elfstrom. 2010. "The Impact of China's Labor Contract Law on Workers." International Labor Rights Forum. May 12.

Beckert, Jens. 2009. "The Great Transformation of Embeddedness: Karl Polanyi and the New Economic Sociology." In *Market and Society: The Great Transformation Today*, edited by Chris Hann and Keith Hart, 38–55. Cambridge: Cambridge University Press.

Behagg, Clive. 1990. *Politics and Production in the Early Nineteenth Century*. London: Routledge.

Bellamy, Joyce. 1952. "Occupations in Kingston Upon Hull, 1841–1949," *Yorkshire Bulletin of Economic and Social Research* 4:33–50.

———. 1963. "A Hull Shipping Firm: The History of C & W. Earle's Shipbuilding and Engineering Co. Ltd." *Business History* 6 (1): 27–47.

———. 1971. *The Trade and Shipping of Nineteenth-Century Hull*. York: East Yorkshire Local History Society.

Berg, Maxine. 1994. *The Age of Manufactures, 1700–1820: Industry, Innovation and Work in Britain*. 2nd ed. London: Routledge.

Bernard, Mitchell. 1997. "Ecology, Political Economy and the Counter-Movement: Karl Polanyi and the Second Great Transformation." In *Innovation and Transformation in International Studies*, edited by Stephen Gill and James H. Mittleman, 75–98. Cambridge: Cambridge University Press.

Biagini, Eugenio F. 1992. *Liberty, Retrenchment and Reform: Popular Liberalism in the Age of Gladstone, 1860–1880*. Cambridge: Cambridge University Press.

Bidet, Jacques. 2007. *Exploring Marx's Capital: Philosophical, Economic and Political* Dimensions. Translated by David Fernbach. Leiden: Brill.

Birchfield, Vicki. 1999. "Contesting the Hegemony of Market Ideology: Gramsci's 'Good Sense' and Polanyi's 'Double Movement.'" *Review of International Political Economy* 6 (1): 27–54.

Blackburn, Sheila. 2007. *A Fair Day's Wage for a Fair Day's Work? Sweated Labour and the Origins of Minimum Wage Legislation in Britain*. Aldershot: Ashgate.

Block, Fred. 1994. "The Role of the State in the Economy." In *the Handbook of Economic Sociology*, edited by Neil Smelser and Richard Swedberg, 691–710. New York: Russell Sage Foundation.

Block, Fred, and Margaret R. Somers. 2014. *The Power of Market Fundamentalism: Karl Polanyi's Critique*. Cambridge, MA: Harvard University Press.

Blomley, Nicholas K. 1994. *Law, Space, and the Geographies of Power*. New York: The Guilford Press.

Boswell, David. 1973. *Sea Fishing Apprentices of Grimsby*. Grimsby: Grimsby Public Libraries and Museum.

Botham, Francis J. 1982. "Working-Class Living Standards in North Staffordshire, 1750–1914." PhD. diss., University of London.

Boyle, John. 1838. "An Account of Strikes in the Potteries, in the Years 1834 and 1836." *Journal of the Statistical Society* 1 (1): 37–45.

Braverman, Harry. 1974. *Labor and Monopoly Capital: The Degradation of Work in the Twentieth Century*. New York: Monthly Review Press.

Bremner, David. 1869. *The Industries of Scotland, Their Rise, Progress, and Present Condition*. Edinburgh: Adam and Charles Black.

Bronstein, Jamie L. 2008. *Caught in the Machinery: Workplace Accidents and Injured Workers in Nineteenth-Century Britain*. Stanford, CA: Stanford University Press.

Brown, Lucy, and C. A. McLaren. 1969. "Modern Hull." In *A History of the County of York East Riding, vol. 1, The City of Kingston Upon Hull*, edited by K. J. Allison, 215–86. Oxford: Institute of Historical Research.

Brown, Raymond. 1972. *Waterfront Organisation in Hull, 1870–1900*. Hull: Hull University Press.

Burawoy, Michael. 1979. *The Manufacture of Consent*. Chicago: University of Chicago Press.

———. 1984. "The Contours of Production Politics." In *Labor in the World Economy*, edited by Charles Berquist, 23–47. Beverly Hills, CA: Sage.

———. 1985. *The Politics of Production*. London: Verso.

———. 2001. "Dwelling in Capitalism, Traveling Through Socialism." In *The Critical*

Study of Work: Labor, Technology and Global Production, edited by Rick Baldoz, Charles Koeber, and Philip Kraft, 21–44. Philadelphia: Temple University Press.

———. 2003. "For a Sociological Marxism: The Complementary Convergence of Antonio Gramsci and Karl Polanyi." *Politics and Society* 31 (2): 193–261.

Burawoy, Michael, and Pavel Krotov. 1992. "The Soviet Transition from Socialism to Capitalism: Worker Control and Economic Bargaining in the Wood Industry." *American Sociological Review* 57 (1): 16–38.

Burawoy, Michael, and Erik Olin Wright. 1990. "Coercion and Consent in Contested Exchange." *Politics and Society* 18 (2): 251–66.

Burchill, Frank, and Richard Ross. 1977. *A History of the Potters' Union*. Hanley: Ceramic and Allied Trades Union.

Burritt, Elihu. 1868. *Walks in the Black Country and Its Green Border-Land*. London: S. Low and Marton.

Burton, Valerie. 1999a. "Apprenticeship Regulation and Maritime Labour in the Nineteenth-Century British Merchant Marine." *International Journal of Maritime History* 1 (1): 29–49.

———. 1999b "'Whoring, Drinking Sailors': Reflections on Masculinity from the Labour History of Nineteenth-Century British Shipping." In *Working Out Gender: Perspectives from Labour History*, edited by Margaret Walsh, 84–101. Aldershot: Ashgate.

Busfield, Deirdre. 1988. "Job Definitions and Inequality: The 'Unskilled' Women Workers of the West Riding Textile Industry." *Textile History* 69 (1): 61–82.

Bythell, D. 1978. *The Sweated Trades: Outwork in Nineteenth-Century Britain*. New York: St. Martin's Press.

Cadle, Clement. 1867. "The Agriculture of Worcestershire." *Journal of the Royal Society of Agriculture* 2nd ser., 28:438–97.

Cain, Maureen, and Alan Hunt. 1979. *Marx on Engels on Law*. London: Academic Press.

Campbell, John L. 2004. *Institutional Change and Globalization*. Princeton, NJ: Princeton University Press.

Cangiani, Michele. 2003. "The Forgotten Institution." *International Review of Sociology* 13 (2): 327–41.

———. 2011. "Karl Polanyi's Institutional Theory: Market Society and Its 'Disembedded' Economy." *Journal of Economic Issues* 45 (1): 177–97.

Caunce, Stephen. 1997. "Farm Servants and the Development of Capitalism in English Agriculture." *Agricultural History Review* 45 (1): 49–60.

Celoria, Francis. 1973. "Ceramic Machinery of the Nineteenth Century in the Potteries and in Other Parts of Britain." *Staffordshire Archaeology* 2:11–48.

Chamber of Commerce. n.d. *The Case of the Manufacturers of China and Earthenware in the Staffordshire Potteries: With Some Account of The Late Turn-out, Its Origin, Proceedings, and Termination, 1836–7*. Hanley: T. Allbut's.

Chan, Jenny. 2009. "Meaningful Progress or Illusory Reform? Analyzing China's Contract Labor Law." *New Labor Forum* 18 (2): 43–51.

Chance, William. 1985. *Children under the Poor Law*. London: Swan Sonnenschein.

Claeys, Gregory. 1987. *Machinery, Money, and the Millennium: From Moral Economy to Socialism, 1815–1850*. Cambridge: Polity.

Clark, Anna. 1995. *The Struggle for the Breeches: Gender and the Making of the British Working Class.* Berkeley: University of California Press.

Clawson, Dan. 1980. *Bureaucracy and the Labor Process.* New York: Monthly Review Press.

Clemens, Elisabeth S. 1997. *The People's Lobby: Organizational Innovation and the Rise of Interest Group Politics in the United States, 1890–1925.* Chicago: University of Chicago Press.

———. 2005. "Afterword: Logics of History? Agency, Multiplicity, and Incoherence in the Explanation of Change." In *Remaking Modernity: Politics, History, and Sociology,* edited by Julia Adams, Elisabeth S. Clemens and Ann Shola Orloff, 493–515. Durham, NC: Duke University Press.

Coates, David. 2005. "Paradigms of Explanation." In *Varieties of Capitalism, Varieties of Approaches,* edited by David Coates, 1–25. London: Palgrave.

Cohen. G. A. 1978. *Karl Marx's Theory of History: A Defense.* Oxford: Oxford University Press.

———. 1988. *History, Labour and Freedom: Themes from Marx.* Oxford: Clarendon Press.

Collins, Hugh. 1982. *Marxism and the Law.* Oxford: Oxford University Press.

Corrigan, Phillip, and Derek Sayer. 1985. *The Great Arch: English State Formation as Cultural Revolution.* Oxford: Blackwell.

Cotterell, Roger. 1981. "The Development of Capitalism and the Formalisation of Contract Law." In *Law, State and Society,* edited by Bob Fryer, Alan Hunt, Doreen McBarnet, and Bert Moorhouse, 54–69. London: Croom Helm.

Cowman, Krista, and Louise A. Jackson. 2005. "Introduction: Women's Work, a Cultural History." In *Women and Work Culture: Britain c. 1850–1950,* edited by Krista Cowman and Louise A. Jackson, 1–24. Aldershot: Ashgate.

Crapper, J. S. 1882. *The Ancient Corporation of Hanley, A Record of Its Proceedings from 1873 to 1900. Being a Revised Version of 'The History of the Ancient Corporation of Hanley.* Hanley: Allbut and Daniel.

Cullenberg, Stephen. 1999. "Overdetermination, Totality, and Institutions: A Genealogy of a Marxist Institutional Economics." *Journal of Economic Issues* 33 (4): 801–15.

Curthoys, Mark. 2004. *Governments, Labour, and the Law in Mid-Victorian Britain: The Trade Union Legislation of the 1870s.* Oxford: Oxford University Press.

Curzon, William D. 1883. *The Manufacturing Industries of Worcestershire.* Birmingham: W. D. Curzon.

Dale, Gareth. 2010. *Karl Polanyi: The Limits of the Market.* Cambridge: Polity.

Davies, Scott. 1990. "Inserting Gender Into Burawoy's Theory of the Labour Process." *Work, Employment and Society* 4 (3): 391–406.

Davis, James Edward. 1868. *The Master and Servant Act, 1867.* London: Butterworth.

D'Cruze, Shani. 1999. "Sex, Violence and Local Courts: Working-Class Respectability in Mid-Nineteenth-Century Lancashire." *British Journal of Criminology* 39 (1): 39–55.

Deakin, Simon. 2009. "Legal Origin, Juridical Form and Industrialization in Historical Perspective: The Case of the Employment Contract and the Joint-Stock Company." *Socio-Economic Review* 7 (1): 35–65.

Deakin, Simon, and Frank Wilkinson. 2005. *The Law of the Labour Market: Industrialization, Employment and Legal Evolution.* Oxford: Oxford University Press.

Deeg, Richard, and Gregory Jackson. 2007. "Towards a More Dynamic Theory of Capitalist Variety." *Socio-Economic Review* 5:149–79.

Dewey, Peter. 2000. "Farm Labour." In *The Agrarian History of England and Wales*, vol. 7, *1850–1914 (Part I)*, edited by E. J. T. Collins, 810–62. Cambridge: Cambridge University Press.

Dickens, Charles. 1852. "Needles." In *Household Words*, 4:540–46. New York: Angell, Engel and Hewitt.

Dodd, J. Phillip. 1979. *Worcestershire Agriculture in the Mid-Nineteenth Century.* Wednesbury: Worcestershire Historical Society.

Dugger, William M., and Howard J. Sherman. 2002. *Reclaiming Evolution: A Dialogue between Marxism and Institutionalism on Social Change.* London: Routledge.

Dunbabin, J. P. D. 1974. *Rural Discontent in Nineteenth-Century Britain.* London: Faber.

Dunlop, O. Jocelyn. 1912. *English Apprenticeship and Child Labour: A History.* New York: Macmillan.

Dunning, T. J. 1860. *Trades' Unions and Strikes: Their Philosophy and Intention.* London.

Dupree, Marguerite W. 1995. *Family Structure in the Staffordshire Potteries, 1840–1880.* Oxford: Oxford University Press.

Dutton, H. I., and S. R. H. Jones. 1983. "Invention and Innovation in the British Pin Industry, 1790–1850." *Business History Review* 57:175–93.

Dutton, H. I., and J. E. King. 1982. "The Limits of Paternalism: The Cotton Tyrants of North Lancashire: 1836–54." *Social History* 7 (1): 59–74.

Edelman, Laura, and Robin Stryker. 2005. "A Sociological Approach to Law and the Economy." In *The Handbook of Economic Sociology*, 2nd. ed., edited by Neil J. Smelser and Richard Swedberg, 527–51. Princeton, NJ: Princeton University Press.

Edgar, A. 1860. "On the Jurisdiction of the Justices of the Peace in Disputes between Employers and Employed Arising from Breach of Contract." *Transactions of the National Association for Political and Social Science, 1859* 3:687–90.

Edwards, P. K. 1986. *Conflict at Work: A Materialist Analysis of Workplace Relations.* Oxford: Basil Blackwell.

Emigh, Rebecca Jean. 2005. "The Great Debates: Transitions to Capitalism." In *Remaking Modernity: Politics, History and Sociology*, edited by Julia Adams, Elizabeth S. Clemens, and Ann S. Orloff, 355–80. Durham, NC: Duke University Press.

Emsley, Clive. 2010. *Crime and Society in England, 1750–1900.* 4th ed. Harlow: Pearson/Longman.

Epstein, James. 1994. *Radical Expression: Political Language, Ritual, and Symbol in England, 1790–1850.* New York: Oxford University Press.

Evans, William. "Art and History of the Potting Business." *Journal of Ceramic History* 3 (1970): 21–43. Originally published as *Art and History of the Potting Business (*Shelton: Examiner, 1846).

Field, Stewart. 1990. "Without the Law? Professor Arthurs and the Early Factory Inspectorate." *Journal of Law and Society* 17 (4): 445–68.

Fine, Bob. 1984. *Democracy and the Rule of Law: Liberal Ideals and Marxist Critiques.* London: Pluto.

Fisk, Catherine. 1994. "Still 'Learning Something of Legislation': The Judiciary and the History of Labor Law." *Law and Social Inquiry* 19 (1): 151–86.

Forbath, William E. 1991. *Law and the Shaping of the American Labor Movement*. Cambridge, MA: Harvard University Press.

Fox, Alan. 1985. *History and Heritage: The Social Origins of the British Industrial Relations System*. London: Allen and Unwin.

Frank, Christopher. 2010. *Master and Servant Law: Chartists, Trade Unions, Radical Lawyers and the Magistracy of England, 1840–1865*. Farnham: Ashgate.

Fraser, W. Hamish. 1974. *Trade Unions and Society: The Struggle for Acceptance, 1850–1880*. Totowa, NJ: Rowman and Littlefield.

Freifeld, Mary. 1986. "Technological Change and the Self-Acting Mule: A Study of Skill and the Sexual Division of Labour." *Social History* 11:319–43.

French, Stanley. 1967a. "The Further History of the Stipendiary Magistrates." *Criminal Law Review* 14:224–30.

———. 1967b. "The Further History of the Stipendiary Magistrates." *Criminal Law Review* 14:269–77.

Friedman, Eli, and Ching Kwan Lee. 2010. "Remaking the World of Chinese Labour: A 30-Year Retrospective" *British Journal of Industrial Relations* 48 (3): 507–33.

Galenson, David W. 1994. "The Rise of Free Labor: Economic Change and the Enforcement of Service Contracts in England, 1351–1875." In *Capitalism in Context: Essays on Economic Development and Cultural Change in Honor of H. M. Hartwell*, edited by John A. James, 114–37. Chicago: University of Chicago Press.

Gallagher, Mary E. 2006. "Mobilizing the Law in China: 'Informed Disenchantment' and the Development of Legal Consciousness." *Law and Society Review* 40 (4): 783–816.

Gallagher, Mary E., and Baohua Dong. 2011. "Legislating Harmony: Labor Reform in Contemporary China." In *From Iron Rice Bowl to Informalization: Markets, Workers, and the State in a Changing China*, edited by Sarosh Kuruvila, Ching Kwan Lee, and Mary E. Gallagher, 36–60. Ithaca, NY: ILR Press.

Garnett, Robert F., Jr. 1999. "Postmodernism and Theories of Value: New Grounds for Institutionalist/Marxist Dialogue?" *Journal of Economic Issues* 33 (4): 817–34.

Gatley, David Alan. 1989. "Hanley in 1851; A Survey Based on the Census Returns." Occasional Paper no. 11. Department of Sociology, Staffordshire Polytechnic, Stoke-on-Trent.

Gaut, R. C. 1939. *A History of Worcestershire Agriculture in and Rural Evolution*. Worcester: Littlebury and Co.

Gemici, Kurtuluş. 2008. "Karl Polanyi and the Antimonies of Embeddedness." *Socio-Economic Review* 6 (1): 5–33.

Gillett, Edward, and Kenneth A. MacMahon. 1989. *A History of Hull*. Hull: Hull University Press.

Godfrey, Barry. 1999a. "Law, Factory Discipline and 'Theft': The Impact of the Factory on Workplace Appropriation in Mid- to Late Nineteenth-Century Yorkshire." *British Journal of Criminology* 39 (1): 56–71.

———. 1999b. "Judicial Impartiality and the Use of Criminal Law against Labour: the Sentencing of Workplace Appropriators in Northern England, 1840–1880." *Crime, History and Societies* 3:57–72.

Greenhow, W. T. 1863. *The Shipping Law Manual; A Concise Treatise on the Law Governing the Interests of Shipowners, Merchants, Masters, Seamen, and Other Persons Connected with British Ships. . . .* London: V. and R. Stevens.

Greenlees, Janet. 2007. *Female Labour Power: Women's Influence on Business Practices in the British and American Cotton Industries, 1780–1860.* Aldershot: Ashgate.

Greenslade, M. W. 1963. "Hanley." In *The Victoria County History of Staffordshire*, vol. 3, edited by J. G. Jenkins, 142–73. London: Institute for Historical Research.

Gritt, A. J. 2002. "The 'Survival' of Service in the English Agricultural Labour Force: Lessons from Lancashire, c. 1650–1851." *Agricultural History Review* 50 (1): 25–50.

Halfpenny, Pat. 1984. "Joseph Clementson: A Potter 'Remarkable for Energy and Character.'" *Northern Ceramic Society Journal* 5:176–206.

Hall, Catherine, Keith McClelland, and Jane Rendall. 2000. "Introduction." In *Defining the Victorian Nation: Class, Race, Gender and the Reform Act of 1867*, edited by Catherine Hall, Keith McClelland and Jane Rendall, 1–70. Cambridge: Cambridge University Press.

Hall, Peter A., and Kathleen Thelen. 2009. "Institutional Change in Varieties of Capitalism." *Socio-Economic Review* 7 (1): 7–34.

Hall, Ray. 1986. "Women in the Labour Force: A Case Study of the Potteries in the Nineteenth Century." Occasional Paper no. 27. Department of Geography and Earth Science, London: Queen Mary College.

Halperin, Sandra. 2004. *War and Social Change in Modern Europe: The Great Transformation Revisited.* Cambridge: Cambridge University Press.

Hann, Chris and Keith Hart, eds. 2009. *Market and Society: The Great Transformation Today.* Cambridge: Cambridge University Press.

Hanson, Susan, and Geraldine Pratt. 1995. *Gender, Work and Space.* London: Routledge.

Harris, F. 1905–6. "Improvements in Potters' Machinery." *Transactions of the English Ceramic Society* 5:45–71.

Harrison, Royden. 1965. *Before the Socialists: Studies in Labour and Politics, 1861–1881.* London: Routledge and Kegan Paul.

Hattam, Victoria C. 1993. *Labor Visions and State Power: The Origins of Business Unionism in the United States.* Princeton, NJ: Princeton University Press.

Hay, Colin, and Daniel Wincott. 1998. "Structure, Agency and Historical Institutionalism." *Political Studies* 46 (5): 951–57.

Hay, Douglas. 1998. "Patronage, Paternalism, and Welfare: Masters, Workers, and Magistrates in Eighteenth-Century England." *International Labor and Working-Class History* 53:27–48.

———. 2000. "Master and Servant in England: Using the Law in the Eighteenth and Nineteenth Centuries." In *Private Law and Social Inequality in the Industrial Age: Comparing Legal Cultures in Britain, France, Germany and the United States*, edited by Willibald Steinmetz, 227–64. Oxford: Oxford University Press.

———. 2004. "England, 1562–1875." In *Masters, Servants and Magistrates in Britain and the Empire, 1562–1955*, edited by Douglas Hay and Paul Craven, 59–116. Chapel Hill: University of North Carolina Press.

Hay, Douglas, and Paul Craven. 2004. "Introduction." In *Masters, Servants and Magistrates in Britain and the Empire, 1562–1955*, edited by Hay and Craven, 1–58. Chapel Hill: University of North Carolina Press.

Haydu, Jeffrey. 1988. *Between Craft and Class: Skilled Workers and Factory Politics in the United States and Britain, 1890–1922.* Berkeley: University of California Press.

———. 1998. "Workplace Governance, Class Formation and the New Institutionalism." *Mobilization.* 3 (1): 69–88.

———. 2001. "Do Capitalists Matter in the Capitalist Labor Process? Collective Capacities, Group Interests, and Management Prerogatives, c. 1886–1904." In *The Critical Study of Work: Labor, Technology and Global Production,* edited by Rick Baldoz, Charles Koeber, and Philip Kraft, 45–68. Philadelphia: Temple University Press.

———. 2008. *Citizen Employers: Business Communities and Labor in Cincinnati and San Francisco, 1870–1916.* Ithaca, NY: Cornell University Press.

———. 2010. "Reversals of Fortune: Path Dependency, Problem Solving, and Temporal Cases." *Theory and Society* 39 (1): 25–48.

Hechter, Michael. 1981. "Karl Polanyi's Social Theory: A Critique." *Politics and Society* 10 (4): 399–429.

Henson, Gravenor, and George White. 1823. *A Few Remarks on the State of the Laws, at Present in Existence, for Regulation Masters and Work People . . .* London.

Hepple, Bob. 2000. "The Historical Development of Collective Labour Law: Comparative Reflections." In *The Rise and Development of Comparative Labour Law,* edited by Marcel van der Linden and Richard Price, 415–35. Bern: Peter Lang.

Herod, Andrew. 2001. *Labor Geographies: Workers and the Landscapes of Capitalism.* New York: Guilford Press.

Hertslet, Charles J. B. 1850. *The Law Relating to Master and Servant . . .* London: John Crockford.

Hindess, Barry. 1987. *Politics and Class Analysis.* Oxford: Blackwell.

Hodgson, Geoffrey M. 2001. *How Economics Forgot History: The Problem of Historical Specificity in Social Science.* London: Routledge.

Holdsworth, Edmund. 1874. *Deep-Sea Fishing and Fishing Boats.* London: E. Stanford.

Hollowood, Bernard. 1951. *The Story of J. and G. Meakin.* Derby: Bemrose Publicity.

Honeyman, Katrina. 2007. *Child Workers in England, 1780–1820: Parish Apprentices and the Making of the Early Industrial Labour Force.* Aldershot: Ashgate.

Hopcroft, Rosemary L. 2001. "Theoretical Implications of Regional Effects." *Sociological Theory* 19 (2): 145–64.

Hopkins, Eric. 1994. *Childhood Transformed: Working-Class Children in Nineteenth-Century England.* Manchester: Manchester University Press.

Horn, Pamela. 1976. *The Changing Countryside in Victorian and Edwardian England and Wales.* London: The Athlone Press.

———. 1984. *Labouring Life in the Victorian Countryside.* Dublin: Gill and Macmillan.

———. 1996. "Pauper Apprenticeship and the Grimsby Fishing Industry, 1870 to 1914." *Labour History Review* 61 (2): 173–94.

Howell, Chris. 2005. *Trade Unions and the State: The Construction of Industrial Relations Institutions in Britain, 1890–2000.* Princeton, NJ: Princeton University Press.

Howell, George. 1905. *Labour Legislation, Labour Movements and Labour Leaders.* 2 vols. London: T. Fisher, Unwin.

Howkins, Alun. 1985. *Poor Labouring Men: Rural Radicalism in Norfolk 1870–1923.* London: Routledge.

———. 1990. "Labour History and the Rural Poor, 1850–1980." *Rural History* 1 (1): 113–22.

Howkins, Alun, and Nicola Verdon. 2008. "Adaptable and Sustainable? Male Farm Service and the Agricultural Labour Force in Midland and Southern England, c.1850–1925." *Economic History Review* 61 (2): 467–95.

Hudson, Pat. 1989. "The Regional Perspective." In *Regions and Industries: A Perspective on the Industrial Revolution in England*, edited by Pat Hudson, 5–38. Cambridge: Cambridge University Press.

———. 1992. *The Industrial Revolution.* London: Edward Arnold.

Humphries, Jane. 2003. "English Apprenticeship: A Neglected Factor in the First Industrial Revolution." In *The Economic Future in Historical Perspective*, edited by Paul A. David, and Mark Thomas, 73–108. Oxford: Oxford University Press.

———. 2010. *Childhood and Child Labour in the British Industrial Revolution.* Cambridge: Cambridge University Press.

Hunter, W. A. 1873. *True Origin of the Criminal Laws Affecting the Working Classes.* Glasgow Tracts for Trades' Unionists—No. 1. Glasgow: Executive for the Repeal of the Criminal Law Amendment Act.

Hyman, Richard. 1987. "Strategy or Structure? Capital, Labour and Control." *Work, Employment and Society* 1 (1): 25–55.

Immergut, Ellen M. 1998. "The Theoretical Core of the New Institutionalism." *Politics and Society* 26 (1): 5–34.

Jacoby, Sanford M. 1982. "The Duration of Indefinite Employment Contracts in the United States and England: An Historical Analysis." *Comparative Labor Law* 5:85–128.

Jaffe, James A. 1991. *The Struggle for Market Power: Industrial Relations in the British Coal Industry, 1800–1840.* Cambridge: Cambridge University Press.

———. 2000. *Striking a Bargain: Work and Industrial Relations in England, 1815–1865.* Manchester: Manchester University Press.

———. 2003. "Industrial Arbitration, Equity, and Authority in England, 1800–1850." *Law and History Review* 18 (3): 525–58.

Jessop, Bob. 2001. "Regulationist and Autopoieticist Reflections on Polanyi's Account of Market Economies and Market Society." *New Political Economy* 6 (2): 213–32.

———. 2008. *State Power.* Cambridge: Polity Press.

Jessop, Bob, and Ngai-Ling Sum. 2006. *Beyond the Regulation Approach: Putting Capitalist Economies in Their Place.* Cheltenham: Edward Elgar.

Jewitt, Llewlellynn. 1878. *The Ceramic Art of Great Britain.* Vol. 2. London: Virtue and Co.

Johnson, Paul. 1993. "Class Law in Victorian England." *Past and Present* 141:147–69.

Jonas, Andrew E. G. 1996. "Local Labour Control Regimes: Uneven Development and the Social Regulation of Production." *Regional Studies* 30 (4): 323–38.

Jones, S. R. H. 1980. "John English & Co., Feckenham: A Study of Enterprise in the West Midlands Needle Trade in the Eighteenth and Nineteenth Centuries," PhD. diss. University of London.

Joyce, Patrick 1990. "Work." In *The Cambridge Social History of Britain, 1750–1850: People and Their Environment*, vol. 2, edited by F. M. L. Thompson, 131–94. Cambridge: Cambridge University Press.

Kaufman, C. J. 1974. "Lord Elcho, Trade Unions and Democracy." In *Essays in Anti-Labour History*, edited by K. D. Brown, 183–207. London: Macmillan.

Kebbel, T. E. 1893. *The Agricultural Labourer.* New ed. London: Swan Sonnenschein and Co.

Kelly, E. R., ed. 1872. *The Post Office Directory of the North and East Ridings of Yorkshire, with the City of York.* London: Kelly and Co.

Kennedy, Duncan. 1985. "The Role of Law in Economic Thought: Essays on the Fetishism of Commodities." *American University Law Review* 34:939–1001.

Kinsey, Richard. 1978. "Marxism and the Law: Preliminary Analyses." *British Journal of Law and Society* 5 (2): 202–17.

Kirby, Peadar. 2002. "The World Bank or Polanyi: Markets, Poverty and Social Well-Being in Latin America." *New Political Economy* 7 (2): 199–219.

Kirk, Neville. 1998. *Change, Continuity and Class: Labour in British Society, 1850–1920.* Manchester: Manchester University Press.

Klarman, Michael J. 1989. "The Judges versus the Unions: The Development of British Labor Law, 1867–1913." *Virginia Law Review* 75 (8): 1487–1602.

Knights, David and Hugh Willmott. 1989. "Power and Subjectivity at Work: From Degradation to Subjugation in Social Relations," *Sociology* 23 (4): 535–58.

Knox, William. 1986. "Apprenticeship and De-Skilling in Britain, 1850–1914." *International Review of Social History* 31 (2): 166–84.

Krippner, Greta R. 2001. "The Elusive Market: Embeddedness and the Paradigm of Economic Sociology." *Theory and Society* 30 (6): 775–810.

Krippner, Greta R., and Anthony S. Alvarez. 2007. "Embeddness and the Intellectual Projects of Economic Sociology." *Annual Review of Sociology* 33:219–40.

Krippner, Gretta, Mark Granovetter, Fred Block, Nicole Biggart, Tom Beamish, Youtien Hsing, Gillian Hart, Giovanni Arrighi, Margie Mendell, John Hall, Michael Burawoy, Steve Vogel and Sean O'Riain. 2004. "Polanyi Symposium: A Conversation on Embeddedness." *Socio-Economic Review* 2 (1): 109–35.

Lamb, A. 1977. "Mechanization and the Application of Steam Power in the North Staffordshire Pottery Industry 1793–1914." *North Staffordshire Journal of Field Studies* 17:50–63.

Lan, Tu, and John Pickles. 2011. "China's New Labour Contract Law: State Regulation and Workers Rights in Global Production Networks." Capturing the Gains, Working Paper 5. Social Science Research Network, http://papers.ssrn.com/sol3/papers.cfm?abstract_id=1987685.

Land, Neville. 1986. *The History of Redditch and the Locality.* 3rd ed. Studley: K. A. F. Brewin Books.

Lane, Joan. 1996. *Apprenticeship in England, 1600–1914.* Boulder, CO: Westview.

Lawrence, Jon. 1998. *Speaking for the People: Party, Language and Popular Politics in England, 1867–1914.* Cambridge: Cambridge University Press.

Lazonick, William. 1979. "Industrial Relations and Technical Change: The Case of the Self-Acting Mule." *Cambridge Journal of Economics* 3:231–62.

———. 1981. "Production Relations, Labor Productivity, and Choice of Technique: British and U.S. Cotton Spinning." *Journal of Economic History* 41 (3): 491–516.

———. 1990. *Competitive Advantage on the Shop Floor.* Cambridge, MA: Harvard University Press.

Lee, Ching Kwan. 2007. *Against the Law: Labor Protests in China's Rustbelt and Sunbelt.* Berkeley: University of California Press.

Leighton, Baldwyn. 1873. "How May the Condition of the Agricultural Labourer Be Improved?" *Transactions of the National Association for the Promotion of Social Science, 1872*, edited by Edwin Pears, 393–416. London: Longmans, Green, Reader and Dyer.

Levi, Leone. 1883. *The Economic Condition of Fishermen.* London: William Clowes and Sons, International Fisheries Exhibition.

Lie, John. 1991. "Embedding Polanyi's Market." *Sociological Perspectives* 34 (2): 219–35.

Littlebury, J. 1873. *Littlebury's Directory and Gazeteer of the County of Worcester.* Worcester: Littlebury.

Littler, Craig. 1990. "The Labour Process Debate: A Critical Review 1974–1988." In *Labour Process Theory*, edited by David Knights, and Hugh Willmott, 46–94. London: Macmillan.

Longe, Francis D. 1860. *An Inquiry into the Law of "Strikes."* London: Macmillan and Co.

Lorenz, Edward H. 1984. "Two Patterns of Development: Labour Process in the British and French Shipbuilding Industries 1880–1930." *Journal of European Economic History* 13 (3): 599–634.

Lyddon, Dave. 1994. "Industrial-Relations Theory and Labor History." *International Labor and Working-Class History* 46:122–41.

Mahoney, James. 2000. "Path Dependency in Historical Sociology," *Theory and Society* 29 (4): 507–48.

———. 2003. "Strategies of Causal Assessment in Comparative Historical Analysis." In *Comparative Historical Analysis in Social Science*, edited by James Mahoney and Dietrich Rueschmeyer, 337–72. Cambridge: Cambridge University Press.

Manchester, A. H. 1980. *A Modern Legal History of England and Wales, 1750–1950.* London: Butterworths.

Malone, Carolyn. 2003. *Women's Bodies and Dangerous Trades in England, 1880–1914.* Woodbridge: Boydell Press.

Marks, Gary. 1989. *Unions in Politics: Britain, Germany, and the United Stated in the Nineteenth and Twentieth Centuries.* Princeton, NJ: Princeton University Press.

Marsden, Richard. 1999. *The Nature of Capital: Marx after Foucault.* London: Routledge.

Martin, Ron. 2003. "Institutional Approaches to Economic Geography." In *A Companion to Economic Geography*, edited by Eric Sheppard and Trevor J. Barnes, 77–94. Oxford: Blackwell.

Marx, Karl. 1965. *Wages, Prices and Profit.* Peking: Foreign Language Press.

———. 1975. "Inaugural Address of the Working Men's International Association." In *Collected Works*, 20:5–13. New York: International Publishers.

———. 1976. *Capital*, vol. 1, Translated by Ben Fowkes. London: Penguin.

———. 1994. "A Critique to the Contribution of Political Economy." In *Collected Works*, 34:7–336. Translated by Ben Fowkes. New York: International Publishers.

MacDonald, Alexander. 1868. *Handybook of the Law Related to Masters, Workmen, Servants, and Apprentices.* London: William MacKenzie.

Massey, Doreen. 1984. *Spatial Divisions of Labour: Social Structure and the Geography of Production.* London: Macmillan.

Maude, Frederic C., and Charles E. Pollock. 1861. *A Compendium of the Law of Merchant Shipping . . .* 2nd. ed. London: H. Sweet.

Maynard, John. 2005. "The Agricultural Labourer in Worcestershire: Responses to Economic Change and Social Dislocation 1790–1841." PhD diss., Coventry University.

McCalman, Iain. 1988. *Radical Underworld: Prophets, Revolutionaries and Pornographers in London, 1795–1840.* Cambridge: Cambridge University Press.

McCann, Michael W. 1994. *Rights at Work: Pay Equity and the Politics of Legal Mobilization.* Chicago: University of Chicago Press.

McCarthy, James F. 1885a. "Pottery and Porcelain. II." In *Great Industries of Great Britain,* 2:162–68. London: Cassell and Co.

———. 1885b. "Pottery and Porcelain. IV." In *Great Industries of Great Britain,* 2:298–302. London: Cassell and Co.

———. 1886. "Pottery and Porcelain. V." In *Great Industries of Great Britain,* 3:14–18. London: Cassell and Co.

McClelland, Keith. 1991. "Masculinity and the 'Representative Artisan' in Britain, 1850–1880." In *Manful Assertions: Masculinities in Britain since 1800,* edited by Michael Roper and John Tosh, 74–91. London: Routledge.

———. 1996. "Rational and Respectable Men: Gender, the Working Class, and Citizenship in Britain, 1850–1867." In *Gender and Class in Modern Europe,* edited by Laura L. Fader and Sonya O. Rose, 280–93. Ithaca, NY: Cornell University Press.

———. 2000. " 'England's Greatness, the Working Man.' " In *Defining the Victorian Nation: Class, Race and Gender and the Reform Act of 1867,* edited by Catherine Hall, Keith McClelland, and Jane Rendall, 71–118. Cambridge: Cambridge University Press.

McClelland, Keith, and Alastair Reid. 1985. "Wood, Iron and Steel: Technology, Labour and Trade Union Organisation in the Shipbuilding Industry, 1840–1914." In *Divisions of Labour: Skilled Workers and Technological Change in Nineteenth-Century England,* edited by Royden Harrison, and Jonathan Zeitlin, 151–84. Brighton: Harvester Press.

McCready, H. W. 1955. "British Labour and the Royal Commission on Trade Unions, 1867–9." *University of Toronto Quarterly* 24 (4): 390–409.

———. 1956. "British Labour's Lobby, 1867–75." *Canadian Journal of Economics and Political Science* 22 (2): 141–60.

McIvor, Arthur. 1998. *Organized Capital: Employers' Associations and Industrial Relations in Northern England, 1880–1939.* Cambridge: Cambridge University Press.

McKendrick, Neil. 1961. "Josiah Wedgwood and Factory Discipline." *Historical Journal* 4 (1): 30–55.

McNally, David. 1993. *Against the Market: Political Economy, Market Socialism and the Marxist Critique.* London: Verso.

Meiksins, Peter. 1994. "*Labor and Monopoly Capital* for the 1990s: A Review and Critique of the Labor Process Debate." *Monthly Review* 46 (6): 45–59.

Miller, Cecilia. 1992. "Master and Man: Farmers and Employees in Nineteenth-Century Gloucestershire." In *Conflict and Community in Southern England: Essays in the Social History of Rural and Urban Labour from Medieval to Modern Times,* edited by Barry Stapleton, 199–209. New York: St. Martin's.

Mjøset, Lars. 1985. "Regulation and the Institutionalist Tradition." In *Introduktion til Reguleringsskolen*, edited by Lars Mjøset and Jan Bohlin, 1–101. Arbejdspapirer fra NSU nr. 21. Ålborg: Nordisk Sommeruniversitet.

Mokyr, Joel. 2008. "The Institutional Origins of the Industrial Revolution." In *Institutions and Economic Performance*, edited by Elhanan Helpman, 64–119 Cambridge, MA: Harvard University Press.

More, Charles. 1980. *Skill and the English Working Class, 1870–1914*. New York: St. Martin's Press.

Morgan, Carol E. 2001. *Women Workers and Gender Identities, 1835–1913: The Cotton and Metal Industries in England*. London: Routledge, 1980.

Morrall, Michael T. 1866. *History and Description of Needle Making*. Manchester: Briddon.

Moses, Gary. 1999. "Proletarian Labourers? East Riding Farm Servants, c. 1850–1875." *Agricultural History Review* 47 (1): 78–94.

Moyes, A. 1979. "Victorian Industrial Structure and Inter-Industry Relationships in the Potteries: A Framework and Exploratory Analysis." *North Staffordshire Journal of Field Studies* 19:39–59.

Munck, Ronaldo. 2007. *Globalisation and Contestation: The New Great Countermovement*. London: Routledge.

Napier, Brian. 1975. "The Contract of Service: The Concept and its Application." D.Phil. diss. University of Cambridge.

Nardinelli, Clark. 1988. "Were Children Exploited During the Industrial Revolution?" *Research in Economic History* 11:243–76.

National Federation of Associated Employers of Labour. 1874. *Report of the Interview on 13 December 1873 between a Deputation from the National Federation of Associated Employers of Labour and the Right Hon. Robert Lowe*. Manchester: A. Ireland and Co.

Newby, Howard. 1977. *The Deferential Worker: A Study of Farm Workers in East Anglia*. London: Allen Lane.

———. 1987. *Country Life: A Social History of Rural England*. Totowa, NJ: Barnes and Noble.

Ngok, Kinglun. 2008. "The Changes of Chinese Labor Policy and Labor Legislation in the Context of Market Transition." *International Labor and Working-Class History* 73:45–64.

Noake, John. 1868. *Noake's Guide to Worcestershire*. London: Longman and Co.

North, Douglass. 1977. "Markets and Other Allocation Systems in History: The Challenge of Karl Polanyi." *Journal of European Economic History* 6 (3): 703–16.

———. 1990. *Institutions, Institutional Change, and Economic Performance*. Cambridge: Cambridge University Press.

Olofsson, Gunnar. 1999. "Embeddedness and Integration." In *Capitalism and Social Cohesion: Essays in Exclusion and Integration*, edited by Ian Gough and Gunnar Olofsson, 38–60. New York: St. Martin's Press.

Orren, Karen. 1991. *Belated Feudalism: Labor, the Law and Liberal Government in the United States*. Cambridge: Cambridge University Press.

Orren, Karen, and Stephen Skowronek. 1996. "Institutions and Intercurrence: Theory

Building in the Fullness of Time." In *Political Order*, edited by Ian Shapiro and Russell Hardin 111–46. New York: New York University Press.

Orth, John V. 1991. *Combination and Conspiracy: A Legal History of Trade Unionism, 1721–1906*. Oxford: Clarendon Press.

Owen, Harold. 1970 [1901]. *The Staffordshire Potter*. Bath: Kingsmead Reprints.

Peck, Jamie. 1996. *Work-Place: The Social Regulation of Labor Markets*. New York: Guilford Press.

———. 2005. "Economic Sociologies in Space." *Economic Geography* 81 (2): 121–75.

Peck, Jamie, and Nik Theodore. 2007. "Variegated Capitalism." *Progress in Human Geography* 31 (6): 731–72.

Pelling, Henry. 1963. *A History of British Trade Unionism*. London: Macmillan.

———. 1968. *Popular Politics and Society in Late Victorian England*. London: Macmillan.

Philips, David. 1976. "The Black Country Magistracy 1835–60." *Midland History* 3 (3): 161–90.

———. 1977. *Crime and Authority in Victorian England: The Black Country 1835–1860*. London: Croom Helm.

Phillips, Paul. 1980. *Marx and Engels on Law and Laws*. Totowa: Barnes & Noble.

Pierson, Paul. 2004. *Politics in Time: History, Institutions, and Social Analysis*. Princeton, NJ: Princeton University Press.

Pinchbeck, Ivy, and Margaret Hewitt. 1969. *Children in English Society*, vol. 2, *From the Eighteenth Century to the Children Act of 1849*. London: Routledge and Kegan Paul.

Polanyi, Karl. 1947. "On Belief in Economic Determinism." *Sociological Review* 39 (1): 96–102.

———. 1957a. *The Great Transformation: The Political Origins of Our Time*. Boston: Beacon Press.

———. 1957b. "Aristotle Discovers the Economy." In *Trade and Market in the Early Empires*, edited by Karl Polanyi, Conrad M. Arensberg, and Harry W. Pearson, 64–97. Chicago: Henry Regnery.

———. 1971a. "Our Obsolete Market Mentality." In *Primitive, Archaic and Modern Economies: Essays of Karl Polanyi*, edited by George Dalton, 59–77. Boston: Beacon Press.

———. 1971b. "The Economy as an Instituted Process" In *Primitive, Archaic and Modern Economies: Essays of Karl Polanyi*, edited by George Dalton, 139–74. Boston: Beacon Press.

———. 1977. *The Livelihood of Man*. Edited by Harry W. Pearson. New York: Academic Press.

Pollard, Sidney. 1965. *The Genesis of Modern Management*. London: Edward Arnold.

———. 1992. "The Concept of the Industrial Revolution." In *Technology and Enterprise in a Historical Perspective*, edited by G. Dosi, G. Renato, and P. A. Toninelli, 29–62. Oxford: Clarendon Press.

Pollard, Sidney, and Paul Robertson. 1979. *The British Shipbuilding Industry, 1870–1914*. Cambridge, MA: Harvard University Press.

Pontusson, Jonas. 1995. "From Comparative Political Policy to Political Economy: Putting Institutions in Their Place and Taking Interests Seriously." *Comparative Political Studies* 28 (1): 117–47.

———. 2005. "Varieties and Commonalties of Capitalism." In *Varieties of Capitalism, Varieties of Approaches*, edited by David Coates, 163–88. Basingstoke: Palgrave.

Price, Richard. 1980. *Masters, Unions and Men: Work Control in Building and the Rise of Labour 1830–1914.* Cambridge: Cambridge University Press.

———. 1982. "Rethinking Labour History: The Importance of Work." In *Social Conflict and the Political Order of Modern Britain*, edited by James E. Cronin and Jonathan Schneer, 179–214. New Brunswick: Rutgers University Press.

———. 1983. "The Labour Process and Labour History." *Social History* 8 (1): 57–75.

———. 1984a. "Conflict and Co-operation: A Reply to Patrick Joyce." *Social History* 9 (2): 217–24.

———. 1984b. "Structures of Subordination in Nineteenth-Century British Industry." In *The Power of the Past*, edited by Pat Thane, Geoffrey Crossick, and Roderick Floud, 119–42. Cambridge: Cambridge University Press.

———.1984c. "Theories of Labor Process Formation." *Journal of Social History* 18 (1): 91–110.

———. 1986. *Labour in British Society: An Interpretive History.* London: Croom Helm.

———. 1991. "The Future of British Labour History," *International Review of Social History* 36 (2): 249–60

Prothero, Iowerth. 1997. *Radical Artisans in England and France, 1830–1870.* Cambridge: Cambridge University Press.

Purdy, Frederick. 1861. "On the Earnings of Agricultural Labourers in England and Wales, 1860." *Journal of the Statistical Society of London* 24 (9): 328–73.

Rainnie, Al, Susan McGrath-Champ, and Andew Herod. 2007. "Spatializing Industrial Relations." *Industrial Relations Journal* 38 (2): 102–18.

———. 2010. "Making Space for Geography in the Labour Process." In *Working Life: Renewing Labour Process Analysis*, edited by Paul Thompson and Chris Smith, 297–315. Basingstoke: Palgrave Macmillan.

Randall, Adrian, and Edwina Newman. 1995. "Protest, Proletarians, and Paternalists: Social Conflict in Wiltshire, 1830–1850." *Rural History* 6 (2): 205–27.

Randles, Sally. 2003. "Issues for a Neo-Polanyian Agenda in Economic Sociology." *International Review of Sociology* 13 (2): 409–34.

Reid, Alastair. 2010. *The Tide of Democracy: Shipyard Workers and Social Relations in Britain, 1870–1950.* Manchester: Manchester University Press.

Richardson, Ralph. 1986. *The Book of Redditch.* Buckingham: Barracuda Books.

Robinson, Robb. 1987. *A History of the Yorkshire Coast Fishing Industry, 1780–1914.* Hull: Hull University Press.

———. 1996. *Trawling: The Rise and Fall of British Trawl Fishery.* Exeter: Exeter University Press.

Rollins, John G. 1981. *Needlemaking.* Princes Risborough: Shire Publications.

———. 1984. *A History of Redditch.* Chichester: Phillimore.

Rose, Mary B. 1989. "Social Policy and Business: Parish Apprenticeship and the Early Factory System 1750–1834." *Business History* 31 (4): 5–32

Rose, Sonya O. 1991. "'From Behind the Women's Petticoats': The English Factory Act of 1874 as a Cultural Production." *Journal of Historical Sociology* 4 (1): 32–51.

———. 1992. *Limited Livelihoods: Gender and Class in Nineteenth-Century England.* Berkeley: University of California Press.

———. 1993. "Gender and Labour History: The Nineteenth-Century Legacy." *International Review of Social History*, suppl., 38:145–62.

Rubin, Gerry R. 2000. "The Historical Development of Collective Labour Law: The United Kingdom." In *The Rise and Development of Comparative Labour Law*, edited by Marcel van der Linden and Richard Price, 291–349. Bern: Peter Lang.

Rule, John. 1976. "The Smackmen of the North Sea: Labour Recruitment and Exploitation in British Deep-Sea Fishing, 1850–1900." *International Review of Social History* 21 (3): 383–411.

———. 1988. "The Property of Skill in the Period of Manufacture." In *The Historical Meaning of Work*, edited by Patrick Joyce, 98–118. Cambridge: Cambridge University Press.

Sabel, Charles, and Jonathan Zeitlin. 1985. "Historical Alternatives to Mass Production: Politics, Markets and Technology in Nineteenth-Century Industrialization." *Past and Present* 108:133–76.

———. 1997. "Stories, Strategies and Structures: Rethinking Historical Alternatives to Mass Production." In *Worlds of Possibilities*, edited by Charles F. Sabel and Jonathan Zeitlin, 1–33. Cambridge: Cambridge University Press.

Samuel, Raphael. 1977. "Workshop of the World: Steam Power and Hand Power in Mid-Victorian England." *History Workshop* 2:6–72.

Savage, Mike, and Andrew Miles. 1994. *The Remaking of the British Working Class, 1840–1940.* London: Routledge.

Sayer, Derek. 1987. *The Violence of Abstraction: The Analytic Foundations of Historical Materialism.* Oxford: Blackwell.

Schneiberg, Marc. 2007. "What's on the Path?: Path Dependence, Organizational Diversity and the Problem of Institutional Change in the US Economy, 1900–1950." *Socio-Economic Review* 5:47–80.

Schneiberg, Marc, and Elisabeth S. Clemens. 2006. "The Typical Tools for the Job: Research Strategies in Institutional Analysis." *Sociological Theory* 24 (3): 195–227.

Schwarzkopf, Jutta. 2004. *Unpicking Cotton: The Social Construction of Gender in the Lancashire Cotton Weaving Industry, 1880–1914.* Aldershot: Ashgate.

Shaw, Charles. 1977 [1903]. *When I Was a Child.* Firle: Caliban Books.

Sheahan, James Joseph. 1864. *General and Concise History and Description of the Town and Port of Kingston-upon-Hull.* London: Simpkin, Marshall and Co.

Silver, Beverly. 2003. *Forces of Labor: Workers' Movements and Globalization since 1870.* Cambridge: Cambridge University Press.

Silver, Beverly, and Giovanni Arrighi. 2003. "Polanyi's 'Double Movement': The Belle Epoques of British and U.S. Hegemony." *Politics and Society* 31 (2): 325–55.

Simon, Daphne. 1954. "Master and Servant." In *Democracy and the Labour Movement*, edited by John Saville, 160–200. London: Lawrence and Wishart.

Skyrme, Thomas. 1994. *History of the Justices of the Peace.* Chichester: Barry Rose.

Smith, Vicki. 1994. "Braverman's Legacy: The Labour Process Tradition at 20." *Work and Occupations* 21 (4): 403–21.

Snell, K. D. M. 1985. *Annals of the Labouring Poor: Social Change and Agrarian England 1660–1900.* Cambridge: Cambridge University Press.

———. 1996. "The Apprenticeship System in British History: The Fragmentation of a Cultural Institution." *History of Education* 25 (4): 303–21.

Somers, Margaret R. 1990. "Karl Polanyi's Intellectual Legacy." In *The Life and Work of Karl Polanyi*, edited by Kari Polanyi-Levitt, 152–58. Montreal: Black Rose Books.

Spain, Jonathan. 1991. "Trade Unionists, Gladstonian Liberals and the Labour Law Reforms of 1875." In *Currents of Radicalism: Popular Radicalism, Organised Labour and Party Politics in Britain, 1850–1914*, edited by Eugenio F. Biagini and Alastair J. Reid, 109–33. Cambridge: Cambridge University Press.

Spencer, David A. 2000. "Braverman and the Contribution of Labour Process Analysis to the Critique of Capitalist Production—Twenty-Five Years On." *Work, Employment and Society* 14 (2): 223–45.

Staples, William G. 1987. "Technology, Control, and the Social Organization of Work at a British Hardware Firm, 1791–1891." *American Journal of Sociology* 93 (1): 62–88.

Staples, William G., and Clifford L. Staples. 2001. *Power, Profits, and Patriarchy: The Social Organization of Work at a British Metal Trades Firm, 1971–1922.* Lanham, MD: Rowman and Littlefield.

Starkey, David. 1996. "Ownership Structures in the British Shipping Industry: The Case of Hull, 1820–1916." *International Journal of Maritime History* 8 (2): 71–95.

Steinberg, Marc W. 1999. *Fighting Words: Working-Class Formation, Collective Action and Discourse in Early Nineteenth-Century England.* Ithaca, NY: Cornell University Press.

Steinfeld, Robert J. 2001. *Coercion, Contract, and Free Labor in the Nineteenth Century.* Cambridge: Cambridge University Press.

Steinmetz, George. 1993. *Regulating the Social: The Welfare State and Local Politics in Imperial Germany.* Princeton, NJ: Princeton University Press.

Steinmetz, Wilibald. 2000a. "Introduction: Towards a Comparative History of Legal Cultures, 1750–1950." In *Private Law and Social Inequality in the Industrial Age: Comparing Legal Cultures in Britain, France, Germany and the United States*, edited by Willibald Steinmetz, 1–41. Oxford: Oxford University Press.

———. 2000b. "Was there a De-juridification of Individual Employment Relations in Britain?" In *Private Law and Social Inequality in the Industrial Age: Comparing Legal Cultures in Britain, France, Germany and the United States*, edited by Willibald Steinmetz, 265–312. Oxford: Oxford University Press.

Stephenson, Nash. 1861. "On the Rise and Progress of the Movement for the Abolition of Statutes, Mops or Feeing Markets." *Transactions of the National Association for the Promotion of Social Science, 1860*, edited by George W. Hastings, 797–805. London: John W. Parker and Son and Bourne.

Stobart, Jon. 2001. "Regions, Localities, and Industrialisation: Evidence from the East Midlands, circa 1780–1840." *Environment and Planning A* 33:1305–25.

Streek, Wolfgang, and Kathleen Thelen. 2005. "Introduction: Institutional Change in Advanced Political Economies." In *Beyond Continuity: Institutional Change in Advanced Political Economies*, edited by Wolfgang Steeck, and Kathleen Thelen, 1–39. Oxford: Oxford University Press.

Stryker, Robin. 2003. "Mind the Gap: Institutional Analysis and Socioeconomics." *Socio-Economic Review* 1:335–67.

Stuart, Denis, ed. 1985. *People of the Potteries: A Dictionary of Local Biography,* vol. 1. Keele: Department of Adult Education, University of Keele.

Sumner, Colin. 1979. *Reading Ideologies: An Investigation into Marxist Theory of Ideology and the Law.* New York: Academic Press.

Taiwo, Olefumi. 1996. *Legal Naturalism: A Marxist Theory of the Law.* Ithaca, NY: Cornell University Press.

Thelen, Kathleen. 1999. "Historical Institutionalism in Comparative Politics," *Annual Review of Political Science* 2:369–404.

———. 2003. "How Institutions Evolve: Insights From Comparative Historical Analysis." In *Comparative Historical Analysis in Social Science,* edited by James Mahoney and Dietrich Rueschmeyer, 337–72. Cambridge: Cambridge University Press.

———. 2004. *How Institutions Evolve: The Political Economy of Skills in Germany, Britain, the United States and Japan.* Cambridge: Cambridge University Press.

Thomas, John. 1971. *The Rise of the Staffordshire Potteries.* Bath: Adams and Dart.

Thompson, E. P. 1966. *The Making of the English Working Class.* New York: Vintage.

———. 1975. *Whigs and Hunters: The Origins of the Black Act.* New York: Pantheon.

Thompson, Noel W. 1984. *The People's Science: The Popular Political Economy of Exploitation and Crisis 1816–1834.* Cambridge: Cambridge University Press.

Thompson, Paul, and Chris Smith, eds. 2010. *Working Life: Renewing Labour Process Analysis.* Basingstoke: Palgrave Macmillan.

Thompson, Paul, and Steve Vincent. 2010. "Labour Process Theory and Critical Realism." In *Working Life: Renewing Labour Process Analysis,* edited by Paul Thompson and Chris Smith, 29–46. Basingstoke: Palgrave Macmillan.

Tilly, Charles. 1997. *Roads from Past to Future.* Lanham, MD: Rowman and Littlefield.

———. 1998. *Durable Inequality.* Berkeley: University of California Press.

———. 2002. *Stories, Identities and Political Change.* Lanham, MD: Rowman and Littlefield.

———. 2008. *Contentious Performances.* Cambridge: Cambridge University Press.

Tilly, Chris, and Charles Tilly. 1998. *Working under Capitalism.* Boulder, CO: Westview.

Tolliday, Steven, and Jonathan Zeitlin. 1991a. "Introduction: Employers and Industrial Relations between Theory and History." In *The Power to Manage? Employers and Industrial Relations in Comparative-Historical Perspective,* edited by Steven Tolliday and Jonathan Zeitlin, 1–31. London: Routledge.

———. 1991b. "Conclusion: National Models and International Variations in Labour Management and Employer Organization." In *The Power to Manage? Employers and Industrial Relations in Comparative-Historical Perspective,* edited by Steven Tolliday and Jonathan Zeitlin, 273–343. London: Routledge.

Tomlins, Christopher. 1985. *The State and the Unions: Labor Relations, Law, and the Organized Labor Movement in America, 1880–1960.* Cambridge: Cambridge University Press.

———. 1993. *Law, Labor and Ideology in the Early American Republic.* Cambridge: Cambridge University Press.

———. 1995a. "How Who Rides Whom. Recent 'New' Histories of American Labour Law and What They May Signify." *Social History* 20 (1): 1–12.

———. 1995b. "Subordination, Authority, Law: Subjects in Labor History." *International Review of Social History* 47:56–90.

———. 2010. *Freedom Bound: Law, Labor and Civic Identity in Colonizing English America, 1580–1865*. New York: Cambridge University Press.

Tosh, John. 1994. "What Should Historians Do with Masculinity? Reflections on Nineteenth-Century Britain." *History Workshop Journal* 39:179–202.

———. 2005. *Manliness and Masculinities in Nineteenth-Century Britain*. Harlow: Pearson/Longman.

The Trade and Commerce of Hull: Its Ships and Shipowners, Past and Present. 1878. 2nd ed. Hull: W. Hunt.

Trainor, Richard H. 1993. *Black Country Elites: The Exercise of Authority in an Industrialised Area, 1830–1900*. Oxford: Oxford University Press.

Tsui, Anna P. Y. 2009. "Labor Dispute Resolution in the Shenzen Special Economic Zone." *China Information* 23 (2): 257–84.

Tuttle, Carolyn. 1999. *Hard at Work in the Factories and Mines: The Economics of Child Labor during the British Industrial Revolution*. Boulder, CO: Westview Press.

Valenze, Deborah. 1995. *The First Industrial Woman*. Oxford: Oxford University Press.

Valverde, Mariana. 1988. "'Giving the Female a Domestic Turn': The Social, Legal and Moral Regulation of Women's Work in the British Cotton Mills, 1820–1850." *Journal of Social History* 21 (4): 619–34.

van der Linden, Marcel, and Richard Price. 2000. "Introduction." In *The Rise and Development of Comparative Labour Law*, edited by Marcel van der Linden, and Richard Price, 7–18. Bern: Peter Lang.

Voss, Kim. 1993. *The Making of American Exceptionalism: The Knights of Labor and Class Formation in the Nineteenth Century*. Ithaca, NY: Cornell University Press.

Walton, John B. 2000. "The Midlands." In *The Agrarian History of England and Wales*, vol. 7, pt. 1, edited by E. J. T. Collins, 384–401. Cambridge: Cambridge University Press.

Wang, Haiyan, Richard P. Appelbaum, Francesca Degiuli, and Nelson Lichtenstein. 2009. "China's New Labor Contract Law: Is China Moving toward Increased Power for Workers?" *Third World Quarterly* 30 (3): 485–501.

Warburton, William H. 1931. *The History of Trade Union Organization in the North Staffordshire Potteries*. London: George Allen and Unwin.

Warde, Alan. 1989. "Industrial Discipline: Factory Regime and Politics in Lancaster." *Work, Employment and Society* 3 (1): 49–63.

Warrilow, E. J. D. 1960. *A Sociological History of Stoke-on-Trent*. Stoke-on-Trent: Etruscan Publications.

Wedgwood, Josiah, and Thomas H. Ormsbee. 1947. *Staffordshire Pottery*. New York: Robert McBride and Co.

Whipp, Richard. 1985. 1987. "'A Time to Every Purpose': An Essay on Time and Work." In *The Historical Meanings of Work, edited by* Patrick Joyce, 210–36. Cambridge: Cambridge University Press.

———. 1990. *Patterns of Labour: Work and Social Change in the Pottery Industry.* London: Routledge.

Willis-Bund, J. W. "Agriculture." 1906. In *The Victoria History of the Counties of England: A History of Worcester,* vol. 2, edited by J. W. Willis-Bund, and William Page, 309–14. London: Constable.

Wood, Ellen Meiksins. 1995. *Democracy against Capitalism: Renewing Historical Materialism.* Cambridge: Cambridge University Press.

———. 2002. *The Origins of Capitalism: A Longer View.* London: Verso.

Woods, David Charles. 1979. "Crime and Society in the Black Country 1860–1900." D.Phil. diss., University of Aston.

Wright, Robert S. 1887. *The Law of Criminal Conspiracies and Agreements.* Philadelphia: Blackstone Publishing.

Yarmie, Andrew H. 1984. "British Employers' Resistance to 'Grandmotherly' Government, 1850–80." *Social History* 9 (2): 141–69.

Yelling, J. A. 1973. "Changes in Crop Production in East Worcestershire, 1540–1867." *Agricultural History Review* 23 (1): 18–34.

Zeitlin, Jonathan. 1985. "Shop Floor Bargaining and the State: A Contradictory Relationship." In *Shop Floor Bargaining and the State: Historical and Comparative Perspectives,* edited by Steven Tolliday, and Jonathan Zeitlin, 1–45. Cambridge: Cambridge University Press.

———. 1987. "From Labour History to the History of Industrial Relations." *Economic History Review,* 2nd ser., 40 (2): 159–84.

———. 1989. "'Rank and Filism' in British Labour History: A Critique." *International Review of Social History* 34 (1): 42–61.

———. 1991. "The Internal Politics of Employer Organization: The Engineering Employers' Federation, 1896–1939." In *The Power to Manage? Employers and Industrial Relations in Comparative-Historical Perspective,* edited by Steven Tolliday and Jonathan Zeitlin, 52–80. London: Routledge.

Zolberg, Aristide R. 1986. "How Many Exceptionalisms?" In *Working-Class Formation: Nineteenth-Century Patterns in Western Europe and the United States,* edited by Ira Katznelson, and Aristide R. Zolberg, 397–455. Princeton, NJ: Princeton University Press.

INDEX